*Advanced Methods of Data
Exploration and Modelling*

Advanced Methods of Data Exploration and Modelling

B. S. Everitt and G. Dunn

Institute of Psychiatry,
University of London

Heinemann Educational Books
London . Exeter (New Hampshire)

Heinemann Educational Books Ltd
22 Bedford Square, London WC1B 3HH

Heinemann Educational Books Inc.
4 Front Street, Exeter, New Hampshire 03833

British Library Cataloguing in Publication Data

Everitt, Brian
   Advanced methods of data exploration and modelling
   1. Social sciences—Data processing
   2. Social sciences—Mathematical models
   I. Title   II. Dunn, G.
   300.1'8   H61
   ISBN 0–435–82294–2
   ISBN 0–435–82295–0 Pbk

Library of Congress Cataloguing in Publication Data

Everitt, Brian
   Advanced methods of data exploration and modelling

   Bibliography: p.
   Includes index.
   1. Social sciences—Statistical methods.
2. Statistics.   3. Multivariate analysis.   I. Dunn,
G. (Graham), 1919–   .   II. Title.
HA29.E825   1983   300'.1'5195   83–286
ISBN 0–435–82294–2

Printed in Great Britain by
Biddles Ltd, Guildford, Surrey

Contents

viii   *Contents*

12 **Structural Equation Models**   211
  12.1 Introduction   211
  12.2 A simple structural equation model   211
  12.3 General structural equation models   214
  12.4 Estimating the parameters of structural
      equation models and testing their fit   216
  12.5 Identification of parameters   217
  12.6 Numerical examples   218
  12.7 Summary   223
  Exercises   224

Appendix A Computer Programs and Packages   226

Appendix B Answers to Selected Exercises   232

Bibliography and References   237

Author Index   244

Subject Index   247

Acknowledgements

The authors and publishers of *Advanced Methods of Data Exploration and Modelling* would like to thank those authors and publishers who have given permission for their material to be reproduced or adapted for use in this book. The original sources of this material are acknowledged throughout the book whenever it is used. Ms. Johanna Beyts, who kindly provided the data given in Table 8.10, wishes to acknowledge the receipt of a Medical Research Council studentship.

Preface

This book is aimed at those interested in the analysis of social or behavioural data, including those actively involved in research and others who are being trained to carry out and understand the results of such research. It has been written as an intermediate text (although it may appear to be rather advanced to the non-mathematically minded reader!) suitable for students who are already familiar with the methods and concepts introduced in introductory statistics texts for social scientists such as *Understanding Data* (Erickson and Nosanchuck, 1979) and *Social Statistics* (Blalock, 1972). We hope that it will also be useful to applied statisticians working as consultants in the behavioural and social sciences. Some familiarity with matrix algebra is assumed, although much of the most important mathematical background needed for this text is reviewed in Chapter 2, which can be used for reference when reading the rest of the book. Non-mathematicians should not be put off the more practical parts of the book by attempting to follow all of the mathematical derivations, particularly in Chapters 11 and 12 which are in this respect more difficult than the rest.

The text comprises four largely self-contained parts. Part I considers particular approaches to data analysis and the mathematical background necessary for understanding the remainder of the text, and should be studied by all readers. Part II covers the exploration of multivariate data, while Parts III and IV introduce linear models for, respectively, manifest (observable) and latent variables. Parts III and IV can be read without any knowledge of Part II, although it might be useful for the reader to study Chapters 4, 7 and 8 before attempting Part IV. The exercises given at the end of each chapter are primarily practical, although a small number of theoretical problems are included, and the solutions to some of these appear in Appendix B.

The statistical analysis of data frequently involves several phases: early analyses might be concerned with the discovery of patterns and structure, later stages with the formulation and testing of hypotheses or models. These are often referred to as *exploratory* and *confirmatory* stages, although the distinction between the two is not as clear-cut as the names imply. In this text we will frequently stress the importance of exploration, leading to the generation of hypotheses and speculation, and will often suggest that significance tests should be used as diagnostic aids rather than as formal decision-making procedures. We hope that in this we will convey to readers a feel for the analysis of real data and that they will then be able to use packages of statistical computer programs correctly and effectively.

It is clear that in many areas of the social sciences scientific activity is dominated by attempts to discover pattern or order in sets of multivariate data. Very rarely can one hope to discover natural laws or actually 'explain' anything. The themes of discovery of patterns, creation of models, and the assessment of their adequacy and plausibility are, therefore, those that have guided the writing of this book.

We wish to thank our colleagues at the Institute of Psychiatry who have helped in some way in the preparation of this text, particularly those who have read the whole book and provided valuable criticism. We also wish to thank those who have provided data for us to include as examples; they are acknowledged individually at appropriate points in the text. Finally, we must express our gratitude to Mrs Bertha Lakey for her careful typing of the manuscript.

B. S. Everitt
G. Dunn
Institute of Psychiatry
London 1982

A Note for Students and Teachers

Most existing textbooks of statistics and data analysis, written at a similar level to the present one, stress hypothesis testing at the expense of data exploration. They also tend to have rather brief descriptions of relatively modern techniques such as multidimensional scaling and cluster analysis (if they mention them at all), these usually following a much fuller account of traditional methods based on the linear model. The authors of the present text, however, are convinced that modern methods should be given much more prominence and have therefore attempted to provide much fuller accounts of them. The ordering of the chapters is also different from that usually encountered in a text of this kind. Instead of discussing more traditional subjects first, and then introducing the newer exploratory methods, we have placed the topics in a logical, rather than historical, order since we are convinced that readers, whether students or research workers, should be able to 'explore' data first, and only then begin to fit the data to more formal statistical models and test specific hypotheses.

List of Figures

List of Tables

PART I
Approaches to Analysing Data

The first two chapters cover essential introductory material. Chapter 1 reviews the authors' approach to the analysis of complex social and behavioural data, and stresses the importance of model building in both the exploratory and hypothesis-testing stages of an investigation. Chapter 2 describes briefly a few mathematical and statistical topics which are needed in the remainder of the text.

---

1. Data and Statistics in the Behavioural Sciences

1.1 Introduction

The methods used in the systematic pursuit of knowledge are the same, or at least very similar, in all branches of science. These involve the recognition and formulation of problems, the collection of relevant empirical data, through passive observation or through experiment, and often the use of mathematical and statistical analysis to explore relationships in the data or to test specific hypotheses about the observations. There are, however, special problems and difficulties in the behavioural sciences which do not, perhaps, exist in disciplines such as physics or chemistry. The complexity and ambiguity of some aspects of human behaviour, for example, create major problems in drawing reliable and valid inferences, which are frequently more difficult than those faced by the physical scientist. Reliable measurement of physical variables is also, in general, much more straightforward than the measurement of behavioural qualities.

Because of these difficulties it has long been recognised by social and behavioural scientists that they will generally need to employ relatively more sophisticated and complex analytical tools to investigate their data. In some cases such tools have been supplied by developments in statistics. Often, however, they have been developed by the behavioural scientists themselves and only later become the concern of statisticians. A classic example of the latter is factor analysis, the basic concepts of which probably originated with Spearman as early as 1904, and were later extended by Burt and Thurstone in the 1920s and 1930s. It was

1

some time after this that Lawley considered the maximum likelihood estimation of the parameters in the factor analysis model, and only comparatively recently that Jöreskog developed suitable algorithms for finding these estimates.

Routine use of many of these methods of analysis has had to await the dramatic revolution in data analysis brought about by the development and increasing availability of the electronic computer. Twenty-five years ago a psychologist wishing to apply factor analysis to a correlation matrix would have been faced with the daunting task of several days or even weeks of hand calculation. Today the equivalent analysis can take a fraction of a second on a modern computer. Well-documented statistical packages such as SPSS, GLIM and CLUSTAN enable even the most complicated of procedures to be performed with ease, often by the mathematically and statistically unsophisticated. This is, of course, not without its problems, and probably results in a number of meaningless research findings in many areas. However, computers and computer packages are here to stay and it would be unrealistic to ignore the fact that they have made a great contribution in removing the necessity for the investigator to be involved in large amounts of tedious arithmetic. But they offer far more than merely a means of short-cutting laborious calculations. The ability to draw graphs, produce geometrical representations of data, and operate in an interactive mode, makes a computer an essential tool at almost all stages of investigation of a set of data. Nevertheless it should not be forgotten that in some circumstances there may be simple 'pencil and paper' techniques that produce a more rewarding result than pages and pages of computer printout.

In this text we will assume that the majority of analyses are to be performed with the aid of a computer, particularly through the use of a computer package, and we will take this as a justification for providing only very few details of the arithmetical calculations involved in the techniques to be described. Instead we shall concentrate on indicating when particular methods are applicable and on the correct interpretation of results. This should, we hope, raise the probability of drawing useful and valid conclusions from the results of an analysis.

1.2   Types of Data

The data with which we shall be primarily concerned in later chapters arise in one of two forms. The first is where a series of measurements or observations have been made on a number of individuals, objects or other entities of interest. Such a data set may be represented by a matrix **X** given by

$$\mathbf{X} = \begin{bmatrix} x_{11} & x_{12} & \cdots & x_{1p} \\ \vdots & & & \\ x_{n1} & \cdots & \cdots & x_{np} \end{bmatrix}$$

where x_{ij} represents the value of the j-th variable for the i-th individual, n is the number of individuals being studied, and p is the number of measurements or observations made on each individual. Table 1.1 gives a hypothetical example of such a *multivariate data* matrix.

Table 1.1 *Data matrix for a hypothetical sample of ten individuals*

Individual	Sex	Age	IQ	Depression	Self-perception health	Weight (lb)
1	Male	21	120	Yes	Very good	150
2	Male	43	87	No	Very good	160
3	Male	22	135	No	Average	135
4	Male	86	150	No	Very poor	140
5	Male	60	92	Yes	Poor	140
6	Female	16	130	Yes	Good	110
7	Female	35	150	Yes	Very good	120
8	Female	43	91	Yes	Average	120
9	Female	22	84	No	Average	105
10	Female	80	70	No	Good	100

In many cases the variables measured will be of different types. For example, in Table 1.1 Sex and Depression are *categorical* variables, Self-perception of health is *ordinal*, and so probably is IQ, while Age has the properties of a *ratio-scale*. (Each of these types is defined in detail in any elementary statistics textbook for the behavioural sciences; see, for example, Siegel, 1956.) As we shall see later, different methods of analysis are generally suitable for different types of variable.

In some cases the variables recorded may fall into two groups, namely *response* and *explanatory* variables. This situation arises when we are interested in investigating the effect of one set of variables (the explanatory variables) on another set (the response variables). For example, in Table 1.1 we might be interested in assessing the effect of age, weight and sex on individuals' perceptions of their own health.

The second type of data with which we shall be concerned is where we have values of the perceived or measured relationship between each pair of individuals, stimuli or variables under investigation. Such data may also be displayed in the form of a matrix, Δ, of the form

$$\Delta = \begin{bmatrix} \delta_{11} & \delta_{12} & \cdots & \delta_{1m} \\ \vdots & & & \\ \delta_{m1} & \cdots & \cdots & \delta_{mm} \end{bmatrix}$$

The most common occurrence of such a matrix is when correlations between variables have been calculated from the raw data matrix X. In such a case, $m = p$, Δ is generally denoted by the letter R, and δ_{ij} represents the correlation between variables i and j. A further situation where such a matrix arises from X is when the elements of this matrix have been used to calculate some measure of distance between individuals. Here $m = n$, Δ is generally denoted by the letter D, and δ_{ij} represents the distance between individuals i and j. Many examples of correlation and distance matrices will be found in later chapters.

In some cases the matrix Δ can arise directly, rather than as a result of calculations involving the elements of X. For example, in psychological experiments subjects may be asked to judge the similarity of two stimuli. Similarly, the number of times that one stimulus is identified as another by a group of subjects may be recorded, leading to a matrix of confusion probabilities. Examples of such data appear in Chapters 5 and 6. Frequently the judgements of the similarity of two stimuli have only ordinal significance, a point which has important implications for their analysis (again, see Chapters 5 and 6).

1.3 Exploratory and Confirmatory Techniques

It is increasingly recognised that the analysis of data often involves two separate stages. The first, particularly in new areas of research, involves the 'exploration' of data in an attempt to recognise any non-random pattern or structure requiring explanation. At this stage, finding the question is often more important than finding the subsequent answer, the aim of this part of the analysis being to generate possibly interesting hypotheses for later study. Here, formal models designed to yield specific answers to rigidly defined questions are not required. Instead, methods are sought which allow possibly unanticipated patterns in the data to be detected, opening up a wide range of alternative explanations. Such techniques are generally characterised by their emphasis on the importance of visual displays and graphical representations, and by the lack of any associated stochastic model, so that questions of the statistical significance of results hardly ever arise.

A confirmatory analysis becomes possible once a research worker has some well-defined hypothesis. It is here that some type of statistical significance test might be considered. Such tests are well known to behavioural scientists and, although their misuse has often brought them into some disrepute they remain of considerable importance.

In this text we have loosely divided the methods of analysis we shall discuss into exploratory (Chapters 3–6) and confirmatory (Chapters 7–10), but this division should not be regarded as much more than a convenient arrangement of the material to be presented, since any sensible investigator will realise the need for both exploratory and confirmatory techniques, and many methods will often be useful in both roles. Linear regression (see Chapter 8), for example, can be both an aid in the search for structure in a set of data via graphical analysis and examination of residuals, and as a formal model for the construction of significance tests. Factor analysis (see Chapter 11), and structural equation models (Chapter 12) can also be used as both exploratory and confirmatory techniques.

Perhaps recent attempts rigidly to divide data analysis into exploratory and confirmatory parts have been misplaced, and what is really important is that research workers should have a flexible and pragmatic approach to the analysis of their data, with sufficient expertise to enable them to choose the appropriate analytical tool and use it correctly.

1.4   The Role of Models

The aim of many of the techniques described in this text is a simplified description of the structure of the observations by means of what is usually referred to as a *model*. This model can range from a fairly imprecise verbal description to a geometrical representation or mathematical equation. The latter is a precise description of what the investigator visualises as occurring in the population of interest, and in many cases may be the basis of a formal test of significance. Geometrical or graphical representations of the data may often, however, have a more powerful impact. The purpose of building a model is to provide the simplest description of the population being studied *that is consistent with the data*. Of course, if one makes the models complex enough they are bound to fit, but a complicated model may have less explanatory power than a simple, more elegant one. Also, the simpler the model, the easier it is to interpret.

In this text then a model is considered to be a way of simplifying and portraying the structure in a set of data, and does not necessarily imply any causal links or explicitly invoke any causal mechanisms. In the physical sciences, of course, the models used often do imply a mechanism, and are often suggested by a particular theoretical framework. A mathematical description or model of planetary movements, for example, can be derived from Newton's laws of motion. The social and behavioural scientist, however, is very rarely in the situation where causal models can be generated from *a priori* theories. Indeed, even when the data can be modelled in this way, the result will very likely have only a restricted area of applicability. Consequently our concern will be to show to workers in these fields how to simplify and describe their data, and how to construct simple *empirical* models rather than mechanistic ones.

The model-building process is summarised in Fig. 1.1. At the first stage a knowledge of the way the data have been collected, the scales of measurement used, and the results of some preliminary exploratory analyses allow the investigator to postulate a very general class of

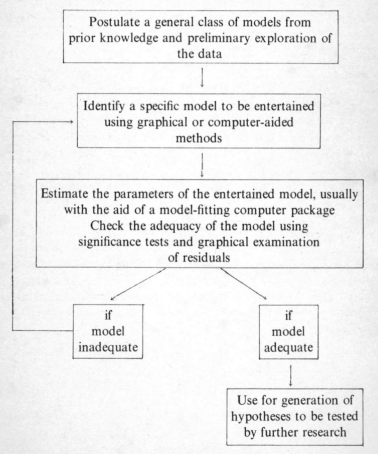

Figure 1.1   *Stages in empirical model building*

models that might prove useful. Exploratory techniques remain important in the second stage, in identifying a particular model that can be entertained by the investigator. Then one moves on to the so-called confirmatory stage in which the parameters of the model are estimated and its goodness-of-fit tested. In addition a graphical or geometrical representation of the supposed structure in the data may be produced. Lastly a series of diagnostic procedures may be used to assess the adequacy of the model, or to check whether the underlying assumptions of the model are sensible and justified, by a re-examination of the original data. If it is decided that the model is not justified, or does not fit the data well enough, then a return to an earlier phase is called for, with a renewed search for alternative models.

Such a procedure can be summarised in terms of the equation

$$data = model + residual$$

The model is the underlying, simplified structure of a set of data that is considered at any particular stage. The residual represents the difference between the model and the observed data points. What is desirable is that the residual should contain no additional pattern or structure. If the residual does contain additional structure then the model associated with the data needs refinement and the process should continue until all parts of this structure can be assumed to be contained within the model.

Most of this text is written from the point of view that there are no rules or laws of scientific inference (Feyerabend, 1975). This implies that we see both exploratory and confirmatory techniques as methods of searching for structure in data rather than as decision-making procedures. For this reason we do not stress the values of significance levels, but merely use them as criteria to guide the modelling process. We believe that in scientific research it is the skilful interpretation of evidence and subsequent development of 'hunches' that are important, rather than a rigid adherence to a formal set of decision rules associated with significance tests.

2. Mathematical and Statistical Background

2.1 Introduction

As we mentioned in the preface, we are assuming that readers of the text have a firm grasp of basic statistics and mathematics, including some familiarity with matrix algebra. Although this should ensure that most of the material in the remaining chapters can be readily understood, we will in this chapter cover briefly the mathematical and statistical concepts most relevant to the remainder of the text.

2.2 Matrices

Examples of matrices have already been given in Chapter 1. They are simply square or rectangular arrangements of numbers or symbols, and we will assume that readers are familiar with the basic concepts of their algebra such as addition, multiplication and inversion. (Readers not familiar with these topics are referred to Maxwell, 1977, Chapter 3.) Here we shall concentrate on describing a number of other aspects of matrices that are particularly relevant at various points in this text.

Rank of a matrix
Consider the three equations

$$2x + y - 5 = 0$$
$$x - 2y \quad = 0 \qquad (2.1)$$
$$3x - y - 5 = 0$$

All three equations are satisfied by the values $x = 2$ and $y = 1$, so they are consistent. The equations can be written as follows:

$$\mathbf{Az} = \mathbf{0}$$

where $\mathbf{A} = \begin{bmatrix} 2 & 1 & -5 \\ 1 & -2 & 0 \\ 3 & -1 & -5 \end{bmatrix}$, $\mathbf{z} = \begin{bmatrix} x \\ y \\ 1 \end{bmatrix}$, $\mathbf{0} = \begin{bmatrix} 0 \\ 0 \\ 0 \end{bmatrix}$. $\qquad (2.2)$

Now, since only two of the original three equations are necessary for solving for x and y, the matrix $\mathbf{A}$ contains redundant information; its rows (or columns) are not all independent.

The number of independent rows (or columns) of a matrix is called the *rank* of the matrix. The rank of a matrix can never exceed the smaller of its two dimensions, i.e. if $e(\mathbf{A})$ is the rank of matrix $\mathbf{A}$ of order $m \times n$ (which we shall sometimes write as $\mathbf{A}(m \times x)$), then

$$r(\mathbf{A}) \leqslant \min(m, n) \qquad (2.3)$$

If $r(\mathbf{A}) = \min(m, n)$ then $\mathbf{A}$ is said to be of *full rank*; if $r(\mathbf{A}) < \min(m, n)$ then $\mathbf{A}$ is of *deficient rank*. For example, consider

$$\mathbf{A} = \begin{bmatrix} 1 & 2 & 2 \\ 1 & 3 & 0 \\ 1 & 2 & 1 \end{bmatrix} \qquad (2.4)$$

This matrix is of full rank, 3, since no column can be expressed as a linear combination of other columns. However, if

$$\mathbf{A} = \begin{bmatrix} 1 & 2 & 1 \\ 1 & 3 & 2 \\ 1 & 2 & 1 \end{bmatrix} \qquad (2.5)$$

then $r(\mathbf{A}) = 2$ since the third column is exactly the difference of columns two and one. Now consider the rectangular matrix $\mathbf{B}$ given by

$$\mathbf{B} = \begin{bmatrix} 1 & 2 & 2 \\ 1 & 3 & 0 \end{bmatrix} \qquad (2.6)$$

The rank of $\mathbf{B}$ cannot exceed 2; the third column is necessarily linearly dependent upon the first two since we can always find values x and y to satisfy

$$\begin{aligned} x + 2y &= 2 \\ x + 3y &= 0 \end{aligned} \qquad (2.7)$$

The matrix is of full rank, 2, as long as the second column (row) is not a linear function of the first.

The rank of a matrix is an indication of how much non-redundant information the matrix contains. The usual multivariate data matrix $\mathbf{X}$, introduced in Chapter 1, is generally of full rank unless any of the variables are linear combinations of others; for example, if subset scores and a total test score are included, or if scores are percentages that add up to 100 for each subject.

The condition of full rank is a prerequisite for the inversion of a square matrix, and also for an operation known as *factoring*, which is important in principal components analysis (see Chapter 4), and factor analysis (see Chapter 11).

Eigenvalues and eigenvectors

If **A** is a square matrix, **x** is a column vector and λ is a scalar quantity such that

$$\mathbf{A}\mathbf{x} = \lambda \mathbf{x} \qquad (2.8)$$

then **x** is said to be an *eigenvector* of **A** and λ to be an *eigenvalue*.

Eigenvalues and eigenvectors arise frequently in statistics, particularly in situations where one wishes to find a linear combination of variables that has maximum variance; see, for example, Chapter 4. Finding the eigenvalues and eigenvectors of a matrix involves laborious calculations but fortunately many very efficient computer programs are now available. In the case of a 2×2 matrix, however, they are relatively easy to obtain as we shall demonstrate using the matrix

$$\mathbf{A} = \begin{bmatrix} 6 & 3 \\ 3 & 4 \end{bmatrix} \qquad (2.9)$$

First it can be shown (see Maxwell, 1977, Chapter 3 for details) that the eigenvalues are obtained as roots of the determinantal equation

$$|\mathbf{A} - \lambda \mathbf{I}| = 0 \qquad (2.10)$$

where **I** is the identity matrix of appropriate order. Expanding the left-hand side of equation (2.10) leads to the following quadratic equation

$$\lambda^2 = 10\lambda + 15 = 0 \qquad (2.11)$$

the roots of which are $\lambda_1 = 8.162$ and $\lambda_2 = 1.838$. To find the eigenvector corresponding to λ_1 we use (2.8) to give

$$\begin{bmatrix} 6 & 3 \\ 3 & 4 \end{bmatrix} \begin{bmatrix} x_1 \\ x_2 \end{bmatrix} = 8.162 \begin{bmatrix} x_1 \\ x_2 \end{bmatrix} \qquad (2.12)$$

i.e.

$$\begin{aligned} -2.162x_1 + 3x_2 = 0 \\ -3x_1 - 4.162x_2 = 0 \end{aligned} \qquad (2.13)$$

It is easy to see from equation (2.8) that the elements of an eigenvector are only determined up to multiplication by a scalar; consequently equations (2.13) only define the ratio of x_1 to x_2, giving

$$\frac{x_1}{x_2} = 1.39 \qquad (2.14)$$

Choosing $x_1 = 1.0$ gives $x_2 = 0.721$. Determination of the second eigenvector is left as an exercise for the reader.

Let us suppose we have a $(p \times p)$ matrix $\mathbf{\Sigma}$ with elements σ_{ij}, eigenvalues $\lambda_1, \lambda_2, \ldots, \lambda_p$ and corresponding eigenvectors $c_1, c_2, \ldots, c_p$. Some useful results are as follows:

(a) $\displaystyle\sum_{i=1}^{p} \sigma_{ii} = \sum_{i=1}^{p} \lambda_i$ (This sum is usually written   (2.15)

as trace(Σ).)

(b) The determinant of Σ is given by

$$|\Sigma| = \prod_{i=1}^{p} \lambda_i \qquad (2.16)$$

(c) For two unequal eigenvalues the corresponding eigenvectors are *orthogonal*, i.e. if c_1 and c_2 are the two eigenvectors, then

$$c_1' c_2 = 0 \qquad (2.17)$$

(d) If we form a $(p \times p)$ matrix, C, whose i-th column is the *normalised* eigenvector c_i, i.e. the eigenvector with its elements scaled so that

$$c_i' c_i = 1 \qquad (2.18)$$

then

$$C'C = I \qquad (2.19)$$

and

$$C'\Sigma C = \Lambda \qquad (2.20)$$

where Λ is a diagonal matrix whose diagonal elements are $\lambda_1, \lambda_2, \ldots, \lambda_p$. (Any matrix satisfying equation (2.19) is known as an *orthogonal* matrix.)

Quadratic forms

A *quadratic form* in p variables $x_1, \ldots, x_p$ is a homogeneous function consisting of all possible second order terms, namely

$$a_{11}x_1^2 + \cdots + a_{pp}x_p^2 + a_{12}x_1x_2 \cdots + a_{p-1, p}x_{p-1}, x_p \qquad (2.21)$$

$$= \sum_{i,j} a_{ij}x_i x_j \qquad (2.22)$$

This expression can be conveniently written as $x'Ax$ where $x' = [x_1, x_2, \ldots, x_p]$ and a_{ij} is the ij-th element of A. A square matrix A and its associated quadratic form is called

(a) *positive definite* if $x'Ax > 0$ for every x not equal to the null vector, or

(b) *positive semidefinite* if $x'Ax \geqslant 0$ for every x not equal to the null vector.

Positive definite quadratic forms have matrices of full rank, the eigenvalues of which are all greater than zero. Positive semidefinite quadratic forms have matrices which are not of full rank, and if their rank is *m* they will have *m* positive eigenvalues and $p-m$ zero eigenvalues.

The matrix, **C**, formed from the normalised eigenvectors of **A** transforms the quadratic form of **A** to the reduced form involving only squared terms, i.e. writing $\mathbf{y} = \mathbf{C}'\mathbf{x}$, we have

$$\mathbf{C}'\mathbf{y} = \mathbf{x} \quad (\text{since } \mathbf{C}'\mathbf{C} = \mathbf{I})$$

and

$$\mathbf{x}'\mathbf{A}\mathbf{x} = \mathbf{y}'\mathbf{C}'\mathbf{A}\mathbf{C}\mathbf{y} \tag{2.23}$$

$$= \mathbf{y}'\Lambda\mathbf{y} \tag{2.24}$$

$$= \lambda_1 y_1^2 + \cdots \lambda_p y_p^2 \tag{2.25}$$

These results are particularly relevant to principal components analysis (see Chapter 4).

2.3 Rotation of Axes

Rotation of axes is a common procedure in principal components analysis (see Chapter 4) and factor analysis (see Chapter 11). If a point P has coordinates (x_1, x_2) with reference to a given set of orthogonal axes and if the axes are rotated about the origin through an angle θ in a clockwise direction, the coordinates (y_1, y_2) of P with reference to the rotated axes are obtained by multiplying the row vector $\mathbf{x}' = (x_1, x_2)$ by an orthogonal matrix **U** where

$$\mathbf{U} = \begin{bmatrix} \cos\theta & \sin\theta \\ -\sin\theta & \cos\theta \end{bmatrix} \tag{2.26}$$

i.e.

$$\mathbf{y}' = \mathbf{x}'\mathbf{U} \tag{2.27}$$

where $\mathbf{y}' = (y_1, y_2)$. Such a rotation is illustrated in Figure 2.1. This rotation preserves Euclidean distances of points from the origin (those readers unfamiliar with the formula for Euclidean distance should refer to page 53).

2.4 Some Basic Topics in Multivariate Statistics

In the univariate case it is often necessary to summarise a data set by calculating its mean and variance. To summarise multivariate data sets we need to find the mean and variance of each of the p variables, together with a measure of the way each pair of variables is related. For

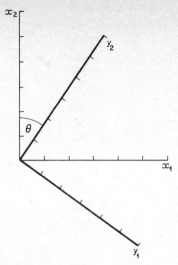

Figure 2.1 *Rotation of axes*

the latter the covariance or correlation of each pair of variables is used. These quantities are defined below.

Means   The population mean vector $\mu' = [\mu_1, \ldots, \mu_p]$, where

$$\mu_i = E(x_i) \tag{2.28}$$

An estimate of μ based on n, p-dimensional observations is $\bar{\mathbf{x}}' = (\bar{x}_1 \cdots \bar{x}_p)$, where $\bar{x}_i$ is the sample mean of variable x_i.

Variance   The vector of population variances is $\sigma' = [\sigma_1^2, \sigma_2^2, \ldots, \sigma_p^2]$ where

$$\sigma_i^2 = E(x_i^2) - \mu_i^2 \tag{2.29}$$

An estimate of σ based on n, p-dimensional observations is $\mathbf{s}' = (s_1^2, \ldots, s_p^2)$, where s_i^2 is the sample variance of variable x_i.

Covariance   The covariance of two variables x_i and x_j is defined by

$$\text{Cov}(x_i, x_j) = E(x_i x_j) - \mu_i \mu_j \tag{2.30}$$

If $i = j$, we note that the covariance of a variable with itself is simply its variance, and there is therefore no need to define variances and covariances independently in the multivariate case.

The covariance of x_i and x_j is usually denoted by σ_{ij}. (So the variance of variable x_i is often denoted by σ_{ii} rather than σ_i^2.)

With p variables, $x_1, \ldots, x_p$, there are p variances and $\frac{1}{2}p(p-1)$

covariances. In general these quantities are arrayed in the $p \times p$ symmetric matrix, Σ, where

$$\Sigma = \begin{bmatrix} \sigma_{11} & \sigma_{12} & \cdots & \sigma_{1p} \\ \sigma_{21} & \sigma_{22} & & \\ \vdots & & & \\ \sigma_{p1} & \cdots & \cdots & \sigma_{pp} \end{bmatrix} \qquad (2.31)$$

(Note that $\sigma_{ij} = \sigma_{ji}$.) This matrix is generally known as the *variance-covariance* matrix or simply as the *covariance* matrix. Σ may be written as

$$= E(\mathbf{x}\mathbf{x}') - \boldsymbol{\mu}\boldsymbol{\mu}' \qquad (2.32)$$

An estimate of Σ based on n sample observations is given by

$$\mathbf{S} = \frac{1}{n-1} \sum_{i=1}^{n} (\mathbf{x}_1 - \bar{\mathbf{x}})(\mathbf{x}_i - \bar{\mathbf{x}})' \qquad (2.33)$$

Correlation The covariance is difficult to interpret because it depends on the units in which the two variables are measured. Thus the covariance is often standardised by dividing by the product of the standard deviations of the two variables to give a quantity called the *correlation coefficient*, ρ_{ij}, where

$$\rho_{ij} = \frac{\sigma_{ij}}{\sigma_i \sigma_j} \qquad (2.34)$$

and σ_i is the standard deviation of variable x_i. ρ_{ij} lies between -1 and 1 and gives a measure of the *linear* relationship of variables x_i and x_j. It is positive if 'high' values of x_i are associated with 'high' values of x_j and negative if 'high' values of x_i are associated with 'low' values of x_j.

With p variables there are $p(p-1)/2$ distinct correlations which may be arrayed in a $p \times p$ matrix, $\mathbf{R}$, whose diagonal elements are unity. This may be written as a function of the covariance matrix as follows:

$$\mathbf{R} = \mathbf{D}^{-1}\Sigma\mathbf{D}^{-1}, \qquad (2.35)$$

where

$$\mathbf{D} = \begin{bmatrix} \sigma_1 & 0 & & 0 \\ 0 & \sigma_2 & & \\ & & \ddots & \\ 0 & & & \sigma_p \end{bmatrix}$$

In most situations we will be dealing with covariance and correlation matrices of full rank, p, so that both matrices will be non-singular. However, in some circumstances variables may be so highly correlated that the covariance or correlation matrix may be 'nearly singular'. (See comments in Chapter 8 on ridge regression.)

Many of the methods of analysis to be described in this text involve linear compounds of the original variables, $x_1, \ldots, x_p$, that is variables constructed thus:

$$y = a_1 x_1 + a_2 x_2 + \cdots + a_p x_p \qquad (2.36)$$

or

$$y = \mathbf{a}'\mathbf{x}$$

where $\mathbf{a}' = [a_1, a_2, \ldots, a_p]$ and y is a univariate variable whose mean is given by

$$E(y) = \mathbf{a}'\boldsymbol{\mu} \qquad (2.37)$$

and whose variance is given by

$$\text{Var}(y) = E[\{\mathbf{a}'(\mathbf{x} - \boldsymbol{\mu})\}^2] \qquad (2.38)$$

Now $\mathbf{a}'(\mathbf{x} - \boldsymbol{\mu})$ is a scalar, and thus is equal to its transpose, so (2.38) may be rewritten as

$$\text{Var}(y) = E\{\mathbf{a}'(\mathbf{x} - \boldsymbol{\mu})(\mathbf{x} - \boldsymbol{\mu})'\mathbf{a}\} \qquad (2.39)$$

$$= \mathbf{a}'\{E(\mathbf{x} - \boldsymbol{\mu})(\mathbf{x} - \boldsymbol{\mu})'\} \cdot \mathbf{a}$$

$$= \mathbf{a}'\boldsymbol{\Sigma}\mathbf{a} \qquad (2.40)$$

2.5 Maximum Likelihood Estimation

Of primary concern in many analyses is the estimation of the parameters of a statistical distribution or of a statistical model. Many methods of estimation have been developed, and for a comprehensive account of this branch of statistics readers are referred to Kendall and Stuart (1963). In this section we shall concentrate on introducing the basic ideas of *maximum likelihood* estimation, perhaps the most widely used of these techniques. To introduce this method let us assume that we have a single random variable, x, whose density function is $f(x; \theta)$ where θ is the parameter to be estimated. For a sample of n observations of this variable, $x_1, x_2, \ldots, x_n$, the *likelihood function*, $\mathscr{L}$ is defined by

$$\mathscr{L} = f(x_1; \theta)f(x_2; \theta) \cdots f(x_n; \theta) \qquad (2.41)$$

$$= \prod_{i=1}^{n} f(x_i; \theta)$$

The maximum likelihood estimate, $\hat{\theta}$, is defined as that value of θ which maximises $\mathscr{L}$. It may be found by solving the equation

$$\frac{d\mathscr{L}}{d\theta} = 0 \tag{2.42}$$

In many cases it may be more convenient to maximise $L = \log_e \mathscr{L}$; this involves solving the equation

$$\frac{dL}{d\theta} = 0 \tag{2.43}$$

Both equations (2.42) and (2.43) will lead to the same value for $\hat{\theta}$.

To illustrate the method let us first consider a random variable with an exponential distribution, that is

$$f(x; \theta) = \theta \, e^{-\theta x} \tag{2.44}$$

The likelihood function for the n observations $x_1, \ldots, x_n$ takes the form

$$\mathscr{L} = \theta \, e^{-\theta x_1} \, \theta \, e^{-\theta x_2} \cdots \theta \, e^{-\theta x_n} \tag{2.45}$$

$$= \theta n e^{-\theta \sum\limits_{i=1}^{n} x_i}$$

Taking logarithms gives

$$L = n \log_e \theta - \theta \sum_{i=1}^{n} x_i \tag{2.46}$$

Differentiating L with respect to θ gives

$$\frac{dL}{d\theta} = \frac{n}{\theta} - \sum x_i \tag{2.47}$$

Setting equation (2.47) equal to zero leads to

$$\hat{\theta} = \frac{n}{\sum\limits_{i=1}^{n} x_i} \tag{2.48}$$

In some cases the distribution of x will depend upon more than a single parameter, that is θ will be a vector rather than a scalar. Perhaps the best-known example is the normal distribution.

$$f(x; \mu, \sigma^2) = \frac{1}{\sqrt{2\pi}\sigma} \exp -\frac{1}{2}\left(\frac{x-\mu}{\sigma}\right)^2 \tag{2.49}$$

For this distribution the log-likelihood function, L, is given by

$$L = -\frac{1}{2\sigma^2} \sum_{k=1}^{n} (x_i - \mu)^2 - \tfrac{1}{2}n \log_e \sigma^2 - \tfrac{1}{2}n \log_e 2\pi \qquad (2.50)$$

So that

$$\frac{\partial L}{\partial \mu} = \frac{1}{\sigma^2} \sum_{i=1}^{n} (x_i - \mu) \qquad (2.51)$$

$$\frac{\partial L}{\partial \sigma^2} = \frac{1}{2\sigma^4} \sum_{i=1}^{n} (x_i - \mu)^2 - \frac{n}{2\sigma^2} \qquad (2.52)$$

Setting equations (2.51) and (2.52) to zero leads to the estimates

$$\hat{\mu} = \frac{1}{n} \sum_{i=1}^{n} x_i, \qquad (2.53)$$

$$\hat{\sigma}^2 = \frac{1}{n} \sum_{i=1}^{n} (x_i - \bar{x})^2. \qquad (2.54)$$

Maximum likelihood estimates (MLE) have a number of desirable properties which are discussed in the aforementioned Kendall and Stuart (1963). One important result which we should note is that the variances and covariances of the estimates are obtained from the inverse of the information matrix, **I**, which has elements given by

$$i_{jj} = E\left(\frac{\partial \log f}{\partial \theta_j^2}\right)^2, \qquad (2.55)$$

and

$$i_{jk} = E\left(\frac{\partial \log f}{\partial \theta_j} \cdot \frac{\partial \log f}{\partial \theta_k}\right) \qquad (2.56)$$

The covariance matrix of the maximum likelihood estimators is given by $(n\mathbf{I})^{-1}$, where n is the sample size. This may be estimated by substituting the MLE themselves for parameter values in **I** (see Exercise 2.4). The information matrix is important for a number of reasons (see Kendall and Stuart, 1963).

In the simple examples given above, the equations defining the MLE (for example, equations (2.51) and (2.52)) may be solved explicitly. In some cases however this is not so, since they involve complex non-linear expressions in the parameters. In such cases the equations must be solved by some type of iterative procedure, of which the most well known is Newton's method (again, see Kendall and Stuart, 1963). Alternatively the maximisation of $\mathscr{L}$ or L may be attacked directly using the alternative optimisation techniques that are described in the next section.

2.6   Optimisation Methods

Optimisation in its simplest form is concerned with finding the maximum or minimum value of a mathematical function. For example, Figure 2.2 shows a plot of the function $f(x) = x^2$, and we can see that this takes its minimum value at $x = 0$. From this figure we can see that if a point x^* corresponds to the minimum value of function $f(x)$, the same point also corresponds to the maximum value of the negative of the function, $-f(x)$. Consequently, without loss of generality, *optimisation* can be taken to mean minimisation, since the maximum of a function can be found by seeking the minimum of the negative of the same function.

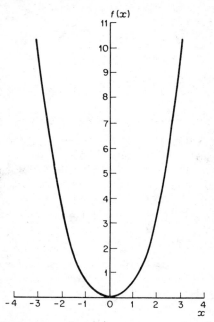

Figure 2.2   *Plot of* $f(x) = x^2$

There is no single method available for solving all optimisation problems efficiently, so that a variety of techniques have been developed for dealing with different types of problem.

The simplest optimisation problems concern functions of a single variable, $f(x)$, and it is easy to show that a *necessary* condition for a minimum of $f(x)$ is that

$$\frac{df}{dx} = 0 \qquad (2.57)$$

A *sufficient* condition for a point satisfying these equations to be a minimum is that

$$\frac{d^2f}{dx^2} > 0 \qquad (2.58)$$

For example, suppose we wish to find the minimum value of the function, $f(x) = (x - a)^2$, where a is some constant.

$$\frac{df}{dx} = 2(x - a) \qquad (2.59)$$

Setting equation (2.59) to zero gives $x = a$. To check that this corresponds to a minimum we need to evaluate the second differential of f with respect to x.

$$\frac{d^2f}{dx^2} = 2 \qquad (2.60)$$

This is always greater than zero so that the point $x = a$ corresponds to a minimum value of $f(x)$.

For a function of several variables corresponding conditions to equations (2.57) and (2.58) can be found for a minimum; details are given in Box, Davies and Swann (1969).

From a practical point-of-view the disadvantages of trying to determine the minimum of a function from consideration of equations such as (2.57) and (2.58) are considerable. A major problem is that in many cases equation (2.57)—or its equivalent in situations involving several variables—will be formidable, and its solution present considerable difficulties. Consequently a different approach is adopted which requires an initial point x_0 to be specified and proceeds by generating a sequence of points $x_1, x_2, \ldots$ which represent improved approximations to the solution, that is

$$f(x_{i+1}) \leqslant f(x_i) \qquad (2.61)$$

Such *iterative techniques* fall into two major classes, *direct search methods* and *gradient methods*. Here we restrict ourselves to a brief description of one technique from the latter class, namely the method of *steepest descent*; details of many other methods from both classes are available in Box *et al.* (1969).

Steepest descent
Suppose we wish to find the minimum of a function of several variables, $x_1, \ldots, x_m$. Starting from a given initial point, $\mathbf{x}_0' = [x_1^0, \ldots, x_m^0]$, we

wish to generate a sequence of points $\mathbf{x}_1, \mathbf{x}_2, \ldots$ such that

$$f(\mathbf{x}_{i+1}) \leqslant f(\mathbf{x}_i) \tag{2.62}$$

The method of steepest descent generates this sequence from the following general iterative rule:

$$\mathbf{x}_{i+1} = \mathbf{x}_i + h_i \mathbf{d}_i \tag{2.63}$$

where h_i is a scalar known as the *step size* and $\mathbf{d}_i$ is the search direction defined by

$$\mathbf{d}_i = \left[-\frac{\partial f}{\partial x_1}, -\frac{\partial f}{\partial x_2}, \ldots, -\frac{\partial f}{\partial x_m} \right] \tag{2.64}$$

evaluated at the current point $\mathbf{x}_i' = [x_1^{(i)}, x_2^{(i)}, \ldots, x_m^{(i)}]$. The rationale behind this procedure is explained in detail in Box *et al.*, Chapter 4. Essentially, however, the greatest change in the function occurs when the components of the search direction are chosen to be proportional to the corresponding $\partial f / \partial x_1$, and for this change to be a decrease the constant of proportionality must be negative.

A basic application of the method would be as follows. Determine the gradient vector at the current point and, using a specified step-length, h_i, obtain a new point by applying the general iterative rule (2.64). This procedure is then repeated using a constant step-length until a step which does not reduce the function value is taken. In this case the step-length is reduced and the procedure continued from the best point. Iteration is continued until some convergence criterion is satisfied; for example, until all the elements of $\mathbf{d}_i$ are almost zero. The

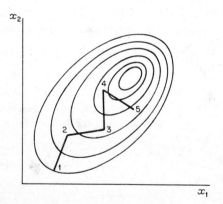

Figure 2.3   *Example of steepest descent*
(Reproduced with permission from Box et al., 1969)

performance of the method for a function of two variables is demonstrated in Figure 2.3. At point 5 the function is greater than at point 4, so a reduction in the step-length is called for before restarting the search from point 4 (see also Exercise 2.6).

Optimisation methods have become of great importance in modern statistics, and are used in many of the techniques discussed in this book.

EXERCISES

2.1   Find the rank of the matrix

$$A = \begin{bmatrix} 1 & 3 & 1 & 2 & 1 \\ 8 & 2 & 1 & 2 & 1 \\ 8 & 6 & 8 & 1 & 1 \\ 1 & 5 & 7 & 4 & 4 \\ 10 & 8 & 3 & 6 & 5 \end{bmatrix}$$

2.2   Find the eigenvalues and normalised eigenvectors of

$$B = \begin{bmatrix} 2 & 1 & 1 \\ 1 & 2 & 1 \\ 1 & 1 & 2 \end{bmatrix}$$

2.3   If A is of order $(m \times n)$, and B and C are square, non-singular matrices of order $(m \times m)$ and $(n \times n)$ respectively show that

$$\text{rank } (A) = \text{rank } (BA) = \text{rank } (AC)$$

2.4   Find the information matrix for the maximum likelihood estimates of the two parameters of a normal distribution.

2.5   Show that the function $f(x) = x^2 + 2x + 3$ has a minimum at $x = -1$.

2.6   Use the method of steepest descent to find the minimum of the function in Exercise 2.5, starting from the point $x = 3$ with step size $h = 0.2$.

2.7   If the random vector $x' = [x_1, x_2, x_3]$ has variance-covariance matrix, Σ, given by

$$\Sigma = \begin{bmatrix} \sigma_{11} & \sigma_{12} & \sigma_{13} \\ \sigma_{21} & \sigma_{22} & \sigma_{23} \\ \sigma_{31} & \sigma_{32} & \sigma_{33} \end{bmatrix}$$

find the covariance of the variables y_1 and y_2 given by

$$y_1 = x_1 + x_2 + x_3,$$

$$y_2 = x_1 - x_3.$$

PART II
Exploring Multivariate Data

Chapters 3 to 6 cover a variety of methods which are primarily of use for the exploration of multivariate data. In a very general sense their aim might be considered to be that of detecting patterns or indicating potentially interesting relationships in the data. Only when some pattern is thought to exist can the further steps be taken of setting up models and hypotheses for future investigation. (In many cases, of course, investigators might feel that an informative description of their data provided by one of the techniques to be discussed in this section completes the analysis.)

A theme common to many of the methods to be described in this part of the text is the production of results in the form of a graph or some other type of visual display. This allows the investigator to get a 'view' of the data that might have an impact impossible or at least difficult to achieve by the mere examination of statistics derived from the data. This aspect of the analysis of data is also relevant to the subsequent presentation of the results to other scientists. This is an area that is often ignored by data analysts so that potentially important findings are sometimes missed through inadequate and uninteresting reporting of the results. The impact of graphical representations of multivariate data can often be enhanced by the use of colour, but unfortunately this is very rarely practicable in research articles or textbooks. But colour can frequently be put to good use in the summary of results on transparencies that are to be used in lectures and seminars.

---

3. Preliminary Data Analysis

3.1 Introduction

Much statistical analysis of data is now carried out with the aid of computers, particularly through the use of computer program packages. This is obviously to be welcomed because it frees the investigator from the burden of large amounts of repetitive arithmetic. Indeed, many analyses now performed routinely could not be attempted at all without the aid of a computer. However, the wide availability of computers and computer packages for complex analyses such as multidimensional scaling (Chapter 5), multiple regression (Chapter 8),

23

or factor analysis (Chapter 11), is not without its problems, since it has fostered in some research workers the unfortunate tendency to rush into the use of complicated methods of analysis without first considering some simple preliminary techniques designed to give them a general 'feel' of their data. Such techniques may serve several purposes. They may, for example, give an early indication of the presence of *outliers* (that is, observations which appear to be inconsistent with the rest of the data). These may be caused by recording or punching errors (in which case they may be corrected and included for further analysis), or they may be genuine observations indicative, perhaps, of an unusual distribution of the data. In either case outliers need to be detected since they can have the effect of greatly distorting the results of analyses carried out by many of the techniques to be discussed in later chapters. A detailed account of the detection of outliers is given in Barnett and Lewis (1978).

In the early phase of an analysis the techniques discussed in this chapter might prove helpful in indicating which of the more complicated exploratory techniques could usefully be applied to the data. For example, an Andrews plot (see Section 3.4) might suggest the presence of distinct 'clusters' of observations, indicating that further investigation via some form of multidimensional scaling (Chapter 5) or cluster analysis (Chapter 6) might be fruitful.

3.2   Rearranging Tables of Numerical Data

The raw data collected in most research investigations will initially consist of a table of numbers. Examples of these are latencies for a number of subjects, examination results for a sample of students, ratings on a number of symptoms for a group of psychiatric patients, and so on. Often these raw data are converted into a further table of numbers, such as a correlation or proximity matrix, depending on the type of question of interest to the investigator. Most investigators would spend little time considering such tables directly, but instead would proceed to apply whatever form of analysis they thought to be appropriate. It is worth considering, however, whether anything might be gleaned from simply examining the original table.

Ehrenberg (1977) argues that many tables appear to be uninformative simply because they are badly presented, and, with the application of some intuitively simple rules, many could be made far more useful. These rules consist of rounding the numbers to two significant or effective digits, placing those numbers that need to be compared in columns rather than rows, and organising the spacing and layout of the table so that the eye does not have too far to travel in making comparisons.

Table 3.1   *Unemployment in Great Britain—original version (Taken with permission from Ehrenberg, 1977.)*

	1966	1968	1970	1973
Total Unemployed (thousands)	330.9	549.4	582.2	597.9
Males	259.6	460.7	495.3	494.4
Females	71.3	88.8	86.9	98.5

Table   3.2   *Unemployment   in   Great   Britain — rearranged table*

	Unemployed (000s)		
GB	Total	Male	Female
1966	330	260	71
1968	550	460	89
1970	580	500	87
1973	600	500	99
Average	520	430	86

Table 3.1, for example, gives some data concerning unemployment in Great Britain over four selected years, as originally presented in a government publication. Rounding the data, and transposing rows and columns, gives Table 3.2. Here it is far easier to detect variations and sub-patterns. Contrary to the total trend, for example, the female figures levelled off only for 1968 and 1970. It is also clear that the 1973 figure is particularly high. When compared with Table 3.1, Table 3.2 gives us a much better 'feel' for the data.

Rounding and a rearrangement of rows and columns can also be useful in dealing with correlation matrices. For example, Table 3.3 (reproduced from Maxwell, 1977) shows a correlation matrix for nine rating scales obtained from a sample of 380 adults. In the case of a relatively small matrix it is often possible, by visual examination of the elements, to discover subsets of variables which correlate relatively highly with each other. For the matrix in Table 3.3 this appears to be the case, since a close examination shows that the variates tend to fall into three groups namely (1, 2, 6), (3, 4, 7) and (5, 8, 9). Rearranging the rows and columns according to these groups and rounding the figures gives Table 3.4, where the three-group pattern is clearly visible. This 'analysis' required nothing more than a little careful thought and a pencil and paper. Nevertheless it makes almost redundant (for this

Table 3.3   *Correlation matrix for nine rating scales*

	1	2	3	4	5	6	7	8	9
1	1.000								
2	0.638	1.000							
3	0.017	0.193	1.000						
4	0.139	0.097	0.616	1.000					
5	0.150	0.245	−0.181	−0.372	1.000				
6	0.704	0.570	0.015	0.179	0.081	1.000			
7	0.114	0.238	0.543	0.476	0.012	0.102	1.000		
8	0.160	0.196	0.302	0.100	0.252	0.007	0.213	1.000	
9	0.228	0.269	0.041	−0.052	0.533	0.172	0.145	0.447	1.000

Table 3.4   *Correlations for rating scales in rearranged order and rounded to one decimal place*

	1	2	6	3	4	7	5	8	9
1	1.0								
2	0.6	1.0							
6	0.7	0.6	1.0						
3	0.0	0.2	0.0	1.0					
4	0.1	0.1	0.2	0.6	1.0				
7	0.1	0.2	0.1	0.5	0.5	1.0			
5	0.1	0.2	0.1	−0.2	−0.4	0.0	1.0		
8	0.2	0.2	0.0	0.3	0.1	0.2	0.4	1.0	
9	0.2	0.3	0.2	0.0	0.0	0.1	0.5	0.4	1.0

particular data set) the more formal methods of looking at the structure or pattern in correlation matrices (factor analysis, for example). Of course, for larger examples this may no longer be the case.

3.3   Simple Plots of Data

Although the preceding section has illustrated that tables of numbers can be made more informative, many research workers are happier when examining representations of their data in the form of diagrams or graphs. Mahon (1977) argues that tables are best for indicating *values* and graphs for indicating *relationships*, although for an effective presentation it is usually necessary to use them in combination. Much, of course, depends on the taste of the individual investigator.

For univariate data a number of simple graphical techniques are available which can provide useful views and summaries of the data. Many of these, such as histograms, frequency polygons and cumulative frequency plots, are well known and are described in all elementary statistical textbooks. Others such as the *stem-and-leaf* display, and the *box-and-whisker* plot, have come into vogue only during the last decade and are associated with the name of Tukey. An excellent introduction to them is given in Hartwig and Dearing (1979).

For bivariate data the standard graphical technique is the *scatter-plot*, which can be useful for indicating various aspects of the relationship between the two variables; for example, whether they are linearly related, whether the scatter of one of the variables is constant over different values of the second variable, and so on. Hartwig and Dearing describe some useful techniques for summarising these relationships; again they are primarily due to Tukey.

With multivariate data the problem of making simple, informative plots is more difficult. Each variable could be examined separately by means of a stem-and-leaf plot and so on, or each pair of variables used to provide a scattergram. Such marginal views of the data may in some cases be very helpful, but could be misleading simply because the marginal distributions of multivariate data do not necessarily reflect adequately its multidimensional structure. An example appears in Figure 3.1, where the univariate marginal distributions do not indicate the complex structure of the bivariate data. Despite this an examination of the distribution of values on each variable, and a selection of bivariate views, might prove very helpful in many situations. Tukey and Tukey (1981a) demonstrate some interesting ideas about how such plots may be arranged so as to be as informative as possible. For example, for data involving three variables the six two-dimensional views could be arranged in the form of a lower triangular matrix.

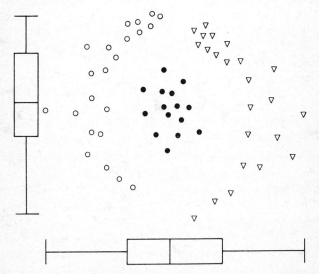

Figure 3.1   *Two-dimensional multimodal data having unimodal marginals (as indicated by the box-and-whisker plots)*

A variety of ingenious suggestions have been made for obtaining simple plots of multivariate data containing information from more than two of the variables. For example, Gower (1967) reports a method due to Ross in which two variables are used to provide a scatterplot of the data. Information on a third variable is now included in this diagram by drawing, from each point, a line with length proportional to that observation's value on this third variable and directed eastwards if this value is positive and westward if negative. Similarly, for a fourth variable the north/south direction could be used and for variables five and six the NE/SW and NW/SE directions. An example of this type of plot is given in Everitt (1978).

In the same vein is a technique known as a *weathervane plot*, introduced by Bruntz *et al.* (1974). These authors were interested in analysing air pollution data, and some of the variables of interest were amounts of solar radiation, wind speed and direction, and temperature. Figure 3.2 taken from Gnanadesikan (1977) shows a weathervane plot for a particular data set. Here the abscissa is used for the total solar radiation from 8 a.m. to noon, while the ordinate is the average ozone level observed from 1 p.m. to 3 p.m. The plot is for a specific site, and the centres of the circles correspond to different days. These points provide information on the relationship between ozone levels and solar radiation. The diameter of the circle surrounding each such point is

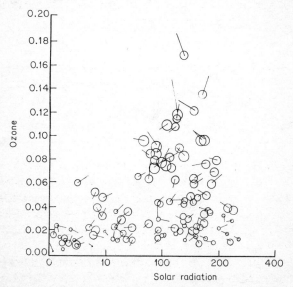

Figure 3.2   *Weathervane plot (Taken with permission from Gnanadesikan, 1977)*

proportional to the observed daily maximum temperature, while the line projecting from the circle is such that its length is inversely proportional to an average wind speed. Also, if the lines are considered as arrows whose heads are at the centres of the circles, then the orientations of these lines correspond to average wind directions.

Figure 3.2 displays the relationships between five variables and enables some overall patterns in the data to be detected. For example, at a given level of solar radiation, ozone seems to increase as temperature increases and wind speed decreases. Wind direction does not appear to play a major influence in these data.

Such plots will clearly become confusing if more than four or five variables are included. Consequently, their use on the raw data is likely to be limited. However, they may prove useful when applied to a reduced number of dimensions obtained from a technique such as principal components analysis (see Chapter 4). (Some other ideas for including extra information on scatterplots are given in Tukey and Tukey, 1981c.)

3.4 Andrews Plots and Chernoff Faces
During the last decade two novel techniques for the graphical display of multivariate data have been introduced. The first, due to Andrews (1972), represents each multidimensional observation as a function of a particular form. The second, due to Chernoff (1973), represents the multivariate observations as cartoon faces.

3.4.1 Andrews plots
This procedure is essentially very simple; each of the p-dimensional observations, $\mathbf{x}' = [x_1, x_2, \ldots, x_p]$, is mapped into a function of the form

$$f_x(t) = x_1/\sqrt{2} + x_2 \sin(t) + x_3 \cos(t) + x_4 \sin(2t)$$

$$+ x_5 \cos(2t) + \cdots \qquad (3.1)$$

This function is then plotted over the range $-\pi \leqslant t \leqslant \pi$. A set of multivariate observations will now appear as a set of lines on the plot. The usefulness of this particular representation lies primarily in the fact that this function preserves Euclidean distances, in the sense that observations close together in the original p-dimensional space will correspond to lines on the plot that remain close together for all values of t; points far apart in the original space will be represented by lines which remain apart for at least some values of t. This property allows the plots to be examined for distinct groups of observations, outlying observations and so on. For example, Figure 3.3 shows an Andrews

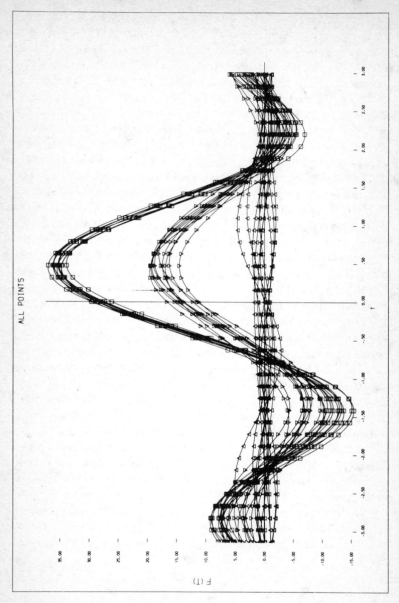

Figure 3.3 *Andrews plot for 30 five-dimensional observations*

plot for 30 five-dimensional observations. This clearly indicates the presence in the data of three well-separated groups of observations. Such a result may lead to the application of some method of cluster analysis (see Chapter 6) to these data in an effort to confirm the presence of the distinct groups, although for this particular data set, the result from the Andrews plot is so clear-cut that further, more complex analysis is really not required.

A problem which arises when using this technique is that only a fairly limited number of observations may be plotted on the same diagram before it becomes too confused to be helpful. Various procedures might be adopted in order to overcome this problem. For example, first a plot of all observations could be produced to assess the general characteristics of the sample. This could be followed by separate plots of each set of, say, ten observations which could be examined and compared to the whole. Alternatively, selected quantiles or percentage points of the distribution of the n values of f could be plotted along with the curves of selected individual observations. An example of such a plot is given in Gnanadesikan (1977).

Examining the form of the function involved in Andrews plots (see equation (3.1)), it is clear that the original variables are not equally weighted. Some are associated with cyclic components having a high frequency, others with components having a low frequency. Since in these plots low frequency components are more informative than those with high frequencies, it may be useful to associate x_1 with the variable considered, in some sense, to be the most important, x_2 with the second most important, and so on. In the absence of any firm ideas as to such an order of variables, it may be useful to apply Andrews' technique not to the raw data but to the transformed variables obtained from principal components analysis (see Chapter 4), since these will automatically be in order of decreasing importance in a particular sense.

Some other possible functions which could be used in place of that in equation (3.1) are given in Andrews (1972) and Gnanadesikan (1977), and an interesting application of the procedure is described by Morgan (1981).

3.4.2 Chernoff faces

Chernoff (1973) describes a method for representing multivariate data in which each multivariate observation has a corresponding face, the features of which are governed by the values taken by particular variables. A sample of multivariate observations is now represented by a collection of such faces and these may then be examined to assess the similarities and differences between observations. Figure 3.4, for example, shows a set of thirty faces representing a sample of multivariate observations generated to contain three distinct groups. These are clearly indicated by an examination of the faces.

This technique has been criticised by a number of statisticians (for example, Chatfield and Collins, 1980) on the grounds of its subjectivity, since different observers are very likely to weight facial features in different ways. Without doubt this is a problem. However, a degree of subjectivity is unlikely to be entirely absent from other graphical techniques, and a set of faces does have the advantage of providing a more interesting representation than many other techniques. Conse-

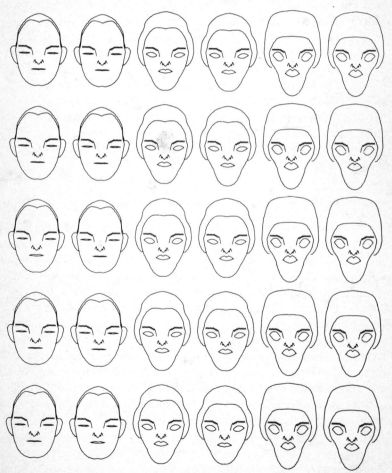

Figure 3.4   *Faces representation of 30 multidimensional observations*

quently investigators may be willing to spend more time and effort in studying faces and this could result in greater insights into the data. Certainly, used in particular ways, a faces representation can provide a dramatic display of multivariate data (see Figure 4.5). A recent addition to the faces technique is the use of asymmetric faces; see Flury and Riedwyl (1981).

3.5 Probability Plots

Probability plots are well known from univariate statistics where they are used to check distributional assumptions and to obtain rough estimates of distribution parameters. The basic procedure involves ordering the observations and then plotting them against the appropriate values of the assumed cumulative distribution function. (Details are given in Everitt, 1978, Chapter 4.) For multivariate data such plots may be used to examine each variable separately. Alternatively the multivariate observation might be converted to a single number in some way. For example, if we were interested in assessing a data set for multivariate normality, we could convert each observation, x_i, into a *generalised distance*, d_i^2, giving a measure of the separation of the particular observation from the mean vector of the complete sample, $\bar{x}$; d_i^2 is given by

$$d_i^2 = (x_i - \bar{x})'S^{-1}(x_i - \bar{x}) \tag{3.2}$$

where S is the sample covariance matrix. If the data do arise from a multivariate normal distribution, then these distances have, approximately, a chi-square distribution with p degrees of freedom. So, plotting the ordered distances against the corresponding quantiles of the appropriate chi-square distribution should lead to a straight line through the origin. Figure 3.5, for example, shows such a plot for 200 observations from a five-dimensional multivariate normal distribution.

Departure from linearity in such plots indicates that the data do not have a multivariate normal distribution. An example of this is seen in Figure 3.6, which is a chi-square plot of 200 five-dimensional observations generated from a population containing two distinct groups. Such plots are often also useful in indicating outliers, as is illustrated for again some five-dimensional data in Figure 3.7.

3.6 Summary

The techniques and procedures described in this chapter are primarily

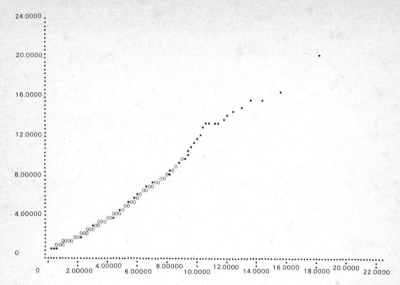

Figure 3.5   *Chi-square plot of generalised distance for 200 observations from a five-dimensional multivariate normal distribution. In Figures 3.5–3.7 the theoretical quantiles are plotted along the x-axis and the ordered generalised distances along the y-axis.*

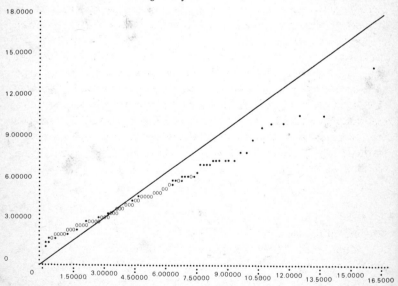

Figure 3.6   *Chi-square plot for five-dimensional data containing two distinct groups*

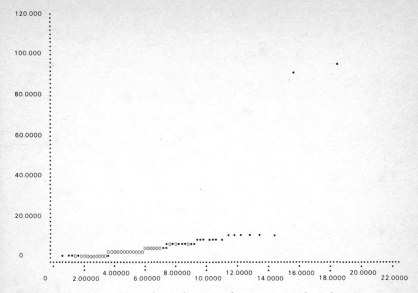

Figure 3.7 *Chi-square plot indicating the presence of outliers*

of use in the early stages of data analysis when the investigator is attempting to gain insights into any interesting patterns or relationships in the data which can be further explored by more complex techniques at some later stage of the analysis. The methods are generally easy to use and do not take up enormous amounts of computer time, and it would be encouraging to see a wider use of these preliminary procedures rather than an increase in the tendency simply to submit the data to a standard (and often irrelevant) procedure via a computer package. (Some very interesting examples of other methods for the preliminary investigation of multivariate data are given in Barnett, 1981, Kleiner and Hartigan, 1981, and Tukey and Tukey, 1981a, b and c.)

EXERCISES
3.1   Yule *et al.* (1969) administered 10 cognitive tests from the Wechsler series to 150 children, graded as good or poor readers. The correlation matrix for good readers on the ten tests is shown below. By suitable rounding and rearrangement of rows and columns show that the tests tend to fall into two groups.

(1)	(2)	(3)	(4)	(5)	(6)	(7)	(8)	(9)	(10)
1.000	0.409	0.332	0.270	0.483	−0.048	0.091	−0.100	0.137	0.106
	1.000	0.285	0.266	0.452	0.138	0.201	−0.055	0.026	0.169
		1.000	0.323	0.360	0.221	0.183	0.094	0.221	0.411
			1.000	0.262	0.262	0.164	0.068	0.222	0.383
				1.000	0.201	0.208	0.165	0.234	0.252
					1.000	0.389	0.315	0.036	0.266
						1.000	0.371	0.127	0.472
							1.000	0.352	0.432
								1.000	0.330
									1.000

3.2   The following data are failure times, in days, of 45 transmissions from caterpillar tractors belonging to the Atkinson Construction Company, South San Francisco.

4381	3953	2603	2320	1161	3286	6914	4007	3168	2376	7498	3923
	9460	4525	2168	1288	5085	2217	6922	218	1309	1875	1023
	1697	1038	3699	6142	4732	3330	4159	2537	3814	2157	7683
	5539	4839	6052	2420	5556	309	1295	3266	6679	1711	5931

Construct a sensible stem-and-leaf display of the data and from it calculate the median and midspread. (See Hartwig and Daring, 1979, and Erickson and Nosanchuk, 1979.)

3.3   The following table shows the hours of work needed to earn the price of the same basket of goods in selected occupations for a number of European cities in 1973.

City	Primary teachers	Bus drivers	Bank tellers	Secretaries
Athens	25	43	30	42
Brussels	19	24	15	20
Copenhagen	25	28	27	31
Düsseldorf	15	26	22	30
Geneva	11	21	18	28
Helsinki	17	26	33	34
Istanbul	36	64	46	39
Lisbon	14	42	18	22
London	18	20	18	20
Luxemburg	10	16	14	25
Madrid	13	38	24	34
Milan	22	23	13	27
Oslo	18	22	21	27
Paris	15	21	20	26
Rome	25	20	15	32
Stockholm	18	25	24	32
Vienna	19	26	22	30
Zurich	11	21	18	26

Construct scatter plots for each pair of occupations and comment on your results.

3.4 Construct a set of Andrews plots for the cities in the above example. Do these suggest that the cities fall into distinct groups?

3.5 The data over relate to the number of crimes of different types prt 100,000 population in several American cities. A representation of these data in terms of cartoon faces is also shown (see Figure 3.8). Does the table of raw data or the set of faces give greater insights into any pattern in these data? (See also Figures 4.4 and 4.5.)

1 Atlanta
2 Boston
3 Chicago
4 Dallas
5 Denver
6 Detroit
7 Hartford
8 Honolulu
9 Houston
10 Kansas City
11 Los Angeles
12 New Orleans
13 New York
14 Portland
15 Tucson
16 Washington

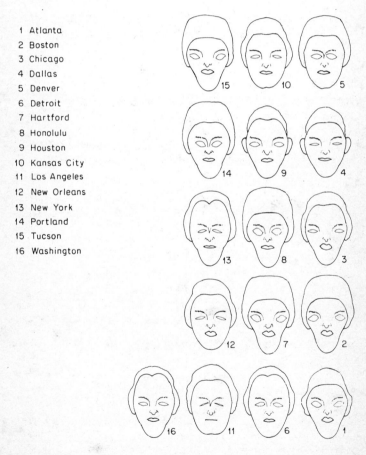

Figure 3.8 *Faces representation of city crime data*

	Murder Man-slaughter	Rape	Robbery	Assault	Burglary	Larceny	Auto Theft
Atlanta	16.5	24.8	106	147	1112	905	494
Boston	4.2	13.3	122	90	982	669	954
Chicago	11.6	24.7	340	242	808	609	645
Dallas	18.1	34.2	184	293	1668	901	602
Denver	6.9	41.5	173	191	1534	1368	780
Detroit	13.0	35.7	477	220	1566	1183	788
Hartford	2.5	8.8	68	103	1017	724	468
Honolulu	3.6	12.7	42	28	1457	1102	637
Houston	16.8	26.6	289	186	1509	787	697
Kansas City	10.8	43.2	255	226	1494	955	765
Los Angeles	9.7	51.8	286	355	1902	1386	862
New Orleans	10.3	39.7	266	283	1056	1036	776
New York	9.4	19.4	522	267	1674	1392	848
Portland	5.0	23.0	157	144	1530	1281	488
Tucson	5.1	22.9	85	148	1206	756	483
Washington	12.5	27.6	524	217	1496	1003	739

(Data taken, with permission, from Hartigan, 1975.)

4. Principal Components Analysis

4.1 Introduction

Principal components analysis is perhaps the most widely used multivariate technique. The basic idea of the method is to describe the variation of the n individuals in p-dimensional space in terms of a set of uncorrelated variables which are linear combinations of the original variables. The new variables are derived in decreasing order of importance so that, for example, the first principal component accounts for as much as possible of the variation in the original data. The usual objective of this type of analysis is to see whether the first few components account for most of the variation in the original data. If they do, then it is argued that they can be used to summarise the data with little loss of information, thus providing a reduction in the dimensionality of the data, which might be very useful in simplifying later analyses.

For example, consider a situation where one has data consisting of several examination results for each of a number of students. A question of interest might be how to construct an informative index of examination achievement. One obvious index is the mean score, although if the possible or observed range of examination scores varies from one subject to another it might be more sensible to produce some kind of weighted mean, or alternatively standardise the results for the separate examinations before attempting to combine them. Another procedure would be to use the first principal component derived from the observed examination results. This would give an index providing maximum discrimination between the students, with examination scores that vary most within the sample of students being given the highest weight.

A further possible application arises in the field of economics, where complex data are often summarised by some kind of index number, for example, indices of prices, wage-rates, cost of living and so on. When assessing changes in prices over time, for instance, the economist will wish to allow for the fact that prices of some commodities are more variable than others, or that the prices of some of the commodities are considered more important than others, and in each case will weight his index accordingly. In such cases the first principal component can often satisfy the investigator's requirements (see Kendall, M. G., 1975).

But often the first principal component will not give an adequate description of the multivariate data, or this component may not be the one that is the most interesting to the investigator. A taxonomist, for example, when investigating variation in morphological measurements on animals, would be more interested in the second principal component since this is likely to be an indication of shape, whereas the first will probably be merely an indicator of the animal's size. Often the first principal component derived from clinical psychiatric scores on patients will provide only an index of the severity of symptoms, and it is the second or subsequent components that gives the investigator information concerning the pattern of symptoms.

Some more detailed applications of principal components analysis are given in Section 4.6, but here we continue with their mathematical derivation.

4.2 Derivation of Principal Components

The first principal component of the observations is that linear combination, y_1, of the original variables,

$$y_1 = a_{11}x_1 + a_{12}x_2 + \cdots + a_{1p}x_p, \tag{4.1}$$

whose sample variance is greatest for all coefficients, $a_{11}, \ldots, a_{1p}$ (which we may write as the vector $\mathbf{a}_1$). Since the variance of y_1 could be increased without limit simply by increasing the elements of $\mathbf{a}_1$, a restriction must be placed on these coefficients, and so it is usually required that the sum of squares of the coefficients, i.e. $\mathbf{a}_1'\mathbf{a}_1$, should be set at a value of unity. The reason for this choice will be seen later.

But how useful is this artificial variate constructed from the observed variables? To answer this question one would first need to know the proportion of the total variance attributable to it. If 87 per cent of the variation in an investigation involving six variables would be accounted for by a simple weighted average of the variable values, it would appear that almost all the variation could be expressed along a single continuum rather than in six-dimensional space. This would provide a highly parsimonious summary of data that could be useful in later analyses.

The second principal component is that linear combination

$$y_2 = a_{21}x_1 + a_{22}x_2 + \cdots + a_{2p}x_p, \tag{4.2}$$

i.e.

$$y_2 = \mathbf{a}_2'\mathbf{x},$$

which has greatest variance subject to the two conditions

$$\mathbf{a}_2'\mathbf{a}_2 = 1 \quad \text{(for the reason indicated previously)}$$

$\mathbf{a}_2'\mathbf{a}_1 = 0$ (this condition ensures that y_1 and y_2
are uncorrelated).

Similarly the j-th principal component is that linear combination

$$y_j = \mathbf{a}_j'\mathbf{x} \tag{4.3}$$

which has greatest variance subject to

$$\mathbf{a}_j'\mathbf{a}_j = 1$$

$$\mathbf{a}_j'\mathbf{a}_i = 0 \quad i < j.$$

To find the first component we need to choose $\mathbf{a}_1$ so as to maximise the variance of y_1 subject to the constraint, $\mathbf{a}_1'\mathbf{a}_1 = 1$. The variance of y_1 is given by

$$v(y_1) = v(\mathbf{a}_1'\mathbf{x})$$

$$= \mathbf{a}_1'\mathbf{S}\mathbf{a}_1 \tag{4.4}$$

where $\mathbf{S}$ is the variance-covariance matrix of the original variables. (This result is derived in Chapter 2, Section 2.4.)

The standard procedure for maximising a function of several variables subject to one or more constraints is the method of *Lagrange multipliers*. Applying this technique to maximise equation (4.4), subject to $\mathbf{a}_1'\mathbf{a}_1 = 1$, leads to the solution that $\mathbf{a}_1$ is the eigenvector of $\mathbf{S}$ corresponding to the largest eigenvalue. (For details see Morrison, 1967 and Chatfield and Collins, 1980.)

To determine the second component, the Lagrange multiplier technique is again used to maximise $v(y_2) = \mathbf{a}_2'\mathbf{S}\mathbf{a}_2$, subject to the two constraints $\mathbf{a}_2'\mathbf{a}_2 = 1$ and $\mathbf{a}_2'\mathbf{a}_1 = 0$. This leads to the solution that $\mathbf{a}_2$ is the eigenvector of $\mathbf{S}$ corresponding to its *second* largest eigenvalue. Similarly the j-th principal component turns out to be the eigenvector associated with the j-th largest eigenvalue.

The eigenvalues of $\mathbf{S}$, that is $\lambda_1, \lambda_2, \ldots, \lambda_p$, give the variances of the derived variables $y_1, y_2, \ldots, y_p$, and so we have that

$$\sum_{i=1}^{p} \lambda_i = \text{trace}\,(\mathbf{S}) \tag{4.5}$$

Consequently the j-th principal component accounts for a proportion

$$t = \lambda_j/\text{trace}\,(\mathbf{S}) \tag{4.6}$$

of the total variation in the original data, and the first p^* components account for a proportion

$$T = \sum_{i=1}^{p^*} \lambda_i \bigg/ \text{trace} (\mathbf{S}) \qquad (4.7)$$

of the total variation.

In many sets of multivariate data the variables will be measured in widely different units and so linear combinations of them will make little sense. In such situations it is usual to calculate the principal components of the variables after they have been standardised to have unit variance. This is equivalent to extracting the components as eigenvectors of the correlation matrix, $\mathbf{R}$, rather than the covariance matrix, $\mathbf{S}$. However, it is important to realise that the eigenvalues and eigenvectors of $\mathbf{R}$ will generally not be the same as those of $\mathbf{S}$, and that choosing to analyse $\mathbf{R}$ rather than $\mathbf{S}$ involves a definite but arbitrary decision to make the variables 'equally important'.

For the correlation matrix, the diagonal terms are all unity. Thus the sum of the diagonal terms is simply p. Consequently the sum of the eigenvalues of $\mathbf{R}$ will also be equal to p, and so now the proportion of the total variation accounted for by the j-th component is simply λ_j/p.

If we were to regard the individuals in our study as a random sample from some population, then the eigenvalues and eigenvectors of $\mathbf{S}$ could be regarded as estimates of the eigenvalues and eigenvectors of the population covariance matrix, $\mathbf{\Sigma}$. Such an approach might lead to the derivation of some sampling theory and possible significance tests for the eigenvalues and the elements of the eigenvectors. For example, the assumption that the observations arise from a multivariate normal distribution leads to a number of interesting asymptotic results; see Morrison (1967) for details. However, the results are used in practice only rarely since the number of observations is generally insufficient for them to be applicable, and in addition the normality assumption is often questionable. Consequently principal components analysis is perhaps best regarded as a mathematical technique, with no underlying statistical model, which can in many cases lead to a useful summarisation of the data.

4.3 Summarising a Data Set

A number of informal suggestions and 'rules of thumb' have been given for deciding on the number of principal components needed to provide an adequate summary of a given data set. Perhaps the most common are:

(1) include just enough components to explain say 80 per cent of the total variation.

(2) exclude those principal components whose eigenvalues are less than the average, i.e. less than one if a correlation matrix has been used.

Another useful way of looking at the contributions of various principal components is to look at a graph of λ_j versus j. Such a diagram can often indicate clearly where 'large' eigenvalues cease and 'small' eigenvalues begin, and an example appears in Figure 4.1.

4.4 Calculating Principal Component Scores

To obtain the scores for an individual on the derived principal component variables we could simply use formulae (4.1), (4.2) and (4.3) on the individuals original variable values. However, it is generally more convenient to arrange matters so that the principal component scores have zero mean, by applying the vectors $\mathbf{a}_1, \ldots, \mathbf{a}_p$ to the vector $(\mathbf{x}_i - \bar{\mathbf{x}})$ where $\mathbf{x}_i$ contains the original variable values for individual i, and $\bar{\mathbf{x}}$ is the vector of mean values of the original variables. The component scores of the i-th individual are thus given by

$$y_{i1} = \mathbf{a}_1'(\mathbf{x}_i - \bar{\mathbf{x}})$$
$$\vdots \qquad \vdots \qquad \vdots \qquad (4.8)$$
$$y_{ip} = \mathbf{a}_p'(\mathbf{x}_i - \bar{\mathbf{x}})$$

If the first p^* components are judged to provide an adequate summary of the data (as indicated by the criteria described in the previous section), then scores for each of the individuals on each of these components may be used in later analyses in place of the original variables.

4.5 Rescaling Principal Components

If the vectors, $\mathbf{a}_1, \ldots, \mathbf{a}_p$, which define the principal components are used to form a $(p \times p)$ matrix, $\mathbf{A} = [\mathbf{a}_1, \ldots, \mathbf{a}_p]$, and the eigenvalues, $\lambda_1, \ldots, \lambda_p$, arrayed in a diagonal matrix $\mathbf{\Lambda}$, then it is easy to show that the covariance matrix, $\mathbf{S}$, of the original variables, $\mathbf{X}$, is given by

$$\mathbf{S} = \mathbf{A}' \mathbf{\Lambda} \mathbf{A}' \qquad (4.9)$$

By rescaling the vectors $\mathbf{a}_1, \ldots, \mathbf{a}_p$ so that the sum of squares of their elements is equal to the corresponding eigenvalue, λ_i, rather than unity, i.e. calculating $\mathbf{a}_i^* = \lambda_i^{\frac{1}{2}} \mathbf{a}_i$, then (4.9) may be written more simply as

$$\mathbf{S} = (\mathbf{A}^*)'(\mathbf{A}^*)' \qquad (4.10)$$

where $\mathbf{A}^* = [\mathbf{a}_1^*, \ldots, \mathbf{a}_p^*]$. The elements of $\mathbf{A}^*$ are such that the coefficients of the more important components are scaled to be generally larger than those of the less important components, and this seems intuitively sensible. The rescaled vectors have a number of other advantages since the elements of A^* are analogous to *factor loadings*, as we shall see in Chapter 11. When they arise from the analysis of a correlation matrix they may be interpreted as correlations between the components and the original variables. Consequently, when a principal components analysis is reported it is quite common to present the vectors $a_1^*, \ldots, a_p^*$ rather than $a_1, \ldots, a_p$.

4.6 Practical Applications of Principal Components Analysis

Principal components analysis is used in a variety of ways in the analysis of multivariate data. It is probably most widely applied in attempting to identify important dimensions of variability in a data set, essentially by examining the variables having high correlations with a particular component, assessing what these variables have in common, and then labelling the component in some intuitively sensible manner. For example, consider the set of data given by Mardia, Kent and Bibby (1979) consisting of a set of five examination scores for each of 88 students. The covariance matrix of these data is shown in Table 4.1, together with its eigenvalues and eigenvectors. The vector defining the first component has fairly high positive elements for all variables and

Table 4.1 *Covariance matrix, eigenvalues and eigenvectors for open (o)/closed (c) book examination scores (Taken from Mardia, Kent and Bibby, 1979, courtesy of Academic Press)*

$$S = \begin{bmatrix} 302.3 & & & & \\ 125.8 & 170.9 & & & \\ 100.4 & 84.2 & 111.6 & & \\ 105.1 & 93.6 & 110.8 & 217.9 & \\ 116.1 & 97.9 & 120.5 & 153.8 & 294.4 \end{bmatrix}$$

Eigenvalues and eigenvectors of S

		Eigenvector			
	1	2	3	4	5
1. Mechanics (c)	0.51	0.75	−0.30	0.30	0.08
2. Vectors (c)	0.37	0.21	0.42	−0.78	0.19
3. Algebra (o)	0.35	−0.08	0.15	−0.00	−0.92
4. Analysis (o)	0.45	−0.30	0.60	0.52	0.29
5. Statistics (o)	0.53	−0.55	−0.60	−0.18	0.15
Eigenvalue:	679.2	199.8	102.6	83.7	31.8

could be labelled simply as an 'average' mark. On the other hand the second component has positive elements for the open book examinations and negative elements for the closed book examinations, and therefore represents some form of 'contrast' between the different types of examination. These first two components account for 80.1 per cent of the variation in the data and would thus provide an excellent summary.

As a further example of this particular use of principal components analysis we shall examine the correlation matrix shown in Table 4.2, which arises in a study concerned with dental calculus reduction. (See Finn, 1974, for details.) The six measures involved in the problem are calculus accumulation measures for six anterior teeth of the lower mandible. The eigenvectors of this matrix, rescaled as described in Section 4.5, are shown in Table 4.3. The first component accounts for about 72 per cent of the variation in the calculus measures, and appears to represent an average calculus accumulation with the contribution to the component increasing as the teeth approach the front of the mouth.

Table 4.2 *Correlations of the calculus measures for the six anterior mandibular teeth (Taken with permission from Finn, 1974)*

	1	2	3	4	5	6
1	1.00					
2	0.54	1.00				
3	0.34	0.65	1.00			
4	0.37	0.65	0.84	1.00		
5	0.36	0.59	0.67	0.80	1.00	
6	0.62	0.49	0.43	0.42	0.55	1.00

$R=$

Table 4.3 *Correlations of principal components with calculus measures for six anterior teeth (Taken with permission from Finn, 1974)*

	Component					
	1	2	3	4	5	6
1. Right canine	−0.49	0.70	−0.07	−0.12	0.42	0.27
2. Right lateral incisor	−0.78	0.36	−0.34	0.36	−0.14	−0.05
3. Right central incisor	−0.91	−0.17	−0.25	−0.25	−0.13	0.08
4. Left central incisor	−0.95	−0.20	0.05	0.05	0.19	−0.09
5. Left lateral incisor	−0.86	0.02	0.44	0.12	−0.18	0.15
6. Left canine	−0.57	0.63	0.24	−0.35	−0.13	−0.28
Eigenvalue	13.82	2.02	1.28	0.88	0.71	0.38

The second component, accounting for an additional 10.6 per cent of the variation, is largely a comparison of the incisors with the canines. The component probably reflects both differential usage in eating and brushing, as well as proximity of the salivary glands.

The third component accounts for an additional 6.7 per cent of score variation and reflects differential calculus formation on the two sides of the mouth. It appears that there exists a tendency for individuals to have a greater calculus formation on one or other side of the mouth. This may reflect lateral favouritism in biting and/or brushing.

The remaining three components account for only a total of 10 per cent of the variation in the data and might safely be ignored.

Figure 4.1 shows a plot of the eigenvalues which clearly indicates the overwhelming importance of the first three components.

Attempting to identify components in this way can be (and often is) a very subjective procedure. Indeed, the identification of components is to a considerable extent arbitrary in that completely different results

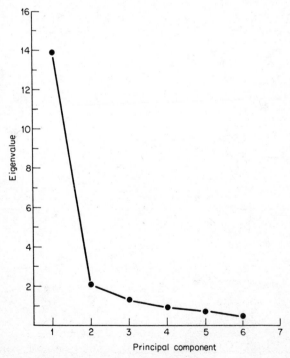

Figure 4.1   *Eigenvalue plot for data of Table 4.2 (sometimes referred to as a 'scree' diagram)*

may be produced by analysing the covariance matrix rather than the correlation matrix. This suggests that it may be dangerous to try to attach too much meaning to components in many situations, and perhaps a more important objective with this type of analysis lies in its possibilities for reducing the dimensionality of the data as a prelude to further investigations, when the question of trying to interpret the components en route will not apply. One area where this may be very useful is that of multiple regression, which we shall discuss in Chapter 8. Another often very helpful application of principal components analysis, not involving any need for interpretation of the components, is in providing low-dimensional plots of the data, which can be an aid in identifying outlying observations, clusters of similar observations, and so on. An example of such a plot is shown in Figure 4.2. This arises from applying principal components analysis to Fisher's iris data (Fisher, 1936), which consists of four measurements on each of 150 iris plants, and plotting the first two principal component scores of each plant. The diagram clearly indicates that the sample consists of separate groups of plants, in accordance with the known fact that the original data consist of measurements from three species of iris. (But note that the plot fails to reveal *all* of the known heterogeneity in this sample.)

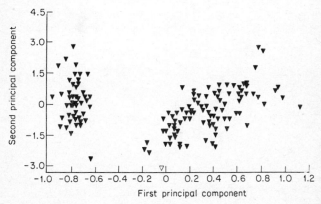

Figure 4.2   *Plot of iris data in the space of first two principal components*

A further example appears in Figure 4.3, which shows a set of five-dimensional observations plotted in the space of its first two principal components. The presence of an outlying observation is clearly indicated, and this observation would need to be examined to decide whether or not it should be removed before attempting further analyses. This particular use of principal components analysis is

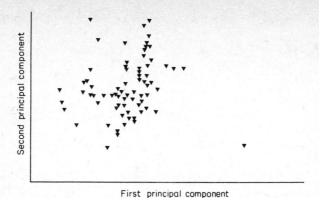

Figure 4.3   *Plot of a set of five-dimensional observations in the space of first two principal components*

analogous to the methods of multidimensional scaling, as we shall see in the next chapter.

Such principal component plots may sometimes be usefully combined with some of the preliminary techniques described in the last chapter. For example, in Exercise 3.5 a table showing the rates of seven different crimes for sixteen American cities is given. Figure 4.4 shows a plot of these cities in the space of the first two principal components; these account for 84 per cent of the total variation in the observations.

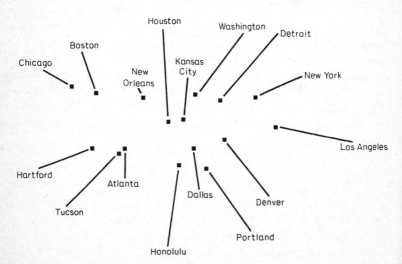

Figure 4.4   *City crime data plotted in the space of first two principal components*

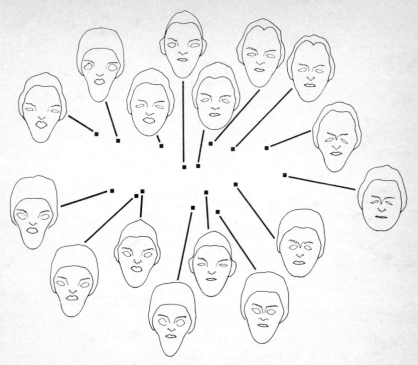

Figure 4.5 *Principal component plot of city crime data enhanced by the addition of faces representation*

Despite this high percentage, however, Figure 4.5, which shows this diagram enhanced by the faces representation of each city plotted at the appropriate points, indicates that some distortion has occurred. For example, the points representing Atlanta and Tucson are very close in Figure 4.4, but Figure 4.5 shows that their crime rate profiles must differ considerably in at least the variable representing the shape of the hair. This variable is the murder/manslaughter rate which is 16.5 in Atlanta and only 5.1 in Tucson.

Some other interesting examples of the use of principal component plots are given in Gower and Digby (1981). A number of other techniques that are related to principal components analysis and may also be used to obtain informative displays of multivariate data are discussed by Gabriel (1981) and Greenacre (1981).

The principal component scores used to display the data are linear functions of the original variables. A number of methods have been developed in which low-dimensional representations of the data are sought but the derived co-ordinates are not restricted to being linearly related to the original variables. An example is the non-linear mapping technique of Sammon (1969).

4.7   Geometrical Interpretation of Principal Components Analysis

In geometrical terms it is easy to show that the first principal component defines the line of best fit (in the least squares sense) to the n p-dimensional observations in the sample. These observations may therefore be represented in one dimension by taking their projection on to this line, i.e. finding their first principal component score. If the n points happened to be collinear this representation would account completely for the variation in the data, and the sample covariance matrix would have only one non-zero eigenvalue. In practice, of course, the points are unlikely to be collinear, and so an improved representation would be given by projecting them on to the plane of best fit, this being defined by the first two principal components. Similarly the first p^* components give the best fit in p^*-dimensions. If the observations fit exactly into a space of p^*-dimensions, this will be indicated by the presence of $p - p^*$ zero eigenvalues of the covariance matrix. This would imply the presence of $p - p^*$ linear constraints on the variables. These constraints are sometimes referred to as *structural* relationships.

4.8   Summary

Principal components analysis looks for a few linear combinations of the original variables that can be used to summarise the data, whilst losing in the process as little information as possible. The derived variables might be useful in a variety of ways, in particular for simplifying later analyses and providing informative plots of the data. The method consists essentially of transforming a set of correlated variables to a new set of uncorrelated variables. Therefore it should be stressed that if the original variables are almost uncorrelated there is little point in carrying out such an analysis, since it will simply find components which are close to the original variables but arranged in decreasing order of variance.

Finally it is important to stress that principal components is, essentially, a straightforward mathematical technique for an orthogonal rotation to principal axes (see Chapter 2). If this is remembered, it might make less likely the exaggerated claims sometimes made for the results obtained from such an analysis.

EXERCISES

4.1   MacDonell (1902) obtained measurements of seven physical characteristics for each of 3000 criminals. The corresponding correlation matrix is shown below:

Variables	1	2	3	4	5	6	7
1	1.000	0.402	0.395	0.301	0.305	0.339	0.340
2	0.402	1.000	0.618	0.150	0.135	0.206	0.183
3	0.395	0.618	1.000	0.321	0.289	0.363	0.345
4	0.301	0.150	0.321	1.000	0.846	0.759	0.661
5	0.305	0.135	0.289	0.846	1.000	0.797	0.800
6	0.339	0.206	0.363	0.759	0.797	1.000	0.736
7	0.340	0.183	0.345	0.661	0.800	0.736	1.000

The seven variables measured were:

1 Head length   5 Left cubit (forearm)
2 Head breadth   6 Left foot
3 Face breadth   7. Height
4 Left finger length

Find the principal components of these data and interpret your results.

4.2   The following (from Spearman, 1904) is a matrix of correlations between 6 examinations taken by 33 children.

		1	2	3	4	5	6
1	Classics	1.00					
2	French	0.83	1.00				
3	English	0.78	0.67	1.00			
4	Mathematics	0.70	0.67	0.64	1.00		
5	Discrimination	0.66	0.65	0.54	0.45	1.00	
6	Music	0.63	0.58	0.51	0.51	0.40	1.00

Carry out a principal components analysis and interpret the results. Compare this interpretation with that of a principal factor analysis (Chapter 11).

4.3   Two standardised variables, x_1 and x_2, have correlation matrix $\mathbf{R}$, given by

$$\mathbf{R} = \begin{bmatrix} 1 & r \\ r & 1 \end{bmatrix}$$

Show that the eigenvalues of $\mathbf{R}$ are $(1+r)$ and $(1-r)$, and find the principal components of $\mathbf{R}$.

4.4   Show that the eigenvectors of a correlation matrix, when scaled so that their sum of squares is equal to the corresponding eigenvalue, contain the correlations between components and original variables.

4.5   If the eigenvectors of a covariance matrix scaled so that their sums of squares are equal to the corresponding latent root are $c_1, \ldots, c_p$, show that

$$S = c_1 c_1' + \cdots + c_p c_p'.$$

(This result is known as the spectral decomposition of S.)

4.6   Suppose that $x' = (x_1, x_2)$ is such that $x_2 = 1 - x_1$ and $x_1 = 1$ with probability p, and $x_1 = 0$ with probability $q = 1 - p$. Find the covariance matrix of x and its eigenvalues and eigenvectors.

5. *Multidimensional Scaling*

5.1 Introduction

In Chapter 1 we mentioned that a frequently encountered type of data in the behavioural sciences is the proximity matrix, arising either directly, from experiments in which subjects are asked to assess the similarity of two stimuli, or indirectly, as a measure of the correlation or covariance of the two stimuli derived from their raw profile data. The investigator collecting such data is interested primarily in uncovering whatever structure or pattern may be present in the observed proximity matrix, and the subject of this chapter is one particularly powerful class of techniques which may prove extremely useful in this search. Members of the class are generally known as *multidimensional scaling techniques*, and the underlying purpose that they share, despite their apparent diversity, is to represent the structure in the proximity matrix by a simple geometrical model or picture.

A geometrical or spatial model for the observed proximity matrix consists of a set of points, $\mathbf{x}_1, \mathbf{x}_2, \ldots, \mathbf{x}_n$, in d-dimensions (each point representing one of the items or stimuli under investigation) and a measure of distance between pairs of points. The object of multi-dimensional scaling is to determine both the dimensionality of the model (that is the value of d) and the position of the points in the resulting d-dimensional space, so that there is, in some sense, maximum correspondence between the observed proximities and the interpoint distances. In general terms this simply means that the larger the dissimilarity between two stimuli (or the smaller their similarity), the further apart should be the points representing the stimuli in the geometrical model. However, in practice more explicit measures of how the proximities agree with the distances are needed, and a variety of such measures have been suggested, giving rise to a variety of multidimensional scaling techniques (see Section 5.4).

A number of interpoint distance measures are possible but by far the most common is Euclidean distance. This measure is illustrated for two-dimensions in Figure 5.1, and for d-dimensions is given by

$$d_{ij} = \left[\sum_{k=1}^{d} (x_{ik} - x_{jk})^2 \right]^{\frac{1}{2}} \tag{5.1}$$

where $x_{i1}, \ldots, x_{id}$ and $x_{j1}, \ldots, x_{jd}$ are the elements of vectors $\mathbf{x}_i$ and $\mathbf{x}_j$ respectively. Some other possible distance measures will be considered briefly in Section 5.7.

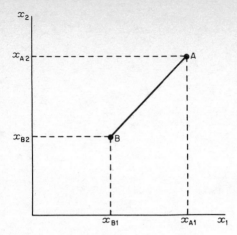

Figure 5.1 *Euclidean distance in two dimensions*

5.2 Simple Examples of Multidimensional Scaling

To clarify just what the techniques of multidimensional scaling attempt
to achieve, and before describing any technique in detail, we shall in
this section look at a few simple examples, beginning with the data
shown in Table 5.1. This is part of a data set collected by Rothkopf
(1957); each entry in the table gives the number of times, expressed as a
percentage, that pairs of morse code signals for two numbers were
declared to be the same by 598 subjects. Application of *classical
multidimensional scaling* (see Section 5.3) results in the two-dimensional
diagram shown in Figure 5.2. At the simplest level the purpose of this

Table 5.1 *Number of times (%) that pairs of morse code signals for
two numbers were declared to be the same by 598 subjects (part of the
data in Rothkopf, 1957)*

	1	2	3	4	5	6	7	8	9	0
($\cdot$——) 1	84									
($\cdot\cdot$——) 2	62	89								
($\cdot\cdot\cdot$——) 3	16	59	86							
($\cdot\cdot\cdot\cdot$—) 4	6	23	38	89						
($\cdot\cdot\cdot\cdot\cdot$) 5	12	8	27	56	90					
(—$\cdot\cdot\cdot\cdot$) 6	12	14	33	34	30	86				
(——$\cdot\cdot\cdot$) 7	20	25	17	24	18	65	85			
(———$\cdot\cdot$) 8	37	25	16	13	10	22	65	88		
(————$\cdot$) 9	57	28	9	7	5	8	31	58	91	
(—————) 0	52	18	9	7	5	18	15	39	79	94

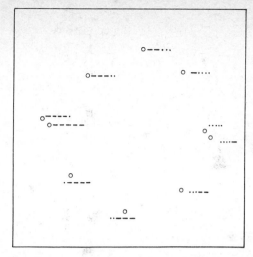

Figure 5.2   *Two-dimensional solution from classical multidimensional scaling applied to the data in Table 5.1 (Adapted from Mardia et al., 1979, courtesy of Academic Press)*

plot is to observe which signals were 'alike' (they are represented by points which are close together), and which were 'not alike' (they are represented by points far from each other). The plot should also indicate the general interrelationships between signals. A possible interpretation of the two axes is that the horizontal one is related to the increasing number of dots in a signal, whereas the vertical one is related to the ordering of dots and dashes in the signal. We shall return to this example later.

As a further example consider the data shown in Table 5.2, which

Table 5.2   *Matrix of mean similarity ratings for eighteen students for twelve nations (Adapted from Kruskal and Wish, 1978, courtesy of Sage Publications)*

	BRZ	ZAI	CUB	EGY	FRA	IND	ISR	JPN	CHI	USSR	USA	YUG
Brazil	—											
Zaire	4.83	—										
Cuba	5.28	4.56										
Egypt	3.44	5.00	5.17	—								
France	4.72	4.00	4.11	4.78	—							
India	4.50	4.83	4.00	5.83	3.44	—						
Israel	3.83	3.33	3.61	4.67	4.00	4.11	—					
Japan	3.50	3.39	2.94	3.83	4.11	4.50	4.83	—				
China	2.39	4.00	5.50	4.39	3.67	4.11	3.00	4.17	—			
USSR	3.06	3.39	5.44	4.39	5.06	4.50	4.17	4.61	5.72	—		
USA	5.39	2.39	3.17	3.33	5.94	4.28	5.94	6.06	2.56	5.00	—	
Yugoslavia	3.17	3.50	5.11	4.28	4.72	4.00	4.44	4.28	5.06	6.67	3.56	—

results from averaging the ratings of eighteen students on the degree of overall similarity between twelve nations on a scale ranging from 1 indicating 'very different' to 9 for 'very similar'. No instructions were given concerning the characteristics on which these similarity judgements were to be made. (Further details of the study are given in Kruskal and Wish, 1978.)

The two-dimensional solution given by non-metric multidimensional scaling (see Section 5.4) appears in Figure 5.3. Kruskal and Wish's subjective interpretation of this solution, obtained by a rotation of the axes (see next section), is also shown.

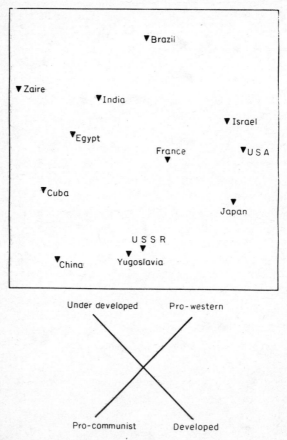

Figure 5.3   *Two-dimensional   solution   from   non-metric   multidimensional scaling applied to the data in Table 5.2 (Adapted from Kruskal and Wish, 1978, courtesy of Sage Publications)*

5.3   Classical Multidimensional Scaling

Given the co-ordinates of n points in p-dimensional Euclidean space it is a simple matter to calculate the Euclidean distance, d_{ij}, between each pair of points. This can be done directly from the data matrix $\mathbf{X}$ using equation (5.1), or via the $(n \times n)$ matrix $\mathbf{B} = \mathbf{X}\mathbf{X}'$ since

$$b_{ij} = \sum_{k=1}^{d} x_{ik} x_{jk} \tag{5.2}$$

so that

$$d_{ij}^2 = b_{ii} + b_{jj} - 2b_{ij} \tag{5.3}$$

Now consider the inverse problem and suppose that we know the distances and wish to determine the co-ordinates. First we must note that there is no unique representation which will give rise to the distances, since these are unchanged by shifting the whole configuration of points from one place to another, or by rotation or reflection of the configuration. In other words, we cannot determine either the *location* or the *orientation* of the configuration. The location problem is usually overcome by placing the mean vector of the configuration at the origin. The orientation problem means that any configuration we obtain may be subjected to an arbitrary orthogonal transformation, i.e. a rigid rotation plus possibly a reflection. Such transformations are often used to facilitate the interpretation of solutions, as we have already seen in the previous section and will meet again in later parts of this chapter.

The procedure used to find the required co-ordinates consists of two stages, the first of which involves finding the elements of the matrix $\mathbf{B}$, introduced above, in terms of the known Euclidean distances, and the second of which consists of simply factorising $\mathbf{B}$ in the form $\mathbf{X}\mathbf{X}'$. To get b_{ij} in terms of d_{ij} involves inverting equation (5.3). No unique solution exists unless we introduce a location constraint which, as indicated previously, is generally taken as $\bar{\mathbf{x}} = \mathbf{0}$, so that $\sum_{i=1}^{n} x_{ij} = 0$, for all j. Using these constraints and equation (5.2) implies that the sum of terms in any row of $\mathbf{B}$, or in any column of $\mathbf{B}$, is zero. Consequently, summing equation (5.2) over i, over j, and finally over i and j leads to the following three equations.

$$\sum_{i=1}^{n} d_{ij}^2 = D + nb_{jj},$$

$$\sum_{j=1}^{n} d_{ij}^2 = nb_{ii} + D, \tag{5.4}$$

$$\sum_{i=1}^{n} \sum_{j=1}^{n} d_{ij}^2 = 2nD.$$

where $D = \sum_{i=1}^{n} b_{ii}$ is the trace of the matrix **B**. Solving equations (5.3) and (5.4), we find that

$$b_{ij} = -\tfrac{1}{2}\left[d_{ij}^2 - d_{i.}^2 - d_{.j}^2 + d_{..}^2\right] \tag{5.5}$$

where $d_{i.}^2 = \dfrac{1}{n}\sum_{j=1}^{n} d_{ij}^2, \quad d_{.j}^2 = \dfrac{1}{n}\sum_{i=1}^{n} d_{ij}^2, \quad d_{..}^2 = \dfrac{1}{n^2}\sum_{i=1}^{n}\sum_{j=1}^{n} d_{ij}^2$

Equation (5.5) now gives us the elements of the matrix **B** in terms of squared Euclidean distances.

To factorise **B** in the form XX' we need to find the eigenvectors of **B** and scale them so that their sums of squares are equal to the corresponding eigenvalues. The matrix **X** is then given by

$$X = [c_1, c_2, \ldots, c_n] \tag{5.6}$$

where $c_1, \ldots, c_n$ are the appropriately scaled eigenvectors of **B**. (This result has been discussed previously in Section 4.5.) **X** now contains the co-ordinates of each point referred to the principal axes.

If we are seeking a configuration in a given number of dimensions, say p^*, then we simply examine the eigenvectors associated with the p^* largest eigenvalues. If we are unsure as to the number of dimensions we should use, then we can assess the adequacy of the first p^* co-ordinates by the criterion, T, given by

$$T = \sum_{i=1}^{p^*} \lambda_i \Bigg/ \sum_{i=1}^{n} \lambda_i \tag{5.7}$$

where $\lambda_1, \ldots, \lambda_n$ are the eigenvalues of **B**. (Since the sum of the elements in each row of **B** is chosen to be zero, **B** will always have at least one zero eigenvalue.)

When **B** arises from *Euclidean* distances it is straightforward to show that it is positive semi-definite, has positive or zero eigenvalues, and when factored as XX' will lead to real (as opposed to imaginary) co-ordinate values. Classical scaling is, however, often applied to dissimilarity measures which are not Euclidean and where the resulting **B** matrix need not be positive semi-definite. Consequently the matrix may have a number of negative eigenvalues, and the factorisation **B** $= XX'$ may now lead to imaginary values for some of the co-ordinates. However, if **B** has only a *small* number of *small* negative eigenvalues, a useful co-ordinate representation of the dissimilarity matrix may still be obtained from the eigenvectors associated with the first few positive eigenvalues. The adequacy of the representation could now be measured by T' given by

$$T' = \sum_{i=1}^{p^*} \lambda_i \bigg/ \sum_{i=1}^{n} |\lambda_i| \qquad (5.8)$$

However, if **B** has a number of large negative eigenvalues, classical scaling of the dissimilarity matrix may be inadvisable, and we may prefer to use one of the methods discussed in Section 5.4.

It is easy to show that classical scaling with Euclidean distances is exactly equivalent to principal components analysis of a covariance matrix, in the sense that the co-ordinates produced by the former will be the same as the principal component scores of each individual. (See Chatfield and Collins, 1980, and Exercise 5.1.) The equivalence of principal components analysis and classical scaling, which is often referred to as principal co-ordinates analysis (see Gower, 1966), means that there is no point in carrying out both analyses. Consequently if $n > p$, then a principal components analysis is to be preferred because it is easier to find the eigenvectors of the $(p \times p)$ matrix $\mathbf{X'X}$ than those of the larger $(n \times n)$ matrix $\mathbf{XX'}$.

5.3.1 Classical scaling – a numerical example

To illustrate how classical scaling might be used in practice we shall apply the method to the matrix of airline distances between the ten American cities shown in Table 5.3. These distances are not Euclidean

Table 5.3 *Airline distances between ten US cities (Kruskal and Wish, 1978, courtesy of Sage Publications)*

Cities	Atla	Chic	Denv	Hous	LA	Mia	NY	Seat	Wash DC
Atlanta									
Chicago	587								
Denver	1212	920							
Houston	701	940	879						
Los Angeles	1936	1745	831	1374					
Miami	604	1188	1726	968	2339				
New York	748	713	1631	1420	2451	1092			
San Fran-									
cisco	2139	1858	949	1645	347	2594	2571		
Seattle	2182	1737	1021	1891	959	2734	2408	678	
Washington									
DC	543	597	1494	1220	2300	923	205	2442	2329

since they relate essentially to journeys along the surface of a sphere. Table 5.4 shows the eigenvalues of the **B** matrix derives from these distances, and the eigenvectors associated with the two largest of these. Since the distance matrix is non-Euclidean, there are a number of negative eigenvalues. However, these are relatively small and Figure 5.4 confirms that the co-ordinates obtained from the first two eigenvectors give a very reasonable representation of the distances.

Table 5.4   *Eigenvalues and eigenvectors arising from classical multi-dimensional scaling applied to the distances in Table 5.3*

	Eigenvalues		First two eigenvectors	
			1	*2*
1	9,582,144.3	Atlanta	718.7	−143.0
2	1,686,820.1	Chicago	382.0	340.8
3	8,157.3	Denver	−481.6	25.3
4	1,432.9	Houston	161.5	−572.8
5	508.7	Los Angeles	−1203.7	−390.1
6	25.1	Miami	1133.5	−581.9
7	0.0	New York	1072.2	519.0
8	−897.7	San Francisco	−1420.6	−112.6
9	−5,467.6	Seattle	−1341.7	579.7
10	−35,478.9	Washington DC	979.6	335.5

The criterion T' given in equation (5.8) takes the value 99 % for the first two eigenvalues of Table 5.4, which again indicates the adequacy of the two-dimensional representation.

5.4   Metric and Nonmetric Multidimensional Scaling

The central motivating concept of multidimensional scaling is that the distances between the points representing the items or stimuli of interest should correspond in some sensible way to the observed proximities. With this in mind various authors, for example, Shepard (1962), Kruskal (1964a) and Sammon (1969), have approached the problem by defining an objective function which measures the discrepancy between the observed proximities and the fitted distances. They then attempt to recover the configuration of points in a particular number of dimensions which minimises this function, using some type of optimisation algorithm.

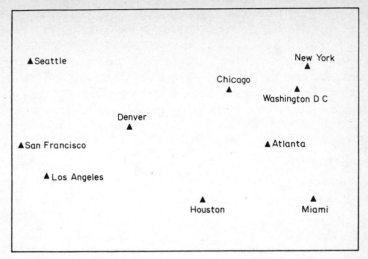

Figure 5.4 *Two-dimensional solution given by classical scaling applied to the data in Table 5.3 (Kruskal and Wish, 1978)*

For example, suppose that the proximity matrix under investigation contains a measure of dissimilarity for each pair of objects, is symmetric, and contains zeros on the main diagonal. (Its elements are represented by δ_{ij}.) What is required is a set of d-dimensional co-ordinates for each object (where d is ideally 2 or 3), with associated Euclidean distances d_{ij} which match the observed dissimilarities. To assess the agreement between distances and dissimilarities we need to define a function which takes the value zero if the pattern of the distances fits that of the dissimilarities perfectly, and increases in value as the fit becomes less good. An intuitively appealing candidate for this function is a sum of squares, SS, given by

$$SS = \sum_{i=1}^{n-1} \sum_{j=i+1}^{n} (\delta_{ij} - d_{ij})^2 \tag{5.9}$$

If the distances are all equal to the corresponding dissimilarities, SS takes the value of zero. As discrepancies between d_{ij} and δ_{ij} increase so does the value of SS. Since the distances d_{ij} are a function of the nd-dimensional co-ordinate values, so also is SS, and by altering the co-ordinate values one changes the value of SS. Since goodness-of-fit increases with decreasing values of SS, we now seek to determine that set of d-dimensional co-ordinates that minimises SS. Various optimisation algorithms, such as the method of steepest descent, might be considered, but the details of these need not concern us here.

The sum of squares criterion is invariant under rigid transformations of the configuration (rotations, translations and reflections). This is clearly desirable. Unfortunately it is not invariant under non-rigid transformations such as uniform stretching and shrinking. In other words, if we stretch the configuration $\mathbf{x}_1, \mathbf{x}_2, \ldots, \mathbf{x}_n$ by the factor k to $k\mathbf{x}_1, k\mathbf{x}_2, \ldots, k\mathbf{x}_n$, then SS changes. Now, purely enlarging or shrinking a configuration should not alter how well it fits the data since the relationships between the distances do not change. Consequently one should introduce a scaling factor which has the same dependence on the scale of the configuration as does SS. Such a scaling factor is easily found, for example:

$$SC = \sum_{i=1}^{n-1} \sum_{j=i+1}^{n} d_{ij}^2. \tag{5.10}$$

A goodness-of-fit measure given by $S = SS/SC$ has all the desirable properties of SS and is, moreover, invariant under changes of scale, that is, uniform stretching or shrinking. The square root of S is generally known as *stress*.

The choice of a goodness-of-fit function based upon SS given by equation (5.9) implies that we may assume that there is the following simple relationship between the observed dissimilarities and the inter-point distances

$$d_{ij} = \delta_{ij} + \varepsilon_{ij} \tag{5.11}$$

where the ε_{ij} represent a combination of errors of measurement and distortion errors arising because the dissimilarities may not exactly correspond to a configuration in d dimensions. It is this rather naive assumption which is essentially the basis of classical multidimensional scaling, discussed in the previous section.

However, in many situations it may be more realistic to postulate a rather less simple relationship between the δ_{ij}s and d_{ij}s. For example, a straightforward extension of equation (5.11) would be the following

$$d_{ij} = a + b\delta_{ij} + \varepsilon_{ij} \tag{5.12}$$

The residual sum of squares criterion would now become

$$SS = \sum_{i=1}^{n-1} \sum_{j=i+1}^{n} (d_{ij} - a - b\delta_{ij})^2 \tag{5.13}$$

Minimisation of stress would now involve a two stage procedure. First, for a given configuration $\mathbf{x}_1, \ldots, \mathbf{x}_n$, and hence a given set of d_{ij} values, one would need to determine values of a and b which minimised equation (5.13). These are obtained from the simple linear regression of the d_{ij}s on the δ_{ij}s. Now, for this value of a and b one would need to apply an optimisation algorithm to find the new values of $\mathbf{x}_1, \ldots, \mathbf{x}_n$ that minimise the stress criterion. These two stages would be repeated until some convergence criterion had been satisfied.

In general, if we postulate a relationship between distances and dissimilarities of the form

$$d_{ij} = f(\delta_{ij}) + \varepsilon_{ij} \tag{5.14}$$

the residual sum of squares would be

$$SS = \sum_{i=1}^{n-1} \sum_{j=i+1}^{n} (d_{ij} - f(\delta_{ij}))^2. \tag{5.15}$$

We would now need first to minimise SS with respect to the parameters of f by some form of regression and then minimise stress with respect to the d-dimensional configuration, $\mathbf{x}_1, \ldots, \mathbf{x}_n$.

In psychological experiments the proximity matrices frequently arise from asking human subjects or observers to assess similarities or distances. These subjects, however, can usually give only ordinal judgements. For example, they can specify that one stimulus is 'larger' than another without being able to attach any value to the exact numerical difference between them. Consequently the proximity judgements do not have strict numerical significance and so one would like, if possible, to use only their ordinal properties, and find a method of multidimensional scaling whose solutions are derived using only the rank order of the proximity values. Such a method would be invariant under monotonic transformations of the proximity matrix. A major breakthrough in multidimensional scaling was achieved in the early 1960s by Shepard (1962) and Kruskal (1964a) when they derived a method which met these requirements by allowing the function f in equation (5.14) to indicate a *monotonic relationship* between distance and dissimilarity. In other words, the distances are now represented as follows:

$$d_{ij} = \hat{d}_{ij} + \varepsilon_{ij} \tag{5.16}$$

where the $\hat{d}_{ij}$'s are a set of numbers which are monotonic with the δ_{ij}'s. That is, if the observed dissimilarities are ranked from lowest to highest as

$$\delta_{i_1 j_1} < \delta_{i_2 j_2} < \cdots < \delta_{i_N j_N}$$

where $N = n(n-1)/2$, then the $\hat{d}_{ij}$'s will satisfy

$$\hat{d}_{i_1 j_1} \leqslant \hat{d}_{i_2 j_2} \leqslant \cdots \leqslant \hat{d}_{i_N j_N}.$$

Stress now becomes

$$
\text{stress} = \sqrt{\left\{ \frac{\displaystyle\sum_{i=1}^{n-1}\sum_{j=i+1}^{n}(d_{ij}-\hat{d}_{ij})^2}{\displaystyle\sum_{i=1}^{n-1}\sum_{j=i+1}^{n}d_{ij}^2} \right\}}
\tag{5.17}
$$

In this case the fitted $\hat{d}_{ij}$ values are obtained from a special type of regression of distance on dissimilarities, known as *monotonic regression*. Details of the technique need not concern us here; they are available in Kruskal (1964b). The important point to emphasise is that the observed dissimilarities now only enter the calculations in terms of their rank order.

As we have seen, minimisation of the stress goodness-of-fit criterion involves two stages. The first is some form of regression analysis, which is straightforward. The second entails the minimisation of a function of nd variables (the d-dimensional co-ordinates of each stimulus). Various optimisation algorithms have been used in this stage (for example, steepest descent and Newton-Raphson) and technical details can be found in Kruskal (1964b) and Ramsay (1977). Essentially, however, all such algorithms start with an arbitrary set of co-ordinate values for each object, move all the points a little to achieve a lower stress and then repeat the procedure until a configuration is reached from which no improvement is possible. Roughly speaking, points $\mathbf{x}_i$ and $\mathbf{x}_j$ are moved closer together if $f(\delta_{ij}) < d_{ij}$ and apart in the opposite case, making d_{ij} more like $f(\delta_{ij})$. Since the stress function may have a number of minima, problems can arise from convergence to a *local* rather than to the *global* minimum. This problem is unavoidable, but can be partially overcome by repeating the calculations with different initial configurations.

5.5 Choosing the Number of Dimensions

The decision about the number of co-ordinates needed for a given data set is as much a substantive question as a statistical one. Even if a reasonable statistical method existed for determining the 'correct' or 'true' dimensionality, this would not in itself be sufficient to indicate how many co-ordinates the researcher needs to use. Since multi-dimensional scaling is almost always used as a descriptive model for representing and understanding a data set, other considerations enter into decisions about the appropriate dimensionality. This point is made by Gnanadesikan and Wilk (1969): 'Interpretability and simplicity are important in data analysis and any rigid inference of optimal dimensionality, in the light of the observed values of a numerical index of goodness-of-fit, may not be productive.'

In the light of such comments, two-dimensional solutions are likely to be those of most *practical* importance since they have the virtue of simplicity, are often readily assimilated by the investigator, and may, in many cases, provide an easily understood basis for the discussion of observed proximity matrices. Nevertheless there may be occasions when two dimensions are just not adequate to contain the full complexity of the structure present and the investigator would like some guidance on a reasonable number of co-ordinates to use to represent the data. Perhaps the most commonly used procedure seeking to give such guidance is that based upon examining stress values for different numbers of dimensions. In his original paper Kruskal (1964a) gave the following advice about stress, based upon his experience with experimental and synthetic data.

Stress (%)	Goodness-of-fit
20	poor
10	fair
5	good
$2\frac{1}{2}$	excellent
0	perfect

Consequently, observed stress values might be 'evaluated' against these comments as an indication of when the fit for a particular number of dimensions is 'good' or better. In addition, it has been suggested that the stress may be plotted against the number of dimensions, and the diagram examined for the presence of an 'elbow' indicating the appropriate number of co-ordinates to use. Examples of such plots are given in the next section. However, Wagenaar and Padmos (1971) indicate that the interpretation of stress is strongly dependent on the number of stimuli involved, and that a simple interpretation in terms of Kruskal's verbal evaluation is often not justified.

Spence (1970 and 1972) and Spence and Graef (1974) have carried out an extensive set of Monte Carlo experiments, the results of which allow a more objective assessment of underlying dimensionality to be made. The simulated data were generated for a wide range of conditions similar to those that might be experienced by a typical user. The number of points was varied from 12 to 36, spaces of true dimensionality from one to four were investigated, and the level of error in the data varied from zero to an infinite amount. An attempt was then made to find the set of simulated values, for some given dimensionality, which best fitted the observed stress values for the data set obtained by the application of multidimensional scaling for different numbers of dimensions. The procedure is described in full detail in Spence and Graef (1974).

5.6   Further Examples of the Application of Multidimensional Scaling Techniques

We will begin by examining in some detail the analysis of the proximity matrix shown in Table 5.5, which arises from minor distortions of the Euclidean distances between the points in Figure 5.5. Here there will be essentially a simple linear relationship between derived distances and

Table 5.5   *Dissimilarity matrix arising from minor distortions of the Euclidean distances between the points in Figure 5.5*

	1	2	3	4	5	6	7	8	9
1	0.0								
2	2.0	0.0							
3	4.0	2.0	0.0						
4	2.0	3.0	4.2	0.0					
5	2.8	2.0	2.9	2.1	0.0				
6	4.5	3.4	2.1	4.3	2.1	0.0			
7	4.0	4.5	5.5	2.0	3.0	4.2	0.0		
8	4.2	4.0	4.3	3.0	2.1	3.1	2.1	0.0	
9	6.0	4.5	4.1	4.5	2.5	2.1	4.1	2.1	0.0

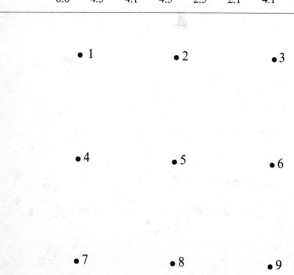

Figure 5.5   *Artificial data set*

dissimilarities, and the analysis of the proximity matrix by the procedures outlined in Section 5.4, with the *assumption* that the function *f* is linear, results in the two-dimensional solution shown in Figure 5.6. As one would expect, the configuration of Figure 5.5 has been completely recovered by this analysis (apart from the orientation of axes, which is, of course, arbitrary). A scatterplot of distances against

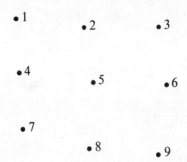

Figure 5.6 *Two-dimensional solution obtained from multidimensional scaling assuming a linear relationship between distances and dissimilarities applied to the data in Table 5.5*

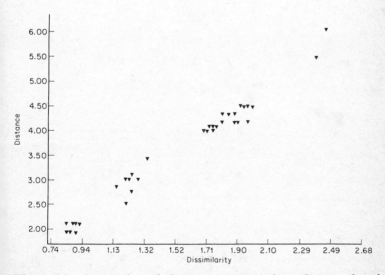

Figure 5.7 *Scatterplot of distances against dissimilarities for the example in Figure 5.6*

dissimilarities (Figure 5.7) confirms that our assumption of a linear relationship for these data is reasonable.

The stress for the two-dimensional sslution is 12.93%, indicating only a 'fair' fit according to Kruskal's ratings. However, the plot of stress against number of dimensions (Figure 5.8) clearly indicates that a two-dimensional solution is appropriate.

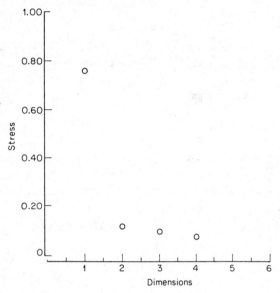

Figure 5.8   *Plot of number of dimensions against stress for multi-dimensional scaling of the artificial data set of Figure 5.5*

Now we shall transform the dissimilarities of Table 5.5 as follows:

$$\delta'_{ij} = \exp(\delta_{ij}) + \delta^2_{ij} \qquad (5.18)$$

Application of the method of multidimensional scaling used above now results in the solution shown in Figure 5.9, which, apart from minor distortions, again recovers the input configuration. In part this is somewhat surprising since the assumption that f is linear is now quite unrealistic. However, this example serves to indicate that metric multidimensional scaling is robust, in the sense that the configuration obtained using one assumption about f will not, in general, be very different from that using an alternative assumption, although, as with this example, the stress may be highly inflated by the inappropriate assumption made about f. (The stress for the configuration in Figure 5.9 is 54.87%.) Examination of the scatterplot of distances against

Figure 5.9 *Two-dimensional solution obtained from multidimensional scaling assuming a linear relationship between distances and dissimilarities applied to the transformed dissimilarities in Table 5.5*

dissimilarities in this case (see Figure 5.10) indicates that the assumption of a linear relationship is wrong. In such cases it is best to reanalyse the data using a more appropriate assumption. Application of nonmetric multidimensional scaling to either the original or the transformed dissimilarities results in the same solution with the same

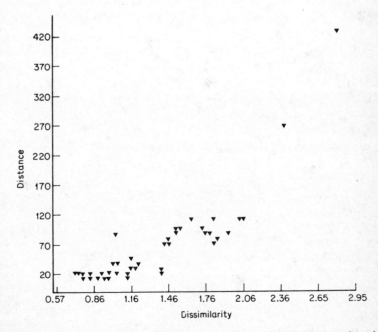

Figure 5.10 *Scatterplot of distances against dissimilarities for the example in Figure 5.9*

stress (2.12%) since δ_{ij} is simply a monotonic transformation of δ_{ij}. This serves to indicate the possible advantages of this method over those specifying a more rigid relationship between distances and dissimilarities.

As a further example we will analyse the similarity matrix shown in Table 5.6, which arises from an investigation into the assessment of pain. The entries in Table 5.6 are the similarities for pairs of adjectives describing pain, derived by a method suggested by Burton (1972). The two-dimensional solution is shown in Figure 5.11. (Two dimensions was suggested by use of the technique of Spence and Graef; see Section 5.5.) The detailed analysis of these data is described in Reading, Everitt and Sledmere (1982), but one interpretation, obtained by a rotation of the axes, is indicated in Figure 5.11. One axis now ranges from words such as 'tingling', 'quivering' and 'pricking' to words such as 'wrenching', 'crushing' and 'pressing', and might be suggestive of a dimension ranging from non-intrusive to intrusive pain. The second axis has adjectives such as 'throbbing', 'beating' and 'pulsing' at one extreme and 'sharp', 'cutting' and 'lancinating' at the other, and could perhaps be a dimension representing non-specific to specific pain. Of course, such interpretations are relatively subjective, and readers might well come up with others which they find more plausible.

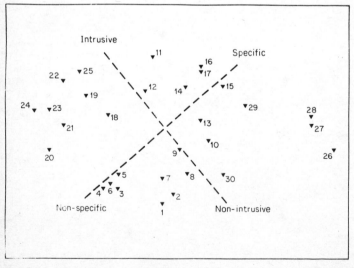

Figure 5.11 *Two-dimensional solution obtained from nonmetric multi-dimensional scaling of the pain adjectives similarity matrix in Table 5.6*

Table 5.6 *Similarities of pairs of adjectives describing pain*

	1	2	3	4	5	6	7	8	9	10	11	12	13	14	15	16	17	18	19	20	21	22	23	24	25	26	27	28	29
2	106.36																												
3	27.72	30.33																											
4	19.45	16.23	144.52																										
5	27.04	13.21	102.95	113.04																									
6	25.06	21.85	130.16	141.26	118.70																								
7	96.13	80.49	31.05	23.00	23.60	23.04																							
8	72.58	49.70	23.71	16.14	17.08	17.64	73.81																						
9	40.17	28.41	16.51	9.39	14.57	12.41	60.16	70.63																					
10	28.03	17.77	-3.61	-5.42	-4.98	-6.94	8.98	9.14	3.27																				
11	-11.40	-5.44	-11.40	-10.10	-10.10	-10.10	-5.88	-11.40	7.50	14.47																			
12	-9.67	-5.48	-1.22	-4.58	-4.58	1.07	-4.46	-2.87	26.46	20.73	100.89																		
13	-3.26	-1.64	3.96	17.63	10.36	11.51	-0.74	2.85	40.82	44.64	23.44	47.08																	
14	-5.44	-7.57	-5.69	-8.29	-4.36	-6.14	-2.14	-3.36	3.44	22.37	15.38	21.54	45.75																
15	-10.29	-10.29	-11.40	-11.40	-6.67	-10.25	-2.49	3.71	10.64	31.03	-4.37	5.84	50.46	39.87															
16	-9.82	-8.95	-9.82	-11.40	-9.43	-10.25	-6.87	-4.71	7.00	2.63	0.57	15.51	34.72	35.16	65.25														
17	-11.40	-11.40	-9.40	-9.40	-5.47	-8.25	-5.85	-3.32	6.89	7.82	-2.47	6.79	27.84	43.73	34.05	118.77													
18	-0.96	-2.17	-7.29	-6.95	-2.10	-6.73	0.98	1.34	-5.42	15.97	-6.99	-2.11	-5.60	-2.67	9.03	4.76	-0.98												
19	-9.27	-3.95	-2.69	-4.14	4.50	0.38	-9.09	-7.30	-4.70	-6.75	-3.97	6.41	-4.48	-2.34	-4.16	-7.30	-4.44	33.09											
20	-7.25	-1.49	-2.67	-0.74	-1.18	-3.30	-6.98	-1.96	-5.40	-5.36	11.01	5.29	-7.14	-7.98	-7.37	-8.62	1.42	-2.37											
21	-2.80	-5.72	-4.02	-3.59	6.92	-1.21	-1.12	-4.82	-4.06	-7.76	-1.48	-2.97	-7.44	-7.07	-4.81	-6.28	-8.12	22.35	21.76	13.61									
22	-9.24	-8.23	-4.19	-6.98	-0.22	1.00	-7.48	-8.33	-3.95	-11.40	-4.72	3.86	-6.61	-6.99	-7.48	-8.56	-2.96	23.24	117.46	-8.55	11.56								
23	-5.91	-9.72	-0.18	-1.67	1.30	0.68	0.15	-11.40	-6.89	-7.92	-5.56	0.73	-9.53	-7.03	-9.60	-2.96	-5.16	11.90	-1.39	6.88	6.01	2.35							
24	-11.40	-10.26	-3.75	0.40	-1.66	-2.90	-3.42	-7.30	-8.73	-10.07	-9.72	-1.29	-8.44	-7.71	-8.55	-5.91	-7.33	16.25	5.45	13.92	10.18	1.19	135.22						
25	-9.87	-8.74	-6.98	-6.71	-6.52	-8.23	-8.50	-6.76	-2.39	-9.87	-1.76	7.97	-9.37	-5.64	-9.20	-0.02	7.25	10.76	6.66	-3.89	36.50	11.92	65.80	63.89					
26	-9.94	-8.34	-9.93	-10.10	-9.31	-10.10	-9.93	-6.91	-11.40	-8.50	-10.10	-11.40	-11.40	-11.40	-7.41	-11.40	-9.96	-9.15	-8.35	-11.40	-11.40	-11.40	-11.40	-11.40	-11.40				
27	-9.67	-9.67	-11.40	-11.40	-10.61	-11.40	-11.40	-6.97	-6.94	-10.01	-11.40	-9.67	-4.47	-11.40	-6.12	-10.06	-8.67	-9.21	-10.10	-11.40	-7.01	-9.67	-8.71	-10.10	-8.71	162.96			
28	-9.67	-8.07	-11.40	-11.40	-10.61	-11.40	-11.40	-8.31	-6.85	-3.85	-10.20	-11.40	-8.48	-4.24	-10.20	-4.80	-7.35	-5.96	-9.41	-8.28	-11.40	-11.40	-9.67	-10.00	-9.89	-10.00	170.71	178.41	
29	-9.02	-9.02	-8.18	-6.88	-4.12	-5.73	-5.25	2.33	13.99	-2.37	-4.86	3.25	7.53	7.72	6.09	25.14	41.90	-9.21	-10.03	8.76	-11.40	-7.21	-6.26	-4.86	9.70	29.66	39.74	38.03	
30	23.12	25.19	-2.31	-5.58	-3.62	-5.58	6.90	17.71	2.81	54.48	-5.76	-7.09	-1.31	-4.20	0.21	-7.19	-4.11	7.33	-8.52	-4.96	-2.56	-9.96	-10.07	-10.07	-11.40	-4.35	-4.22	-7.51	-7.06

Key

1	Flickering	11	Boring	21	Cramping
2	Quivering	12	Drilling	22	Crushing
3	Pulsing	13	Stabbing	23	Tugging
4	Throbbing	14	Lancinating	24	Pulling
5	Beating	15	Sharp	25	Wrenching
6	Pounding	16	Cutting	26	Hot
7	Jumping	17	Lacerating	27	Burning
8	Flashing	18	Pinching	28	Scalding
9	Shooting	19	Pressing	29	Searing
10	Pricking	20	Gnawing	30	Tingling

The search for meaningful dimensions is often one of the main aims of scaling and Kruskal and Wish (1978) suggest that multiple linear regression between some direction in the configuration and various characteristics of the points may be useful in trying to interpret the dimensions.

5.7   Non-Euclidean Metrics

Up to now we have considered only the use of Euclidean distances in multidimensional scaling procedures. In principle, however, there is no reason why the goodness-of-fit function, stress, could not be used with almost any kind of distance. For example, Kruskal (1964a) has considered a class of distances known as *Minkowski metrics* which are defined as follows:

$$d_{ij} = \left[\sum_{k=1}^{d} |x_{ik} - x_{jk}|^r \right]^{1/r} \tag{5.19}$$

When $r = 1$ we have the fairly well-known *city block metric*; and when $r = 2$, equation (5.19) reduces to the Euclidean distance. Kruskal (1964a) gives an example of using such metrics on a set of experimental data obtained by Ekman (1954), from the judgement of similarities of fourteen colour stimuli. Figure 5.12 shows the different values of stress

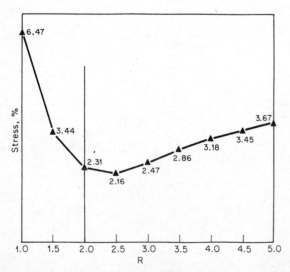

Figure 5.12   *Plot of stress against value of* r *in Minkowski metrics formula for colour stimulus data (Taken from Kruskal and Wish, 1978, courtesy of Sage Publications)*

obtained for different values of r, in equation (5.19), for a two-dimensional solution. From this we see that a value of $r = 2.5$ gives the best fit, indicating perhaps, that subjective distance between colours may be slightly non-Euclidean. The actual two-dimensional solution obtained in each case was very similar in general terms, although the precise shape, spacing and angular orientation varied with r.

The Minkowski metrics differ sharply from Euclidean distance in not being invariant under rigid rotation of the co-ordinate axes. Thus, while a configuration may be freely rotated when Euclidean distances are being used, it may not be when more general distances are employed.

In most applications of multidimensional scaling, Euclidean distance is likely to be of greatest use, but non-Euclidean distances such as those specified in equation (5.19) may be worth considering in some situations.

5.8 Three-Way Multidimensional Scaling

The methods of multidimensional scaling discussed in Sections 5.3 and 5.4 are designed essentially for the analysis of *two-way* matrices of proximities. In many situations the investigator may have several such matrices for the same set of objects, for example, one from each subject, and these may be thought of as forming a *three-way matrix* (see Figure 5.13). A method such as nonmetric multidimensional scaling could be used to analyse such data by simply averaging the proximities over subjects (see, for example, the similarity of nations example in Section

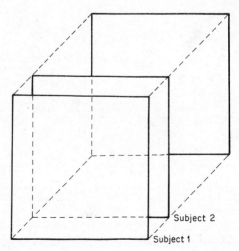

Figure 5.13   *Three-way data matrix*

5.2). Such an approach, however, implicitly assumes that differences between subjects are simply due to random error, and this may be unrealistic. Consequently we would prefer a method capable of dealing with such three-way data which allows for the possibility of large systematic differences among the observed proximity matrices of different subjects. Several methods have been suggested by, amongst others, Tucker (1964 and 1972), Harshman (1972) and Tucker and Messick (1963). However, the most successful approach would seem to be the INDSCAL model, proposed by Carroll and Chang (1970), which is the focus of our attention here. (INDSCAL stands for individual scaling or individual differences scaling.)

This model assumes that there is a set of d dimensions *common* to all subjects in which the n objects or stimuli may be represented, but that the distances between points in this space differ from subject to subject according to the importance, or *weight*, attached to each dimension by a particular subject. So the 'modified' Euclidean distance between points i and j for the l-th subject is given by

$$d_{ij}^{(l)} = \left[\sum_{k=1}^{d} w_{lk}(x_{ik} - x_{jk})^2 \right]^{\frac{1}{2}} \tag{5.20}$$

where the weights w_{lk}, $k = 1, \ldots, d$ represent the differing importance attached to each dimension by subject l. Another way of looking at formula (5.20) is to say that the $d_{ij}^{(l)}$'s are ordinary Euclidean distances computed in a space whose co-ordinates are

$$y_{ik}^{(l)} = w_{lk}^{\frac{1}{2}} x_{ik}, \tag{5.21}$$

that is, a space like the x space except that the configuration has been expanded or contracted (differentially) in directions corresponding to the co-ordinate axes. The model is illustrated in Figure 5.14. An important point to note about the INDSCAL model is that it produces a *unique* orientation of the axes of the space in which the stimuli or objects are represented as points. This arises because subjects are permitted to stretch or shrink axes differentially, whereas only a uniform stretching preserves distances. Consequently it is not permissible to rotate the axes here as it was for the methods of scaling described in Sections 5.3 and 5.4. Fortunately it has usually been found that the recovered dimensions are fairly readily interpretable. A linear relationship is assumed between the distances given by equation (5.20) and the observed dissimilarities, and the first step in fitting this model is to convert the dissimilarity matrix of each subject into a corresponding **B** matrix, using equation (5.5). Least squares estimates of the required weights and co-ordinates are then found by a procedure which Carroll

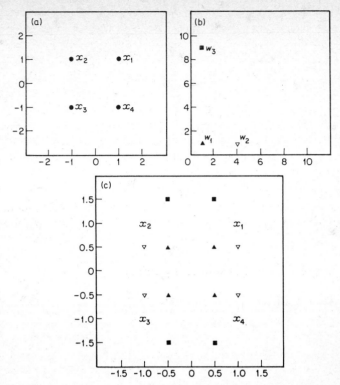

Figure 5.14 *Illustration of the* INDSCAL *model: (a) common stimulus space; (b) subject weights for two-dimensions; (c) 'private' stimulus space for the three individuals with weights as in (b). (Adapted from Kruskal and Wish, 1978, courtesy of Sage Publications)*

and Chang call the canonical decomposition of N-way tables. This involves an iterative procedure in which, for given initial estimates of the co-ordinates, least squares estimates of the weights are determined. These are then used to find revised least squares estimates of the co-ordinates and the procedure is repeated until some convergence criterion is satisfied. For details the reader is referred to the original paper by Carroll and Chang (1970).

We will now examine an application of this technique to some actual data, arising from dissimilarity ratings made by a number of subjects on politicians prominent at the time of the Second World War. The ratings were made on a nine point scale from 1, indicating very similar, to 9, indicating very dissimilar. Two of the dissimilarity matrices collected are shown in Table 5.7.

Table 5.7 *Dissimilarity ratings of World War II politicians by two subjects*

Subject 1 in lower triangle,   Subject 2 in upper triangle

		1	2	3	4	5	6	7	8	9	10	11	12
1	Hitler		2	7	8	5	9	2	6	8	8	8	9
2	Mussolini	3		8	8	8	9	1	7	9	9	9	9
3	Churchill	4	6		3	5	8	7	2	8	3	5	6
4	Eisenhower	7	8	4		8	7	7	3	8	2	3	8
5	Stalin	3	5	6	8		7	7	5	6	7	9	5
6	Attlee	8	9	3	9	8		9	7	7	4	7	5
7	Franco	3	2	5	7	6	7		5	9	8	8	9
8	De Gaulle	4	4	3	5	6	5	4		6	5	6	5
9	Mao Tse Tung	8	9	8	9	6	9	8	7		8	8	6
10	Truman	9	9	5	4	7	8	8	4	4		4	6
11	Chamberlain	4	5	5	4	7	2	2	5	9	5		8
12	Tito	7	8	2	4	7	8	3	2	4	5	7	

The two-dimensional INDSCAL solution obtained from the dissimilarity matrices of eight subjects is shown in Figure 5.15. One possible interpretation of the two-dimensions is that the first is some indication of the 'historical impact' of the politician ranging from Attlee at one end to Hitler at the other. The second might tentatively be

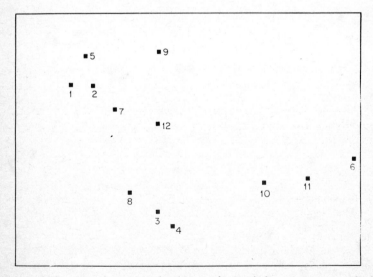

Figure 5.15 *Two-dimensional solution obtained from* INDSCAL *applied to dissimilarity ratings of World War II politicians*

labelled as a 'democracy' dimension, ranging from Eisenhower, Churchill and De Gaulle through Tito, to Mao Tse Tung.

In addition to the diagram in Figure 5.15, INDSCAL produces a set of weights for each subject on each dimension. With a two-dimensional solution the pairs of weights for each subject may be further plotted to give the 'subject space'. This is shown in Figure 5.16. From this we can see that, for example, subject 1 weights the historical impact dimension rather more than the democracy dimension, whilst for subjects 6 and 8 the reverse situation holds. It is often useful to relate these weights to other characteristics of the subjects. For example, if some biographical

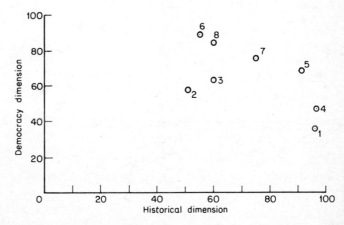

Figure 5.16   *Subject weights from* INDSCAL

or attitudinal information is available, we could investigate whether subjects having high weights on a dimension differ from those with low weight on any of the background variables. By applying a subject's weights to the respective dimensions of Figure 5.15, one obtains the 'private' stimulus space of that subject. The private spaces of subjects 1 and 6 are shown in Figure 5.17. This example demonstrates how the INDSCAL model can accommodate large differences between individuals, and although the model is likely to be perhaps an oversimplification for many data sets, it can still prove extremely useful in identifying and characterising important variation in such data structures.

5.9   The Analysis of Asymmetric Proximity Matrices
In most applications of multidimensional scaling the observed proximity matrix is symmetric, that is

$$\delta_{ij} = \delta_{ji} \tag{5.22}$$

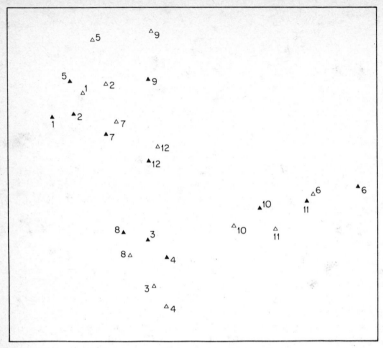

Figure 5.17   *'Private' spaces of individuals 1 and 6*

However, situations can arise in which there are asymmetric relationships between pairs of objects so that the equality (5.22) no longer holds. Take, for example, the data described in Section 5.2 concerning morse code signals, which is shown in its complete form in Table 5.8. This table is not symmetric since the percentage of times that signal i followed by signal j was said to be the same is not necessarily the same as when the signals are presented in the reverse order. Constantine and Gower (1978) suggest a number of other applications where assymetry may arise, including diallel cross experiments giving the number of progeny or yield when a male of line i is crossed with a female of line j; the number of people who live in location i and work in location j and the frequency with which journal i cites journal j. Such asymmetric matrices are frequently made suitable for analysis by one of the methods described previously by the transformation

$$\delta'_{ij} = \tfrac{1}{2}(\delta_{ij} + \delta_{ji}) \qquad (5.23)$$

However, this ignores departures from symmetry which may be

Second signal

First signal

	A	B	C	D	E	F	G	H	I	J	K	L	M	N	O	P	Q	R	S	T	U	V	W	X	Y	Z	1	2	3	4	5	6	7	8	9	∅
A	92	04	06	13	03	14	10	13	46	05	22	03	25	34	06	06	09	35	23	06	37	13	17	12	07	03	02	07	05	05	08	06	05	06	02	03
B	05	84	37	31	05	28	17	21	05	19	34	40	06	10	12	22	25	16	18	02	18	34	08	84	30	42	12	17	14	40	32	74	43	17	04	04
C	04	38	87	17	04	29	13	07	11	19	24	35	14	03	09	51	34	24	14	06	06	11	14	32	82	38	13	15	31	14	10	30	28	24	18	12
D	08	62	17	88	07	23	40	36	09	13	81	56	08	07	09	27	09	45	29	06	17	20	27	40	15	33	03	09	06	14	09	08	08	10	05	06
E	06	13	14	06	97	02	04	04	17	01	05	06	04	04	05	01	05	10	07	67	03	03	03	02	05	06	04	03	05	05	02	04	02	03	03	03
F	04	51	33	19	02	90	10	29	05	33	16	50	07	06	10	42	12	35	14	02	21	27	25	19	27	13	08	16	47	25	26	24	21	05	05	05
G	09	18	27	38	01	14	90	87	10	10	09	29	08	87	14	13	62	52	21	05	03	15	14	32	21	23	39	15	14	05	10	04	10	17	23	11
H	03	45	23	25	09	32	08	10	10	09	06	12	93	03	05	16	13	30	07	03	05	19	35	16	10	59	09	33	14	11	03	09	18	05	20	11
I	64	07	07	13	10	08	87	10	11	09	02	05	04	85	22	31	08	03	21	63	47	11	02	09	09	09	02	28	67	66	33	15	43	70	35	12
J	07	09	38	09	02	24	18	05	04	85	27	91	33	10	27	86	02	11	15	20	09	18	06	01	01	07	12	15	26	36	16	07	09	01	02	02
K	05	24	38	73	01	17	25	11	05	27	91	33	10	27	86	06	37	36	16	02	23	17	33	63	16	18	05	09	17	15	26	29	36	16	07	03
L	02	69	43	45	10	24	12	26	09	30	27	83	26	07	21	33	14	12	29	07	16	19	20	31	25	59	12	13	17	15	29	36	16	07	10	04
M	24	12	05	14	07	17	29	08	08	11	21	33	14	12	21	05	17	06	06	11	04	21	18	08	05	02	03	04	04	06	06	18	14	11	20	12
N	31	04	13	30	08	12	10	16	13	03	16	08	12	59	93	09	05	09	28	12	10	16	04	12	04	06	11	05	02	02	10	02	02	07	01	02
O	07	07	20	06	05	09	76	07	02	39	26	10	16	13	03	16	08	59	93	05	27	09	35	35	27	11	41	30	34	32	07	09	01	02	12	02
P	05	22	33	12	05	36	22	12	03	78	14	34	21	07	02	78	11	83	43	09	04	11	02	04	02	05	27	09	11	06	09	05	03	05	05	02
Q	08	20	38	11	04	15	10	05	02	27	83	26	33	11	06	20	21	11	06	32	92	17	57	35	10	10	06	16	34	10	09	08	07	04	03	01
R	13	14	16	23	05	34	26	15	07	12	21	33	14	15	15	12	29	08	87	16	06	32	04	19	20	86	22	25	22	10	22	19	16	05	01	05
S	17	24	05	30	11	26	05	59	16	03	13	10	05	17	17	06	06	24	09	05	17	86	14	57	12	21	24	24	40	11	06	03	09	05	05	02
T	13	10	01	05	46	03	06	06	14	07	10	05	17	44	32	11	13	06	06	04	09	11	20	22	10	84	12	20	15	16	57	29	16	17	06	06
U	14	29	12	32	04	12	34	21	07	44	17	34	21	09	11	06	24	13	21	03	12	21	91	48	26	63	20	24	27	05	26	32	23	15	19	02
V	05	17	24	16	09	29	06	39	05	11	26	43	04	01	09	20	32	61	10	04	17	48	21	16	21	89	44	40	15	09	47	10	01	01	05	07
W	09	21	30	22	09	36	25	15	04	25	29	18	15	06	24	32	61	10	24	03	21	16	48	21	91	22	36	15	08	11	29	16	17	06	03	07
X	07	64	45	15	04	20	03	28	11	06	01	35	50	42	10	08	24	32	60	14	30	13	21	91	48	16	42	12	23	33	25	66	47	15	16	15
Y	09	23	62	15	04	26	22	09	08	11	06	01	12	44	05	06	14	30	05	05	37	29	11	12	36	22	44	86	42	44	47	15	15	32	57	55
Z	03	46	45	18	02	22	17	10	07	23	21	19	03	03	02	17	59	72	14	04	55	08	12	14	17	84	63	13	08	20	10	16	20	11	16	11
1	02	05	10	03	03	05	13	04	02	45	51	11	25	26	09	07	14	30	28	03	09	11	12	14	19	22	89	54	20	05	14	20	21	16	11	02
2	07	14	22	05	04	20	13	03	25	26	09	14	02	44	25	16	42	13	17	06	11	12	26	44	22	84	62	89	05	23	41	16	17	08	10	03
3	03	08	21	05	04	32	06	12	02	12	16	42	05	18	26	13	06	05	37	04	55	12	14	87	42	18	64	25	26	41	32	10	03	03	03	04
4	06	19	12	18	12	05	14	14	07	21	13	19	14	04	14	05	02	15	29	02	55	14	17	22	44	89	44	26	44	44	42	24	10	06	05	05
5	08	45	15	14	02	45	04	67	07	14	04	41	04	02	00	04	13	07	09	27	14	45	07	19	10	22	30	14	10	03	05	24	17	14	05	14
6	07	80	30	17	04	23	04	14	06	02	45	04	67	07	16	30	11	14	03	02	03	12	30	09	58	38	39	15	14	26	24	17	88	69	14	06
7	06	33	22	14	05	25	06	04	06	24	13	32	07	06	04	07	36	39	17	02	02	03	13	09	30	30	50	22	29	18	15	12	61	85	70	13
8	03	23	40	06	03	15	15	06	02	33	10	14	03	06	04	14	12	45	02	06	04	06	13	05	24	35	50	42	29	16	16	09	30	60	89	61	26	8
9	03	14	23	03	01	06	14	05	07	30	06	07	16	11	10	31	32	05	06	03	17	21	11	21	24	57	39	09	12	04	11	42	56	91	78	9
∅	09	03	11	02	05	07	14	04	05	08	03	03	04	05	07	14	29	02	03	04	05	03	02	12	15	20	26	09	11	05	22	17	52	81	94	∅

informative, and Gower (1977) suggests a number of other methods which may be used directly on asymmetric matrices to obtain a spatial representation. Here we shall concentrate on just one of these, namely *multidimensional unfolding*, which derives from the 'unfolding' method of Coombs (1964), originally designed to scale preference data.

To introduce the method suppose that one has a number of subjects, say n, who are asked to rank a number of stimuli, say m, in order of preference. So the data matrix consists of n rows each containing an ordering of the m stimuli. (Note that there is no need for n to equal m.) Multidimensional unfolding attempts to find a set of co-ordinates for the subjects and a set of co-ordinates for the stimuli such that the ordering of the Euclidean distances between a given individual and each of the stimuli corresponds to the observed preference order for that individual in the sense that small distances will correspond to the most preferred stimuli.

The problem of finding the co-ordinates is approached in a manner very similar to non-metric multidimensional scaling as described in Section 5.4. In the case however the goodness-of-fit criterion to be minimised takes a different form namely

$$S_2 = \sqrt{\left\{ \frac{1}{n} \sum_{i=1}^{n} \frac{\sum_{j=1}^{m} (d_{ij} - \hat{d}_{ij})^2}{\sum_{j=1}^{m} (d_{ij} - \bar{d}_{i.})^2} \right\}} \qquad (5.24)$$

where d_{ij} is the Euclidean distance between the point representing subject i and that representing stimuli j; $\bar{d}_{i.} = (1/m) \sum_{j=1}^{m} d_{ij}$ is the mean distance of subject i from the m stimuli; and the numbers $\hat{d}_{ij}$ are such that $\hat{d}_{ij} < \hat{d}_{ik}$ when subject i prefers stimuli j over stimuli k. In other words the $\hat{d}_{ij}$ $(j = 1, \ldots, m)$, will have the same rank order as does is preferences for the m stimuli. S_2 is again seen to be essentially a sum-of-squares criterion, but now involving only those squared deviations relevant to each subject.

When the data matrix is square $(n = m)$, with its rows and columns similarly classified (as with the morse signal data), multidimensional unfolding will lead to n points representing the row objects and n points representing the columns. Interpretation of the data lies mainly in investigating the distances *between* the two sets, and there is only secondary interest in the within-set distances.

We will now examine an example of the application of this technique using the data shown in Table 5.9, taken from Hartigan (1975). The percentages given in this table may be thought of as defining a rank

Table 5.9 Numbers of persons (%) claiming to speak a language 'enough to make yourself understood (adapted from Hartigan, 1975)

	Language											
Country	1 Ger	2 Ital	3 Fr	4 Dch	5 Flem	6 G.B.	7 Port	8 Swed	9 Dan	10 Nor	11 Finn	12 Spn
1 West Germany	100	2	10	2	1	21	0	0	0	0	0	1
2 Italy	3	100	11	0	0	5	0	0	0	0	0	1
3 France	7	12	100	1	1	10	1	2	3	0	0	7
4 Netherlands	47	2	16	100	100	41	0	0	0	0	0	2
5 Belgium	15	2	44	0	59	14	0	0	0	0	0	1
6 Great Britain	7	3	15	0	0	100	0	0	0	0	0	2
7 Portugal	0	1	10	0	0	9	100	0	0	0	0	2
8 Sweden	25	1	6	0	0	43	0	100	10	11	5	1
9 Denmark	36	3	10	1	1	38	0	22	100	20	0	1
10 Norway	19	1	4	0	0	34	1	25	19	100	0	0
11 Finland	11	1	2	0	0	12	0	23	0	0	100	0
12 Spain	1	2	11	0	0	5	0	0	0	0	0	100

order of the 'preferences' of a country for a particular language. The two-dimensional solution obtained from multidimensional unfolding appears in Figure 5.18. The main interest in this diagram lies in the distances apart of points representing countries and those representing languages. Of particular note are the fairly marked discrepancies between the points representing Sweden and Swedish and Finland and Finnish, this reflecting the fact that a large number of Swedes and Finns speak languages other than their own, whereas there are few nationals of other countries who speak either Swedish or Finnish.

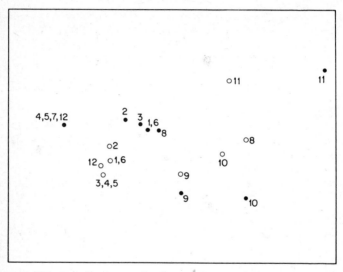

Figure 5.18   *Two-dimensional solution from multidimensional unfolding of the language data in Table 5.9*

5.10   Summary

The literature of multidimensional scaling is now vast and continues to grow at a considerable rate. It has been possible in this chapter to discuss only a small number of the many methods which have been suggested. Nevertheless it is hoped that the examples presented have demonstrated that the techniques of multidimensional scaling provide powerful possibilities for the analysis of proximity matrices. Many other interesting applications are described in Romney, Shepard and Nerlove (1972).

Recent work in this area, for example, Ramsay (1977), has considered possible error models and included the application of maximum likelihood techniques to the estimation of co-ordinates. Such an approach allows confidence regions to be found for the points in a solution configuration, and although the introduction of stochastic models into this area may not be welcomed by all, it does indicate perhaps a maturing of the technology of this type of data analysis.

EXERCISES

5.1 The *Consumer Reports Buying Guide* (1969) gives information on the frequency of different types of car repairs for various makes of car; part of these data is reproduced below. Construct a dissimilarity matrix for the ten cars using (a) the simple matching coefficient; (b) Jaccard's coefficient, both of which are defined below the table.

	BR	FU	EL	EX	ST	EM	RS	RA	RU	SA	TC	WA	OT
					Frequency of Car Repairs								
Buick Special 6	−	−	−	−	−	−	+	−	+	−	−	−	+
Chevy 11	−	+	−	−	+	−	+	+	+	−	−	+	−
Chrysler Newport	+	−	−	−	−	−	−	−	−	−	−	−	−
New Yorker	+	−	−	−	−	−	−	+	−	−	−	−	+
Fairlane 6	−	−	−	−	−	−	+	−	−	−	−	−	−
Ford, Full Size	−	−	−	+	+	−	−	−	−	+	−	+	+
Thunderbird	−	−	+	−	+	+	−	−	−	−	−	+	+
Pontiac Tempest	−	+	−	−	−	−	+	−	+	+	−	+	−
Mercedes	−	−	−	−	−	−	−	−	−	+	−	−	−
MG 1100	−	−	+	+	−	−	−	−	−	−	−	−	−

BR = brake system   ST = steering   RU = rust
FU = fuel system   EM = engine mechanical   SA = shock absorbers
EL = electrical   RS = rattles and squeaks   TC = transmission, clutch
EX = exhaust   RA = rear axle   WA = wheel alignment
OT = other

A + means greater than average frequency of repair in 1962–1967.

(The simple matching coefficient is defined as the total number of matches for two cars over the total number of variables, e.g. Buick Special 6 and Chevy 11 S = 8/13. Jaccard's coefficient is defined as the number of + matches over the total number of variables (excluding the negative matches), e.g. Buick Special 6 and Chevy 11 S = 2/7.)

5.2 Apply both classical and nonmetric multidimensional scaling to each of the dissimilarity matrices computed in Exercise 5.1 and compare the four, two-dimensional solutions.

5.3   Using the distance matrix shown below (from Baum, 1977) apply principal co-ordinate analysis, metric multidimensional scaling (using two or more transformations of the data) and nonmetric multidimensional scaling. What can you conclude from the results? (See Dunn and Everitt, 1982.)

Distance matrix for 28 points (Baum, 1977)

```
2  911
3  806 936
4  950 711 962
5  969 835 923 788
6  959 877 921 810 665
7  959 877 948 875 833 831
8  975 928 923 946 876 863 875
9  900 912 830 926 886 836 924 814
10 964 902 902 864 862 826 927 825 710
11 891 897 858 934 840 856 910 860 759 865
12 951 765 867 792 728 800 784 857 838 826 902
13 926 756 903 711 766 790 875 881 871 794 889 779
14 900 815 807 845 754 800 822 901 849 869 898 688 723
15 884 810 834 907 844 857 904 919 809 892 767 849 889 832
16 850 947 764 964 943 921 940 882 811 906 862 899 916 886 862
17 934 891 865 931 921 886 849 817 841 865 843 883 935 934 830 876
18 980 917 956 936 931 938 914 863 905 908 905 942 857 949 914 936 894
19 967 864 928 742 786 808 829 890 848 804 882 765 781 822 885 945 913 935
20 959 791 946 640 818 805 890 954 929 882 945 803 701 816 945 953 943 955 792
21 915 782 864 815 899 811 882 887 828 778 866 752 815 832 814 880 744 937 858 825
22 913 883 903 873 875 810 888 699 698 790 846 816 881 884 888 809 799 896 831 868 790
23 933 832 841 809 764 781 823 916 866 879 883 717 678 543 872 869 939 938 805 719 833 902
24 941 881 869 875 846 884 901 901 865 888 752 876 908 934 818 896 786 831 889 913 835 855 908
25 939 877 870 894 877 875 905 767 710 743 869 758 800 805 853 840 879 919 848 912 814 762 824 913
26 955 872 924 872 884 776 917 868 710 713 876 834 851 893 842 880 853 932 841 892 779 781 866 915 783
27 928 928 872 883 806 738 896 872 660 650 859 862 802 851 855 805 881 893 841 849 842 754 851 887 812 746
28 736 921 703 909 908 919 933 944 842 896 781 904 879 852 824 829 864 941 922 934 859 926 854 819 897 918 881
```

5.4   **Suggest** how Kruskal's method of nonmetric multidimensional scaling may be adapted for the situations (a) when there are missing values in the observed proximity matrix; (b) when there are ties in this matrix.

5.5   **What** is meant by the horseshoe effect in multidimensional scaling? (See Kendall, D. G., 1975.)

5.6   The following data show the co-ordinates of fifteen points in two dimensions. Calculate the Euclidean and city-block distances between each pair of points.

Point	x	y
1	2.0	1.0
2	13.0	1.0
3	1.0	2.0
4	3.0	2.0
5	12.0	2.0
6	14.0	2.0
7	2.0	3.0
8	13.0	3.0
9	7.0	4.0

	x	y
10	7.0	6.0
11	3.0	5.0
12	5.0	7.0
13	7.0	8.0
14	9.0	7.0
15	11.0	5.0

5.7 Apply metric multidimensional scaling to the two distance matrices from Exercise 5.6, assuming a linear relationship between derived and observed distances.

5.8 Using the following similarity matrix (from Woese, 1981) apply metric multidimensional scaling (using a linear transformation of the data) and nonmetric multidimensional scaling to produce configurations of the sixteen points in 2, 3 and 4 dimensions. This illustrates the problem of degeneracy (see Kruskal and Wish, 1978).

```
.29
.33  .36
.05  .10  .06
.06  .05  .06  .24
.08  .06  .07  .25  .22
.09  .10  .07  .28  .22  .34
.11  .09  .09  .26  .20  .26  .23
.08  .11  .06  .21  .19  .20  .21  .31
.11  .10  .10  .11  .06  .11  .12  .11  .14
.11  .10  .10  .12  .07  .13  .12  .11  .12  .51
.08  .13  .09  .07  .06  .06  .09  .10  .10  .25  .25
.08  .07  .07  .12  .09  .12  .10  .10  .12  .30  .24  .32
.10  .09  .11  .07  .07  .10  .10  .13  .12  .34  .31  .29  .28
.07  .07  .06  .07  .05  .07  .06  .10  .06  .17  .15  .13  .16  .19
.08  .09  .07  .09  .07  .09  .09  .10  .07  .19  .20  .21  .23  .23  .13
```

5.9 What are the main assumptions of the INDSCAL model? Explain why the positions of the axes produced by the method of scaling are determined uniquely.

5.10 What is an asymmetric matrix? Suggest four possible methods of analysis for asymmetric proximity matrices and, if possible, apply each method to the following data, which arise from children's ratings of other children in their class. (See Chatfield and Collins, 1980, for details.)

Dissimilarity matrix (Taken from Chatfield and Collins, 1980, courtesy of Chapman & Hall)

Child	1	2	3	4	5	6	7	8
1	0	25	3	25	1	1	2	3
2	1	0	4	25	2	1	3	4
3	1	25	0	25	1	2	1	2
4	1	25	2	0	2	1	1	2
5	1	25	2	25	0	1	1	2
6	1	25	3	25	2	0	2	3
7	2	25	1	25	1	2	0	1
8	1	25	2	25	2	2	1	0

6. Cluster Analysis

6.1 Introduction

An important component of virtually all scientific research is the classification of the phenomena being studied. In the behavioural sciences, for example, these may be individuals or societies or even patterns of behaviour or perception. The investigator is usually interested in finding a classification in which the items of interest are placed into a small number of homogeneous groups or clusters. These are usually mutually exclusive, but this is not obligatory. At the very least the classification may provide a convenient summary of the multivariate data on which it is based, but often it will yield much more than this. It will be an aid to memory and the understanding of the data, and will facilitate communication between different groups of research workers. Often it will have important theoretical or practical implications. In psychiatry, for example, the classification of mental disturbances should help in the search for their causes and lead to improved methods of therapy.

The simplest approach to discovering distinct groups or clusters is by the examination of scattergrams. These may be obtained by plotting the first two or three principal components (see Chapter 4) or from the results of multidimensional scaling (see Chapter 5). Other exploratory methods useful in the search for clustering are the use of Andrews plots and Chernoff 'faces' (see Chapter 3). Once evidence of clustering has been found it will often be useful to provide some sort of explicit classification using one or more *cluster analysis* algorithms. This is the subject covered in the present chapter. There are now very many different methods of cluster analysis and only a selection of the most widely used methods will be introduced here. Comprehensive reviews of clustering techniques are provided by Cormack (1971) and Everitt (1980).

6.2 Examples of the Application of Cluster Analysis

Before proceeding to describe any particular method of cluster analysis in detail it may be useful to look at some examples of their application in order to illustrate their utility.

The first example is of an analysis of a set of data consisting of eight scores for each of 86 long-term prisoners in a British prison. The eight scores were derived from the Buss–Durkee hostility questionnaire (Buss and Durkee, 1957), which consists of 75 questions having an answer 'true' or 'false'. Some typical questions are shown in Table 6.1. The eight scores used in this investigation are subtotals of different sets of the original seventy-five answers; the scores measure various aspects of hostility, these being as follows:

1	Assault	5	Resentment
2	Indirect Hostility	6	Suspicion
3	Irritability	7	Verbal Hostility
4	Negativism	8	Guilt

Table 6.1   *Some typical questions from the Buss–Durkee questionnaire*

I seldom strike back, even if someone hits me first.	TRUE/FALSE
I know that people tend to talk about me behind my back.	TRUE/FALSE
I demand that people respect my rights.	TRUE/FALSE

The method of cluster analysis to be described in Section 6.4 was applied to these data and a three-cluster solution obtained. Table 6.2 shows the within-cluster means for the eight scores and the number of individuals in each cluster.

Table 6.2   *Means on the eight variables for each of three clusters derived from the mixture of multivariate normal clustering technique*

	No. in cluster	Variable							
		1	*2*	*3*	*4*	*5*	*6*	*7*	*8*
Cluster 1	43	5.5	3.5	5.0	2.9	2.9	3.3	6.4	3.9
Cluster 2	17	5.8	6.6	7.2	2.7	4.8	5.6	9.5	6.2
Cluster 3	26	6.4	3.1	4.5	3.0	4.6	5.1	7.0	5.3

The first cluster is characterised by low mean scores on all eight variables, indicating rather low hostility. This could perhaps be termed an essentially 'non-aggressive' group who, on the whole, are likely to be less troublesome for prison authorities. The other two groups show more hostility and could perhaps both be termed 'aggressive' groups. However, they differ in the manner in which their aggression is displayed. Group 2 seem more likely to show verbal hostility rather than to resort to physical assault; in group 3 hostility is likely to manifest itself more violently. Such findings may have important practical implications for the management of prisoners.

A second example concerns a classification of attempted suicide by cluster analysis reported by Paykel and Rassby (1978). The subjects here were 236 suicide attempters presenting at the main emergency service for one city in the USA. From the pool of available variables, fourteen were selected as especially relevant to classification and were used in the cluster analysis. The variables included age, sex, previous suicide history, recent suicidal feelings, and so on. Prior to cluster analysis, a principal components analysis was carried out on the inter-correlation matrix of the fourteen variables, and the first twelve principal component scores used in the cluster analysis rather than the original variables. (This indicates a further possible use of principal components analysis.) Several of the agglomerative hierarchical clustering techniques to be described in the next section were applied to the data and the most satisfactory results were obtained from Ward's method, which indicated that suicide attempters could be classified into three groups. The largest group comprises patients taking overdoses, with less risk to life and a predominance of inter-personal motivations. A second smaller group is distinguished by the use of violent methods with higher risk to life. A third and very striking group comprises recurrent attempters, with previous histories of many attempts, relatively low risk to life, and overtly hostile behaviour. Whilst not claiming that these findings provide a definitive classification of suicide attempters, the authors do suggest that it has the virtue of simplicity, and may be worthy of further exploration.

6.3 Agglomerative Hierarchical Clustering Techniques

This family of methods includes some of the oldest and most frequently used clustering techniques. They all operate in essentially the same way, proceeding sequentially from the stage in which each object is considered to be a single member 'cluster', to the final stage in which there is a single group containing all *n* objects. At each stage in the procedure the number of groups is reduced by one by joining together or *fusing* the two groups considered to be the most similar or to be the closest to each other. The variety of techniques available arises because of the different possibilities for defining inter-group distance or similarity, as we shall see later.

Since the clusters at any stage are obtained by the fusion of two clusters from the previous stage, these methods lead to a hierarchical structure for the objects. One useful visualisation of such a hierarchy is a *tree diagram*, more commonly known as a *dendrogram*. Examples of such diagrams will be given later. Before discussing any of these techniques in detail, however, we should perhaps consider briefly the implications of imposing a hierarchical structure of this kind on data.

The concept of the hierarchical representation of a data set was developed primarily in biology. The structures output from a hierarchical clustering method resembles the traditional hierarchical structure of Linnaean taxonomy with its graded sequence of ranks. Although any numerical taxonomic exercise with biological data need not replicate the structure of traditional classification, there nevertheless remains a strong tendency among biologists to prefer hierarchical classifications. These methods are now used, however, in many other fields in which hierarchical structures may not be the most appropriate, and the logic of their use in such areas needs careful evaluation. For example, in their biological application questions concerning the optimal number of groups do not arise—here the investigator is often specifically interested in the complete tree structure. Such questions, however, are often raised by other users of these techniques, who consequently require a decision regarding the stage of the hierarchical clustering process at which an optimum partitioning of the items to be classified is obtained. This important and difficult question will be discussed in Section 6.3.3.

6.3.1   *Measuring inter-cluster dissimilarity*

Agglomerative hierarchical techniques differ primarily in how they measure the distance or similarity of two clusters (where a cluster may, at times, consist of only a single object). Perhaps the simplest inter-group measures are

$$\text{(a)} \quad d_{AB} = \min_{\substack{i \in A \\ j \in B}} \{d_{ij}\} \tag{6.1}$$

$$\text{(b)} \quad d_{AB} = \max_{\substack{i \in C \\ j \in B}} \{d_{ij}\} \tag{6.2}$$

where d_{AB} is the dissimilarity between two clusters, A and B, and d_{ij} is the dissimilarity between objects i and j. (This, of course, could be one of a large variety of measures, including, for example, Euclidean and city block distances.) The dissimilarity measure in equation (6.1) is the basis of *single linkage* clustering and that in (6.2) the basis of *complete linkage* clustering. Both these techniques have the often desirable property that they are invariant under monotone transformations of the original inter-object dissimilarities (cf. non-metric multidimensional scaling, Section 5.4). To illustrate the operation of agglomerative hierarchical clustering techniques we shall apply both single and complete linkage to the dissimilarity matrix shown in Table 6.3.

Table 6.3 *Dissimilarity matrix for five individuals*

$$
\mathbf{D} = \begin{array}{c} \\ 1 \\ 2 \\ 3 \\ 4 \\ 5 \end{array}
\begin{array}{ccccc}
1 & 2 & 3 & 4 & 5 \\
\left[\begin{array}{ccccc}
0.0 & & & & \\
2.0 & 0.0 & & & \\
6.0 & 5.0 & 0.0 & & \\
10.0 & 9.0 & 4.0 & 0.0 & \\
9.0 & 8.0 & 5.0 & 3.0 & 0.0
\end{array} \right]
\end{array}
$$

6.3.2 Single linkage clustering

At stage one of the procedure individuals 1 and 2 are merged to form a cluster, since d_{12} is the smallest entry in the dissimilarity matrix $\mathbf{D}$. The distances between this group and the three remaining single individuals 3, 4 and 5 are obtained from $\mathbf{D}$ as follows:

$$d_{(12)3} = \min \{d_{13}, d_{23}\} = d_{23} = 5.0,$$

$$d_{(12)4} = \min \{d_{14}, d_{24}\} = d_{24} = 9.0,$$

$$d_{(12)5} = \min \{d_{15}, d_{25}\} = d_{25} = 8.0.$$

We may now form a new distance matrix $\mathbf{D}$, giving inter-individual dissimilarities, and cluster-individual dissimilarities:

$$
\mathbf{D}_1 = \begin{array}{c} \\ (12) \\ 3 \\ 4 \\ 5 \end{array}
\begin{array}{cccc}
(12) & 3 & 4 & 5 \\
\left[\begin{array}{cccc}
0.0 & & & \\
5.0 & 0.0 & & \\
9.0 & 4.0 & 0.0 & \\
8.0 & 5.0 & 3.0 & 0.0
\end{array} \right]
\end{array}
$$

The smallest entry in $\mathbf{D}_1$ is d_{45} and so individuals 4 and 5 are now merged to form a second cluster, and the dissimilarities now become

$$d_{(12)3} = 5.0 \quad \text{(as before)},$$

$$d_{(12)(45)} = \min \{d_{14}, d_{15}, d_{24}, d_{25}\} = d_{25} = 8.0,$$

$$d_{(45)3} = \min \{d_{34}, d_{35}\} = d_{34} = 4.0.$$

These may be arranged in a matrix $\mathbf{D}_2$, where

$$
\mathbf{D}_2 = \begin{array}{c} \\ (12) \\ 3 \\ (45) \end{array}
\begin{array}{ccc}
(12) & 3 & (45) \\
\left[\begin{array}{ccc}
0.0 & & \\
5.0 & 0.0 & \\
8.0 & 4.0 & 0.0
\end{array} \right]
\end{array}
$$

The smallest entry is now $d_{(45)3}$, and so individual 3 is added to the groups containing individuals 4 and 5. Finally, fusion of the two groups at this stage takes place to form a single group containing all five individuals. The dendrogram illustrating this series of mergers is shown in Figure 6.1.

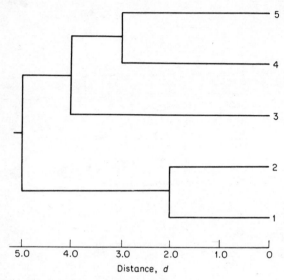

Figure 6.1   *Single linkage dendrogram*

This technique seems first to have been described by Florek *et al.* (1951) under the title 'dendritic method'. McQuitty (1957) and Sneath (1957) independently introduced slightly different versions of it, and it was the subject of further discussion in Johnson (1967).

6.3.3   *Complete linkage clustering*
As with single linkage this method begins by merging individuals 1 and 2. The dissimilarities between this cluster and the three remaining individuals 3, 4 and 5 are obtained from **D** as follows:

$$d_{(12)3} = \max \{d_{13}, d_{23}\} = d_{13} = 6.0,$$

$$d_{(12)4} = \max \{d_{14}, d_{24}\} = d_{14} = 10.0,$$

$$d_{(12)5} = \max \{d_{15}, d_{25}\} = d_{15} = 9.0.$$

The final result is the dendrogram shown in Figure 6.2.
A further possibility for measuring inter-cluster dissimilarity is the

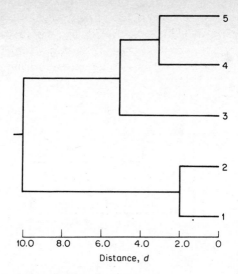

Figure 6.2 *Complete linkage dendrogram*

following

$$d_{AB} = \frac{1}{n_A n_B} \sum_{i \in A} \sum_{j \in B} d_{ij} \qquad (6.3)$$

where n_A and n_B are the number of individuals in clusters A and B. This measure is the basis of a very widely used procedure known as *group average clustering*. Another very popular technique is that introduced by Ward (1963), who proposed that at any stage of the analysis the loss of information which results from the grouping of objects into clusters can be measured by the total sum of squared deviations of every object's variable values from their respective cluster means. At each step in the analysis, union of all possible pairs of clusters is considered, and the two clusters where fusion results in the minimum increase in the sum of squares are combined. A numerical example illustrating group average clustering is given in Everitt (1977b), and one for Ward's technique in Everitt (1980). It is important to note that neither of these techniques is invariant to monotone transformations.

6.3.4 *An example of the application of single linkage, complete linkage, and group average clustering*
Each of these methods was applied to the similarity matrix of thirty adjectives describing pain given in Table 5.6. The resulting dendrograms appear in Figures 6.3, 6.4 and 6.5.

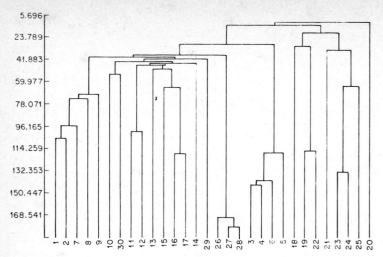

Figure 6.3   *Single linkage dendrogram for pain adjectives similarity matrix*

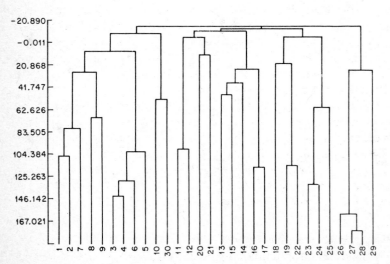

Figure 6.4   *Complete linkage dendrogram for pain adjectives similarity matrix*

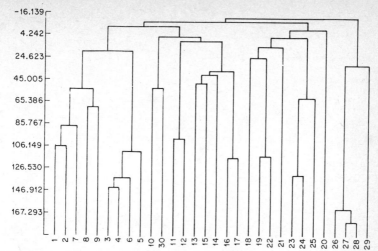

Figure 6.5 *Group average dendrogram for pain adjectives similarity matrix*

For these data the results given by each of the three methods are very similar and the clusters of adjectives appear intuitively sensible, with, for example, words such as flickering, quivering, jumping and flashing forming one group, and hot, burning and scalding forming another. The detailed analyses of these data, and a comparison of the cluster analysis groupings with those proposed originally by Melzack (1975), are given in Reading, Everitt and Sledmere (1982).

These results can usefully be combined with those obtained from a multidimensional scaling of the same data (see Section 5.6) by indicating part of the hierarchical cluster structure on the two-dimensional solution obtained from the scaling procedure. Figure 6.6 shows the single linkage solution displayed in this way, and provides a convenient and informative display of the relationships between the adjectives as indicated by their similarities.

6.3.6 Measuring goodness-of-fit

Once a dendrogram has been obtained from some particular hierarchical technique it is important to consider how well it 'fits' the original similarity or dissimilarity matrix. In this way we might be able to assess whether the derived hierarchical structure is suitable for the data set under investigation. Essentially there are two aspects of fit that require attention. The first is the global fit of the dendrogram for the input

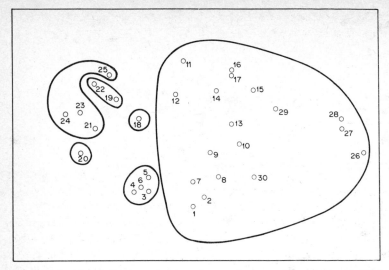

Figure 6.6   *Single linkage cluster solution for pain adjectives embedded in two-dimensional non-metric multidimensional scaling solution*

similarities or dissimilarities. The second is concerned with which particular partition obtained from the hierarchy is, in some sense, optimal. In other words, what is the best number of groups?

The usual way to assess the global fit of the dendrograms is by use of the *cophenetic correlation coefficient* (CPCC). This is simply the product moment correlation between the entries of the dissimilarity matrix and those of the so-called *cophenetic matrix*, the latter being the fusion level at which a pair of objects appear together in the same cluster for the first time. For example, the cophenetic matrix arising from the application of single linkage to the dissimilarity matrix in Table 6.3 is given in Table 6.4. The cophenetic correlation for this example takes the value 0.82.

In general, 'large' values of the CPCC are taken as indicating that the dendrogram provides a reasonable summary of the observed similarities or dissimilarities. However, the question obviously arises as to what, exactly, constitutes a 'large' value. In an attempt to answer this question Rohlf and Fisher (1968) studied the distribution of the CPCC under the null hypothesis of a single cluster versus the alternative hypothesis of a system of nested clusters. They found that a value of the CPCC above 0.8 is needed for rejecting the null hypothesis, although in a later paper, Rohlf (1970) warns that even a CPCC near 0.9 does not

Table 6.4 *Cophenetic matrix obtained by applying single linkage clustering to Table 6.3*

$$
\mathbf{C} = \begin{array}{c}
 \\
1 \\
2 \\
3 \\
4 \\
5
\end{array}
\begin{array}{ccccc}
1 & 2 & 3 & 4 & 5 \\
\hline
0.0 & & & & \\
2.0 & 0.0 & & & \\
5.0 & 5.0 & 0.0 & & \\
5.0 & 5.0 & 4.0 & 0.0 & \\
5.0 & 5.0 & 4.0 & 3.0 & 0.0
\end{array}
$$

guarantee that the dendrogram provides an adequate summary of the observed dissimilarities. In other words, very high values of the CPCC are needed before it can be safely assumed that a hierarchical cluster structure is suitable for the data under investigation. When one is only willing to assume that the observed similarities or dissimilarities have ordinal significance, then a coefficient of rank correlation is used to measure the global fit of the dendrogram in place of the CPCC; for example, Hubert (1974) proposed the Goodman–Kruskal γ statistic for this purpose.

With hierarchical clustering, partitions for a particular number of groups are obtained by selecting one of the clusterings in the nested sequence of groupings that comprise the hierarchy. Many investigators will be interested in selecting that partition which best fits the data in some sense and a number of possible methods for this have been suggested. Perhaps the most common is to examine the dendrogram for large changes between adjacent fusion levels; such a change in going from, say, j to $j-1$ groups might be indicative of a j group solution. For example, Figure 6.7 shows a dendrogram rather suggestive of three groups.

Such a procedure may, of course, be rather subjective as some of the examples in Everitt (1980), Chapter 5, indicate. Mojena (1977) suggests a more objective procedure based upon the relative sizes of the different fusion levels. His proposal is to select the number of groups corresponding to the first stage in the dendrogram satisfying

$$\alpha_{j+1} > \bar{\alpha} + k s_\alpha \tag{6.4}$$

where $\alpha_0, \alpha_1, \ldots, \alpha_{n-1}$ are the fusion levels corresponding to stages with $n, n-1, \ldots, 1$ clusters, $\bar{\alpha}$ and s_α are, respectively, the mean and unbiased standard deviation of the α values, and k is a constant. As given in (6.4) the stopping rule is for fusion levels arising from the analysis of dissimilarity matrices; in the case of similarities where $\alpha_0 > \alpha_1 \cdots$

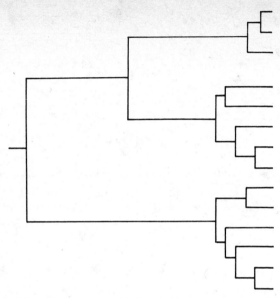

Figure 6.7 *Dendrogram suggestive of three groups*

$> \alpha_{n-1}$, the corresponding inequality is $\alpha_{j+1} < \alpha - ks_\alpha$. Mojena suggested that values of k in the range 2.75 to 3.50 gave the best overall results. If no value of α satisfies inequality (6.4) then the data are regarded as consisting of a single cluster. Mojena gives a number of examples which indicate that his suggested procedure may prove very useful and have many practical applications.

6.3.6 Some properties of agglomerative hierarchical clustering techniques

Single linkage often does not give satisfactory results if intermediates are present between clusters, due to the phenomena known as *chaining*, which refers to the tendency of a method to incorporate these intermediate points into an existing cluster rather than initiating a new one. A set of two-dimensional data which might give rise to chaining is shown in Figure 6.8. Because of this problem single linkage tends to lead to the formation of long straggly clusters.

Group average, complete linkage and Ward's method often find spherical clusters even when the data appear to contain clusters of other shapes. Consequently they may impose a structure on the data rather than extract the actual structure present. This problem is illustrated for some two-dimensional data in Figure 6.9.

In the late 1960s there were several attempts at constructing a

Figure 6.8 *Data illustrating chaining effect*

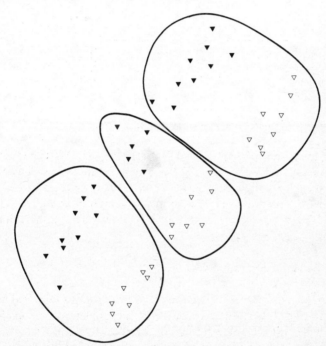

Figure 6.9 *Two-dimensional data illustrating type of solution given by group average, Ward's method and complete linkage for elliptical groups*

theoretical framework within which to study the properties of hierarchical clustering techniques. For example, Johnson (1967) showed that the entries in the cophenetic matrices derived from such methods satisfy the *ultrametric inequality*,

$$d(x, y) \leqslant \max \{d(x, z), d(y, z)\} \qquad (6.5)$$

(see Exercise 6.1). Johnson showed that each hierarchical clustering scheme gives rise to this particular kind of metric, and, conversely, that given such a metric we may recover the hierarchical structure from it.

Jardine and Sibson (1968) took this as their starting point and argued that since the input proximities are. not generally ultrametric (and only occasionally metric), then a cluster method which transforms a proximity matrix into a hierarchic dendrogram should be regarded as a method whereby the ultrametric inequality is imposed on a proximity measure. They then specify a number of criteria which, they argue, should be met by any such transformation. The first three criteria are as follows:

(a) A unique result should be obtained from a given proximity matrix; that is, the transformation should be *well defined.*

(b) Small changes in the data should produce small changes in the resultant dendrograms; that is, the transformation should be *continuous.*

(c) If the dissimilarity coefficient is already ultrametric it should be unchanged by the transformation.

Jardine and Sibson show that these criteria are satisfied only by the single linkage method and, consequently, suggest that other hierarchical techniques are unacceptable. Since single linkage has never proved to be a very popular or successful method in practice, this recommendation has led to some controversy, the most severe criticism coming from the so-called 'Australian school' of Williams, Lance, Dale and Clifford (1971).

Consider first the criterion that the transformation should be well defined; that is, that a unique result should be obtained from a given proximity matrix. Methods other than single linkage will fail this test only when there are equal proximity values which are arbitrarily resolved. Williams *et al.* suggest that in practice such ambiguities are rare, but where they are encountered propose an alternative to making an arbitrary choice, involving reference to information outside the ambiguity under consideration, in particular to the relationships with all other entities in the proximity matrix.

Williams *et al.* also produce fairly convincing arguments against the need for these techniques to satisfy the criteria of being continuous and leaving an ultrametric unchanged by transformation. Essentially they are more concerned with a pragmatic approach to numerical classification and have obviously found methods other than single linkage useful in practice. Gower (1975) also feels that Jardine and Sibson's rejection of all but single linkage clustering is too extreme and that their criteria may be too stringent. He concludes that some of the criteria are not essential.

It must be said that the approach taken by Jardine and Sibson appears to have had little impact on the majority of users of cluster analysis. Single linkage is not popular with most investigators employing clustering methods, and the alternative mathematically acceptable method provided by these two authors is applicable only to small data sets, and the solutions given are generally rather difficult to interpret.

An alternative to setting up a series of mathematical criteria for studying and evaluating the numerous agglomerative hierarchical techniques is to compare their effectiveness across a variety of data sets generated to have a particular structure. In this way the solutions obtained by a particular technique may be compared with the generated structure. A number of studies of this type have been undertaken (for example, Cunningham and Ogilvie, 1972). Whilst the results are dependent on the data generated, group average clustering and Ward's method of clustering appear to perform fairly well overall. (These Monte Carlo studies are reviewed by Milligan, 1981.)

6.4 Mixture Models for Cluster Analysis

Although cluster analysis techniques have generally been considered to be part of exploratory data analysis where stochastic models are not considered essential, a number of attempts have been made to introduce a more formal probabilistic approach. For example, Ling (1973) and Smith and Dubes (1980) consider various probability models for proximity matrices. However, here we shall consider an approach to clustering the raw data matrix **X**, which uses a particular type of probability density function, known as a *finite mixture distribution*, as its model. One great advantage of this approach is that it completely disposes of the need for a similarity measure between individuals.

To introduce the approach let us suppose that we have measured a single variable, x, on a number of individuals from some population of interest. We suspect that in the population there are two distinct types of individual and that for one type x has a normal distribution with mean μ_1 and standard deviation σ_1, and that for the second type, x also has a normal distribution but with mean μ_2 and standard deviation σ_2. Taking the population as a whole, we may then say that the density function of x is as follows:

$$f(x; \theta) = p \frac{1}{\sqrt{2\pi}\,\sigma_1} \exp-\tfrac{1}{2}\left(\frac{x-\mu_1}{\sigma_1}\right)^2$$

$$+ (1-p) \frac{1}{\sqrt{2\pi}\,\sigma_2} \exp-\tfrac{1}{2}\left(\frac{x-\mu_2}{\sigma_2}\right)^2 \qquad (6.6)$$

where $\theta' = [\mu_1, \mu_2, \sigma_1, \sigma_2, p]$ and p and $(1-p)$ are the relative sizes of the two clusters in the population; p is known as the *mixing proportion* and f is a normal mixture density with two components. Given a sample of observations $x_1, \ldots, x_n$ from this population we would like to be able to estimate the parameter vector θ, since this would give us the information sought on the constituent clusters.

Density functions such as (6.6) that assume normal component densities are suitable models for continuous variables and could be extended in a straightforward way to the multivariate situation by using multivariate normal components; the number of components might also be altered to allow for, say, c clusters. (The problem of assessing the value of c from the data is discussed briefly a little later.) Such mixture distributions have been studied by Wolfe (1970), Day (1969) and Duda and Hart (1973). Estimation of the considerable number of parameters is a formidable computational problem but can be handled fairly successfully by maximum likelihood methods. A numerical example of the application of this approach to cluster analysis is described below.

If the variables being recorded are binary rather than continuous then a mixture density based upon normal components would obviously not be realistic. However, the approach may still be used with a suitable choice of component density. One possibility is to assume that, within each cluster, responses to individual binary items are independent, with probabilities which are constant within clusters but different between clusters. We would then want to estimate the mixing proportions and the probability of a positive response on each variable in each cluster, and again maximum likelihood estimation may be used; details are given in Everitt and Hand (1981). Finite mixture distributions based upon such components are essentially equivalent to the *latent class model* proposed by Lazarsfeld and Henry (1968). The assumption that within clusters the variables are independent is difficult to verify in practice, but is directly analogous to the assumption in the factor analysis model that observed variables are conditionally independent given the factors (see Chapter 11). So, in a latent class model any observed correlations between the binary items are considered to be due to the clustered nature of the population.

Maximum likelihood estimation for both mixtures of multivariate normal densities and for latent class analysis assume that c, the number of components in the mixture (or the number of clusters in the population), is known *a priori*. In many applications, however, this will not be so and, consequently, we would need to construct some kind of hypothesis test for c. One test, considered by a number of authors, including Wolfe (1971) and Binder (1978), is a likelihood ratio test of c $= c_0$ against $c = c_1$. The test statistic, λ, is given by

$$\lambda = 2(L_{c_1} - L_{c_0}) \tag{6.7}$$

where L_{c_0} and L_{c_1} are the log-likelihoods under the hypothesis of c_0 and c_1 groups. Under the null hypothesis that $c = c_0$, λ is generally assumed to be asymptotically distributed as chi-square, with degrees of freedom equal to the difference in the number of parameters between the two hypotheses. However, in the context of finite mixtures various authors, for example Wolfe (1971), Binder (1978) and Everitt (1981), have shown that λ does not have such a null distribution, and have suggested various small amendments to the test. For example, with normal mixtures, Wolfe (1971) has suggested the modified test statistic

$$\lambda' = \frac{2}{n}\left(n - 1 - d - \frac{c_1}{2}\right)(L_{c_1} - L_{c_0}) \tag{6.8}$$

to be tested as a chi-square with $2d(c_1 - c_0)$ degrees of freedom. This appears to work reasonably well in practice. We will now move on to consider some examples of the application of this approach to cluster analysis.

6.4.1 Some numerical examples of the application of mixture distributions

The first example concerns the application of multivariate normal mixture distributions to a set of four test scores obtained from 86 aphasic cases. The four variables were measures of auditory disturbance, visual and reading disturbances, speech and language disturbances and visuomotor and writing disturbances. The data are described in detail in Powell, Clark and Bailey (1979).

Fitting mixtures of multivariate normal distributions to these data, assuming equal variance–covariance matrices in each group, resulted in a four group solution (as indicated by the likelihood ratio test). Figure 6.10 shows the means of each group for each of the four variables. Essentially the four groups differ only in severity, and could be contrasted with the original classification of aphasia described by

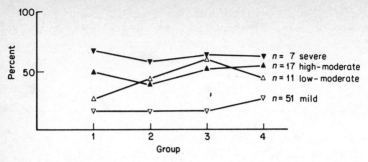

Figure 6.10   *Mean error scores (as % of total possible errors) for four cluster solution on aphasic patients (Taken with permission from Powell et al., 1979)*

Schuell (1965) in which it was claimed there were seven groups differing in the pattern of symptoms.

The next example consists of the application of latent class analysis to data collected by Bennett (1976) on school teachers' responses to a questionnaire concerned with various aspects of classroom behaviour, classroom management and organisation, and teacher control. In total the questionnaire consisted of 38 items each having a yes–no answer. Aitken, Anderson and Hinde (1981) applied latent class analysis to the answers from 468 teachers in an attempt to discover evidence for different teaching styles. Table 6.5 presents the results for a two-class solution. Class 1 teachers almost all restrict children's movement and talking in the classroom, while a large majority organise their work by timetable, emphasise separate subject teaching and talk to the whole class, and many have pupils working individually on tasks chosen by the teacher. Class 2 teachers are much less restrictive in their classroom organisation, emphasise integrated subject teaching, and are likely to have pupils working individually or in groups on work of their own choice. Marking or grading of pupils' work is very uncommon in Class 2. The identification of Class 1 with a formal and Class 2 with an informal teaching style is very clear. Aitken *et al.* also fitted a three-class model, and readers are referred to the original paper for details.

6.5   Graphical Aids to Cluster Analysis
It has been stressed in the introduction to this text that, in the exploratory stage of data analysis, graphs and diagrams have an important role to play. This is particularly so in applications where graphs and diagrams of various kinds can facilitate the understanding and interpretation of the results obtained from clustering algorithms.

Table 6.5 *Parameter estimates for latent class model fitted to data obtained from teachers' questionnaire (with permission from Aitken et al. 1981) (decimal point omitted)*

Variable		Class 1	Class 2
1	Pupils have choice of where to sit	22	43
2	Pupils sit in groups of three or more	60	87*
3	Pupils allocated to seating by ability	35	23
4	Pupils stay in same seats for most of day	91	63*
5	Pupils not allowed freedom of movement in classroom	97	54*
6	Pupils not allowed to talk freely	89	48*
7	Pupils expected to ask permission to leave room	97	76*
8	Pupils expected to be quiet	82	42*
9	Monitors appointed for special jobs	85	67
10	Pupils taken out of school regularly	32	60
11	Timetable used for organising work	90	66*
12	Use own materials rather than textbooks	19	49
13	Pupils expected to know tables by heart	92	76
14	Pupils asked to find own reference materials	29	37
15	Pupils given homework regularly	35	22
16	Teacher talks to whole class	71	44
17	Pupils work in groups on teacher tasks	29	42
18	Pupils work in groups on work of own choice	15	46*
19	Pupils work individually on teacher tasks	55	37
20	Pupils work individually on work of own choice	28	50
21	Explore concepts in number work	18	55*
22	Encourage fluency in written English even if inaccurate	87	94
23	Pupils' work marked or graded	43	14*
24	Spelling and grammatical errors corrected	84	68
25	Stars given to pupils who produce best work	57	29
26	Arithmetic tests given at least once a week	59	38
27	Spelling tests given at least once a week	73	51
28	End of term tests given	66	44
29	Many pupils who create discipline problems	09	09
30	Verbal reproof sufficient	97	95
31	Discipline—extra work given	70	53
32	Smack	65	42
33	Withdrawal of privileges	86	77
34	Send to head teacher	24	17
35	Send out of room	19	15
36	Emphasis on separate subject teaching	85	50*
37	Emphasis on aesthetic subject	55	63
38	Emphasis on integrated subject teaching	22	65*

* Indicates an item with large differences in response probability between Classes 1 and 2.

Some of these aids have already been discussed (for example, scattergrams, Andrews plots and principal component plots). A number of others will be described in this section.

6.5.1   *Some simple plots for examining cluster solutions*

Cohen *et al.* (1980) describes a number of potentially useful *ad hoc* methods for evaluating cluster analysis solutions, some involving very simple plotting procedures. For example, they suggest a plot of squared distances from certain cluster centroids to entities that are near that centroid might be useful for examining the internal cohesiveness of a cluster. For each cluster centroid, the distances of every entity from that centroid are plotted above the cluster identification shown on the *x*-axis. The symbol plotted is the cluster to which the entity was assigned. Such a plot is shown in Figure 6.11. The information obtainable from this very simple plot includes the following: clusters F and H are extremely well separated from neighbouring entities; an entity not assigned to cluster E is still reasonably close to cluster E, and there is a large distance between the members of cluster A farthest from their centroid and the next closest entities not assigned to A.

Another simple graphical aid described by these authors can be used for examining the clusters in terms of either variables used to form the clusters or other variables of interest. Here the clusters are again identified along the *x*-axis, and above each label the values on a certain variable for each entity in that cluster are plotted. The median for the cluster is plotted as a star. This enables one to use the variable in question to compare several entities grouped in the same cluster and to make multiple comparisons across clusters. An example of such a plot appears in Figure 6.12. This shows that clusters A and B are quite similar on this variable except for one entity, A1, in cluster A; cluster E tends to have large entities with moderate spread while cluster M has much smaller values with small spread.

6.5.2   *Canonical variate plots*

A useful method of displaying a set of clusters obtained from the application of some clustering technique is by means of a *canonical variate* plot. Essentially this involves a principal components type analysis of the matrix **G** given by

$$\mathbf{G} = \mathbf{W}^{-1}\mathbf{B} \qquad (6.9)$$

where **W** is the $(p \times p)$ pooled *within groups* covariance matrix and **B** is the $(p \times p)$ *between groups* covariance matrix. Such an analysis leads to a new set of variables (the canonical variates) which are linear

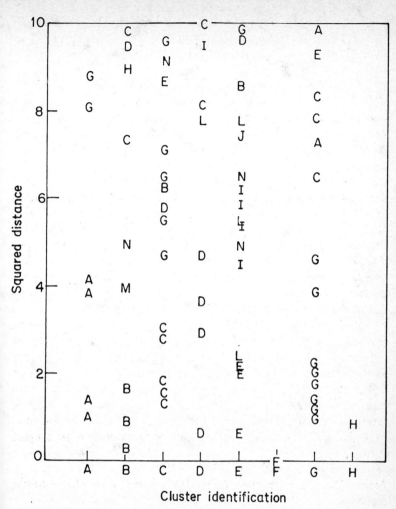

Figure 6.11 *Plot of squared distances of selected individuals from their cluster centroids (Taken with permission from Cohen et al., 1977)*

transformations of the original variates that have the properties of being orthogonal and maximising the between-group variation relative to that within groups. The number of canonical variates that can be derived is equal to the smaller of $(g-1)$ and p where g is the number of clusters.

Plots of the data in the space of the first few canonical variates allow a visual inspection of the separation between groups, relative to the

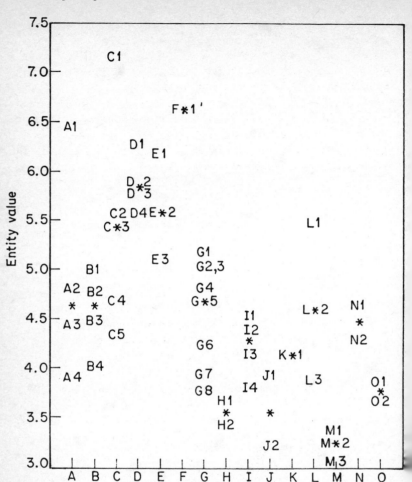

Figure 6.12   *Plot of values of a single variable for selected individuals in various clusters (Taken with permission from Cohen et al., 1977)*

variation within groups. For example, Figure 6.13 shows a plot in the space of the two canonical variates of the three groups obtained by applying normal mixture cluster analysis (see Section 6.4) to the 'prisoners' data described in Section 6.2. The major impression gained from this plot is of a 'cloud' of points, with little evidence of any clear-cut 'gaps' between the clusters. The diagram suggests perhaps that this cluster solution has not identified really distinct groups of prisoners,

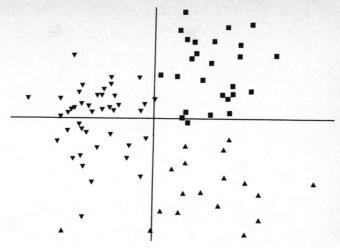

Figure 6.13 *Canonical variate plot for 'prisoners' data*

but has merely 'dissected' a homogeneous data set into three parts.

When there are just two groups only one canonical variate is possible, and this is then equivalent to the *linear discriminant function*, originally derived by Fisher. This function is often used as an aid to classification and diagnosis. For example, suppose a disease can only be diagnosed without error by means of a post-mortem examination. If a number of patients are measured on variables considered to be indicative of the disease, and these patients are then subjected to post-mortem examination upon death, then Fisher's discriminant function may be computed for the two groups—'with disease' and 'without disease'. Now, given a new patient measured on the same variables, a discriminant function score may be calculated; this may then be compared with a threshold value to judge whether the patients' scores are indicative that the disease is present or not. If the distribution of the scores in each group is multivariate normal with the same variance-covariance matrix, then it can be shown that Fisher's discriminant function is optimal in the sense of minimising the misclassification rate. Details of this technique and many other methods of classification are to be found in Hand (1981b).

6.6 Summary

Cluster analysis is potentially a very useful method for the exploration of complex multivariate data. Its use, however, requires considerable care if misleading solutions are to be avoided, and much attention needs to be given to the evaluation and validation of results. Mixture models present a more 'statistical' approach to the area and in many respects this is to be welcomed; more details of finite mixture distributions are given in Everitt and Hand (1981). Since clustering techniques will generate a set of clusters even when applied to random, unclustered data, the question of validating and evaluating solutions becomes of great importance. A number of generally *ad hoc* procedures for this purpose have been suggested, details of which may be found in Anderberg (1973) and Dubes and Jain (1979).

Finally, we should perhaps comment briefly on the differences between the tree representations of dissimilarity and similarity matrices given by the hierarchical clustering techniques described in this chapter, and the spatial representations given by the methods of multidimensional scaling. Sattath and Tversky (1977) give some examples where such data are better described by a tree representation rather than by a spatial configuration, but also concede that for some data the opposite will be true. In general, the appropriateness of a tree or a spatial representation will depend upon the nature of both the task and the structure of the stimuli. Some object sets suggest a natural dimensional structure, for example, emotions in terms of intensity and pleasure, and sound in terms of intensity and pitch. Other object sets may suggest a hierarchical structure that results, for example, from an evolutionary process in which all the objects have an initial common structure and later develop additional distinctive features. Perhaps the two approaches are, in general, appropriate for different data, or for capturing different aspects of the same data.

EXERCISES

6.1   Show that the entries of the cophenetic matrix satisfy the ultrametric inequality.

6.2   Show that the inter-cluster distances used by single linkage, complete linkage and group average clustering satisfy the formula

$$d_{k(ij)} = \alpha_i d_{ki} + \alpha_j d_{kj} + \gamma |d_{ki} - d_{kj}|$$

with

$\alpha_i = \alpha_j = \frac{1}{2};\quad \gamma = -\frac{1}{2}$ (single linkage)

$\alpha_i = \alpha_j = \frac{1}{2};\quad \gamma = \frac{1}{2}$ (complete linkage)

$\alpha_i = n_i(n_i + n_j);\quad \alpha_j = n_j/(n_i + n_j);\quad \gamma = 0$ (group average).

($d_{k(ij)}$ is the distance between a group k and a group (ij) formed by the fusion of groups i and j, and d_{ij} is the distance between groups i and j.)

6.3   Apply Ward's hierarchical clustering method to the following set of univariate data on five individuals:

Individual	Variable value
1	1
2	2
3	7
4	9
5	12

6.4   Consider Ward's hierarchical clustering procedure in which clusters are merged so as to produce the smallest increase in the sum-of-squared error at each step. If the i-th cluster contains n_i objects with sample mean vector $\mathbf{m}_i$ and the j-th cluster contains n_j objects with sample mean vector $\mathbf{m}_j$, show that the smallest increase results from merging the pair of clusters for which

$$\frac{n_i n_j}{(n_i + n_j)} d_{ij}^2$$

is a minimum where d_{ij} is the Euclidean distance between the means of cluster i and cluster j.

6.5   For the 'city crime' data of Exercise 3.5 apply several different methods of cluster analysis and compare the results. Are the cluster analysis solutions more informative than the principal components and faces representations of Chapters 3 and 4?

PART III
Explanatory and Response Variables

A distinction is made between response and explanatory variables, and a convenient system of models introduced with which to examine the effects of the latter type of variable on the former. The reader should bear in mind that the distinction between the two types of variable is not always clear cut, and that one particular variable might be considered as an explanatory variable for one analysis, yet be the response variable in another. The case where one is interested in modelling the variation of a quantitative response variable in terms of the variation in one or more quantitative explanatory variables will be familiar to most readers as *multiple regression*. Readers should also be familiar with models for the *analysis of variance* (ANOVA) and *covariance* (ANCOVA). The generalised linear model incorporates all of these, as well as *log-linear models* for contingency tables, *linear-logistic* models for binary response variables, and *hazard* models for response, failure or survival times.

---

7. *The Generalised Linear Model*

7.1 Introduction

When analysing data using factor analysis (see Chapter 11) or principal components analysis (Chapter 4) no distinction is made between the observed variables, and it is the interrelationships between all of these, and the structure or pattern of these relationships, which is of most interest. However, in many situations the observed variables will be of two types, usually designated as *response* and *explanatory* and, in such cases, interest focuses on how the response variable is related to the explanatory variables. For example, one might be interested in investigating how an animal's response to a drug changes as the dosage of the drug increases, or in how achievement test scores are related to measures of academic performance. In this chapter we shall discuss an extremely useful approach to such problems via the application of *linear models*, confining ourselves to the situation where we have a single response variable and multiple explanatory variables.

7.2 Linear Models

Consider a situation where we are interested, for example, in describing the number of times people visit their doctor annually as a function of their age. There is, of course, considerable variation in the number of times people of a given age visit their doctor and so only population means or *expected values* for the number of visits will be considered in this section. After the relevant data have been analysed, suppose it is found that the average number of visits is predicted by the following equation:

$$\text{Visits} = 2 + \tfrac{1}{20} \times \text{Age} \tag{7.1}$$

This means that, on average, a person aged 40 will visit a doctor four times a year, a person aged 80, six times, and so on. A general (algebraic) form of this equation is:

$$y = \beta_0 + \beta_1 x \tag{7.2}$$

where y is the *response variable* (here, visits) and x the *explanatory variable* (age). The terms β_0 and β_1 are called *parameters* of the model. The latter have fixed, but usually unknown values which have to be estimated from data obtained from a sample of the population of interest. The parameters of a linear model such as (7.2) are called *regression coefficients*; they are merely numbers that describe the way in which the response variable is dependent on the explanatory variable. Graphically, equation (7.2) can be represented as a single straight line (Figure 7.1). It can be seen that the parameter β_0 is the point where the line intercepts the vertical axis, and β_1 is the slope of the line.

It may now be asked whether, after allowing for the effect of age, a person's sex has any influence on the frequency of visits to a physician. On the assumption that it has, the model appropriate to this situation might be the following:

$$\text{Visits} = \beta_0 + \beta_1 \times \text{Age} + \beta_2 \times \text{Sex} \tag{7.3}$$

or, in general,

$$y = \beta_0 + \beta_1 x_1 + \beta_2 x_2 \tag{7.4}$$

This description is not quite so straightforward as before because the variable 'sex' cannot have the same quantitative meaning as measurement of a person's age. It is here defined to be a *dummy variable* that

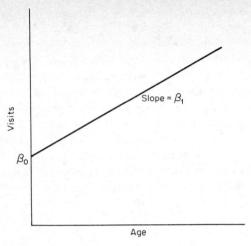

Figure 7.1   *Graphical representation of the model specified by equation*
(7.2)

takes the value 0 for men, and 1 for women; it is merely a way of
distinguishing between males and females. The model in equation (7.3)
describes two lines as is shown in Figure 7.2. These lines are parallel,
with their slope equal to the value of β_1. The parameter β_0 is the
intercept of the male line on the vertical axis, and β_2 is the distance
between the two lines. The parameter β_2 (which could, of course, be

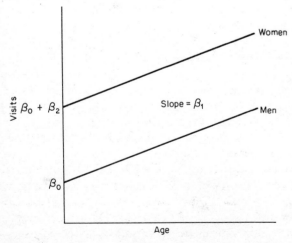

Figure 7.2   *Graphical representation of the model specified by equation*
(7.3)

negative) is a measure of the influence of a person's sex on the expected annual number of visits to a doctor. The fact that the two lines are parallel means that the effect of age on frequency of visits is the same for both sexes, or that the known effect of a person's sex is the same for all age groups. These are merely different ways of saying that there is no *interaction* between the effects of age and sex.

Now consider a situation where there is interaction between the effects of age and sex. How could this be incorporated into our model? An interaction between the two effects indicates that the two lines describing the effect of age on doctor-visits for the two sexes are not parallel. A convenient way of expressing this fact algebraically is to create a new variable (Int, or x_3) which is defined as the product of the variables Age and Sex (or, in general, x_1 and x_2). The model describing this situation now becomes:

$$\text{Visits} = \beta_0 + \beta_1 \times \text{Age} + \beta_2 \times \text{Sex} + \beta_3 \times \text{Int} \qquad (7.5)$$

or, in general,

$$y = \beta_0 + \beta_1 x_1 + \beta_2 x_2 + \beta_3 x_3 \qquad (7.6)$$

Each time a new variable is introduced into the model an additional parameter is added (here β_3). To understand what equation (7.5) means, we first consider the number of visits by men. Here both Sex and Int are equal to 0, and equation (7.5) reduces to

$$\text{Visits} = \beta_0 + \beta_1 \times \text{Age} \qquad (7.7)$$

For women, however, Sex = 1 and Int takes the same values as Age, so that (7.5) now becomes

$$\text{Visits} = \beta_0 + \beta_1 \times \text{Age} + \beta_2 + \beta_3 \times \text{Age} \qquad (7.8)$$

or

$$\text{Visits} = (\beta_0 + \beta_2) + (\beta_1 + \beta_3) \times \text{Age} \qquad (7.9)$$

Clearly the parameter β_3 is a measure of the difference between the slopes of the two lines (Figure 7.3).

This process is an example of *model building*, and provides an approach by which we can find a mathematical or geometrical description of the structure in the values of the response variable. (The question of how well the model describes the data is taken up in later chapters.) All the models discussed above involve a *linear combination* of the parameters $\beta_0, \beta_1, \beta_2, \ldots$, and consequently are known as *linear models*. In other words, such models are defined in terms of their parameters, not in terms of the explanatory variables, so models such as

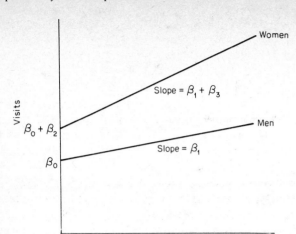

Figure 7.3 *Graphical representation of the model specified by equation* (7.5)

$$y = \beta_0 + \beta_1 x + \beta_2 x^2 + \beta_3 x^3 \tag{7.10}$$

and

$$y = \beta_0 + \beta_1 x_1 x_2 + \beta_3 x_3 x_4 \tag{7.11}$$

are also linear models, a fact which is, at times, confusing to the beginner.

Returning to our expected-number-of-visits example, let us suppose that we wish to consider, now, the effect of a person's social class (with, for example, five classes coded as 1, 2, 3, 4 and 5), on our response variable. A possible linear model would be

$$\text{Visits} = \mu + \alpha_i \tag{7.12}$$

where μ is an overall mean for the number of visits, and α_i represents the effect of the i-th social class on the number of visits. Equation (7.12) should be familiar as the usual *one-way analysis of variance model*. As written it appears to be somewhat different from models such as (7.2) and (7.3), but by extending the concept of dummy variables met earlier, it may easily be rearranged into an essentially similar form. To represent the variable social class, five dummy variables are introduced coded as indicated in Table 7.1. In terms of the five dummy variables, equation (7.12) may be rewritten as

$$\text{Visits} = \mu + \alpha_1 x_1 + \alpha_2 x_2 + \alpha_3 x_3 + \alpha_4 x_4 + \alpha_5 x_5 \tag{7.13}$$

Equation (7.13) is now of the same general form as (7.2), (7.3) and

Table 7.1   *Coding of social class in terms of binary dummy variables*

Social class	Dummy variables				
	x_1	x_2	x_3	x_4	x_5
1	1	0	0	0	0
2	0	1	0	0	0
3	0	0	1	0	0
4	0	0	0	1	0
5	0	0	0	0	1

others met earlier in the discussion. As we shall see in more detail in Chapter 8, other analysis of variance models may also be rearranged in this manner.

Linear models are postulated far more often than non-linear ones because they are mathematically easier to manipulate and usually easier to interpret. Fortunately they appear to provide an adequate description of many data sets. However, there are many other types of mathematical model that could be postulated. For example, a relationship of the following form might be assumed between age, sex and expected number of visits

$$\text{Visits} = e^{\beta_0 + \beta_1 \times \text{Age} + \beta_2 \times \text{Sex}} \qquad (7.14)$$

or perhaps

$$\text{Visits} = \beta_0 + \beta_1 e^{\beta_2 \times \text{Age}} + \beta_3 e^{\beta_4 \times \text{Sex}} \qquad (7.15)$$

Often these non-linear models can be converted into a linear form by some transformation of the data. For example, if we take natural logarithms of equation (7.14), we obtain

$$\log(\text{Visits}) = \beta_0 + \beta_1 \times \text{Age} + \beta_2 \times \text{Sex} \qquad (7.16)$$

which is now a linear model for the transformed response, $\log(\text{Visits})$.

A class of linear models which are of particular interest and derive from such a transformation are those for data arising in the form of *a contingency table*, where a sample of individuals are cross-classified with respect to two or more qualitative variables. The observations are counts for each cell of the table. A two-dimensional contingency table appears in Table 7.2. For such a table the model of most interest is that of the independence of the two classifying variables, which is generally formulated as

$$p_{ij} = p_{i.} p_{.j} \qquad (7.17)$$

where p_{ij} is the probability of an observation falling in the ij-th cell of

Table 7.2   *A two-dimensional contingency table involving severity of depression and suicidal intent in a sample of 500 psychiatric patients*

	Not depressed	Moderately depressed	Severely depressed	Totals
Attempted suicide	26	39	39	104
Contemplated or threatened suicide	20	27	27	74
Neither	195	93	34	322
	241	159	100	500

the table, and $p_{i.}$ and $p_{.j}$ are row and column marginal probabilities. (This is the hypothesis usually tested by means of the familiar chi-square test of independence (see, for example, Everitt, 1977, Chapter 3).) Equation (7.17) may be rewritten in terms of expected cell frequencies, m_{ij}, as

$$m_{ij} = N p_{i.} p_{.j} \qquad (7.18)$$

where N is the sample size. By taking logs, this may be written as

$$\log (m_{ij}) = \log N + \log p_{i.} + \log p_{.j} \qquad (7.19)$$

From here it is a relatively simple matter to show that log (expected count in the ij-th cell) may be expressed in the form

$$\log (m_{ij}) = \beta_0 + \text{Row} (i) + \text{Col} (j) \qquad (7.20)$$

where Row (i) and Col (j) are parameters representing the effects of row and column categories. (For details of how to express equation (7.19) in the form of (7.20), see Everitt, 1977, Chapter 5; see also Exercise 7.1.) The model in (7.20) is now very similar to that in (7.12) and by a comparable use of dummy variables could be expressed in the same general form as (7.2) and (7.3). Such models are generally known as *log-linear models*, and will be the subject of detailed discussion in Chapter 9.

In many contingency tables there is one variable of particular interest and it is the effects of the remaining variables on this that is of primary interest. (Some examples of such contingency tables appear in Chapter 9.) If the former variable is dichotomous, then we might be interested in modelling the probability of an observation falling into one of its categories, p, or the ratio of the probabilities for the two categories, $p/(1-p)$. These quantities might then be modelled as linear functions of the effects of other variables. For example,

$$p = \beta_0 + \text{Var}(i) \qquad (7.21)$$

where Var (i) represents the effect of the i-th category of some variable on p. However, such models have a number of difficulties, the foremost being that estimated parameter values may lead to fitted p values outside the range $(0, 1)$. (Other problems are described by Cox, 1970.) Consequently, p is not modelled directly but via the *logistic transformation*, that is

$$\lambda = \log(p/1 - p) \qquad (7.22)$$

The rationale behind this transformation is that as p varies between 0 and 1, λ will vary between $-\infty$ and ∞; consequently there are now no difficulties with fitted values of λ being outside its possible range. Models for λ are known as *linear-logistic models*, or logistic models for short, and these are also discussed in Chapter 9. (The ratio, $p/(1-p)$ is often referred to as the 'odds' in favour of the first category of the dichotomous response variable. Since it involves population rather than sample values it will often be referred to in the remainder of the text as 'true odds'.)

The general form of the models discussed in this section is now seen to be

$$y = \beta_0 + \sum_{j=1}^{p} \beta_j x_j \qquad (7.23)$$

where y is the expected value of the response variable, or in some cases the expected value transformed in some way, and $x_1, x_2, \ldots, x_p$ are explanatory variables; by introducing the vector $\boldsymbol{\beta}' = [\beta_0, \beta_1, \ldots, \beta_p]$ and the vector $\mathbf{x}' = [1, x_1, \ldots, x_p]$, equation (7.22) may be rewritten as

$$y = \mathbf{x}'\boldsymbol{\beta} \qquad (7.24)$$

7.3 Link Functions and Error Models in the Generalised Linear Model

In equations (7.1) and (7.2) we describe the variation in the expected values of a response variable as a function of a single explanatory variable. The relationship between the two quantities has an exact functional form; there is a one-to-one mapping from the person's age to the expected number of visits. If we were now, however, to consider a single individual, equation (7.2) would no longer be expected to hold, since we know that all men aged, say, 57 will not visit a physician the same number of times in a year, simply because of *random variation* in the population of patients. The model applicable to the number of visits for individuals must contain some account of this variation. This is usually dealt with by introducing a random disturbance term into the model to give, for example,

$$y_i = \beta_0 + \beta_1 x_i + \varepsilon_i \qquad (7.25)$$

where y_i is now the number of visits for the i-th member of the population and ε_i measures the deviation of y_i from the appropriate expected value; β_0 and β_1 are regression coefficients, as before, and x_i represents the age of the i-th individual. The disturbance term, ε_i, is often called an *error* term, although in many cases it may not have anything to do with measurement error. In the present example there would still have to be a disturbance term in the model even if one knew that all measurement errors had been eliminated. The term ε merely represents that part of the response variable y that is not accounted for by the explanatory variable, x.

The problem of fitting a linear regression model such as (7.22), or other more complex linear models, is to select a sample of individuals from the population of interest, measure the response variable and the corresponding explanatory variables for each individual, and then *estimate* the parameters in the model. Then follows the question of assessing the fit of the model.

Before we can consider the estimation of parameters and the assessment of fit, however, we must decide on an appropriate distributional form for the disturbance terms. The most common assumption, of course, is that these follow a normal distribution generally, with zero mean and constant variance. Models assuming such an error structure are considered in Chapter 8.

For contingency table data a more realistic assumption is that the observed count in the ij-cell, n_{ij}, is a Poisson variable with expected value, m_{ij}, so that

$$n_{ij} = m_{ij} + \varepsilon_{ij} \qquad (7.26)$$

where the random disturbance term ε_{ij} now represents Poisson random deviation from the expected value. When interest centres on one particular binary variable in the table, as discussed on page 158, random disturbance terms are considered to be *binomial* (see Chapter 9).

Both of equations (7.25) and (7.26) can be written in the form

observed response = expected response + random component

$$(7.27)$$

The random component is assumed to have a particular type of distribution (Normal, Poisson, etc.), and the expected response, *or some transformation of it*, to be a linear function of the explanatory variables, $x_1, \ldots, x_p$. For example, in linear and multiple linear regression (see Chapter 8),

$$\text{expected response} = \mathbf{x}'\boldsymbol{\beta} \qquad (7.28)$$

and for contingency tables

$$\log(\text{expected count}) = \mathbf{x}'\boldsymbol{\beta} \qquad (7.29)$$

$$\text{expected count} = e^{\mathbf{x}'\beta} \qquad (7.30)$$

The transformation of the response variable equated to the linear sum of explanatory variables is generally known as the *link function*.

The formulation of linear models in terms of the distribution of the random disturbances and the form of the link function was suggested by Nelder and Wedderburn (1972), who also give details of how such models could be fitted to data using maximum likelihood methods. Details of the general fitting procedure are outside the scope of this book, but some comments on fitting specific models will be found in Chapters 8 to 10.

An important feature of the model-building process is to assess how many parameters are required in the model to provide an adequate description of the data. Since a smaller number of parameters means easier interpretation our aim will be to find the simplest model which represents the data adequately. For this purpose Nelder and Wedderburn (1972) suggest a goodness-of-fit criterion based on the maximised value of the log-likelihood and known as the *deviance*. For normally distributed random disturbance terms the deviance is related to the familiar sums of squares met in regression and the analysis of variance, as we shall see in Chapter 8. For contingency table data the deviance is much like the Pearson chi-square statistic, which we will consider in Chapter 9.

A number of special models need to be noted, the first of which is one containing as many parameters as observations. This is known as the *full* or *saturated* model and reproduces the data exactly, but without any simplification of interpretation. Furthest removed from the saturated model is the *null model* which proposes a common value for all observations; this is, of course, a very simple model, and one that in most cases will not adequately represent the structure of the data. Also of importance in some cases, particularly in dealing with contingency tables, is the *minimal model*, which arises in those situations where certain parameters must be included in any sensible model. For example, in a two-way contingency table, equation (7.20) would be the minimal model, since it allows for differences in cell frequencies that are attributable simply to differences in row and column marginal totals.

A point which should be noted here is that some of the models, as formulated in this chapter, are *over parameterised*. For example, the model in equation (7.12) contains six parameters, μ, α_1, α_2, α_3, α_4, and α_5. Since, however, we have observations on only five social classes, we can estimate a maximum of five parameters in any model; we cannot produce independent estimates of all the factor-level effects in the presence of a parameter μ, representing the grand mean. The possible methods of dealing with this problem are discussed in the next chapter.

Nelder and Wedderburn's very general formulation of linear models leads naturally to the idea of a general computer package for fitting such models, estimating their parameters, and so on. Such a program has been developed by Nelder and his co-workers, and is known as GLIM which stands for Generalised Linear Interactive Modelling (Baker and Nelder, 1978). By allowing a number of possible error distributions, and a variety of 'link functions', a large number of models can be accommodated in the general framework. Since the program is designed to be used primarily in an interactive mode, it allows the possibility of exploring a large number of alternative models reasonably quickly, and this can be of considerable advantage in the model building process outlined in Chapter 1.

EXERCISES

7.1   By summing equation (7.19) over i, over j, and finally over i and j, show that it may be expressed in the form of equation (7.20). How could the model in (7.20) be extended to allow for a possible interaction between the row and column variables forming the table?

7.2   In a two-way analysis of variance design with r levels of one factor and c levels of the other factor, and n observations per cell, the usual model considered is

$$y_{ijk} = \mu + \alpha_i + \beta_j + (\alpha\beta)_{ij} + \varepsilon_{ijk}$$

(See, for example, Winer, 1971.) How could this model be coded in terms of dummy variables?

7.3   In a three-way contingency table what would be the usual form of the minimal model and the saturated model?

8. Regression and the Analysis of Variance

8.1 Introduction

Regression and the analysis of variance are both topics which are familiar to most social and behavioural scientists. They are covered in all but the simplest statistical textbooks, and the literature surrounding them is enormous. Consequently, it would be impossible to provide a comprehensive account of them in a single chapter such as this. What we shall attempt instead, however, is to show the essential equivalence of the two techniques and how each may be regarded as an aid to model building for particular types of data. (For a much more comprehensive treatment of the two topics readers are referred to Draper and Smith, 1981, Wonnacott and Wonnacott, 1981, Chatterjee and Price, 1977, and Finn, 1974. In addition a lot may be learnt from the very stimulating book by Mosteller and Tukey, 1977.)

8.2 Least Squares Estimation for Regression and Analysis of Variance (ANOVA) Models

Suppose we have several measurements for each of a sample of n individuals. For the i-th individual there is a measurement of a continuous response variable, y_i, and the values of p explanatory variables $x_{i1}, x_{i2}, \ldots, x_{ip}$. (Some of the latter may be dummy variables.) To investigate the effect of the explanatory variables on the response variable we shall assume a linear model of the form

$$y_i = \mathbf{x}_i' \boldsymbol{\beta} + \varepsilon_i \quad (i = 1, \ldots, n) \qquad (8.1)$$

where $\mathbf{x}_i' = [1, x_{i1}, x_{i2}, \ldots, x_{ip}]$ and $\boldsymbol{\beta} = [\beta_0, \beta_1, \ldots, \beta_p]$, the vector of the parameters that require estimating. If we assume that the random disturbance terms, ε_i, are normally distributed with constant variance σ^2, then the method of maximum likelihood estimation mentioned in Chapter 7 is equivalent to the more familiar least squares estimation procedure. In the latter we choose estimates of the parameters that minimise the sum of squares criterion, $\sum_{i=1}^{n} \varepsilon_i^2$. If we introduce the vector $\mathbf{y}' = [y_1, \ldots, y_n]$, and an $n \times (p+1)$ matrix $\mathbf{X}$, given by

$$\mathbf{X} = \begin{bmatrix} 1 & x_{11} & x_{12} & \cdots & x_{1p} \\ 1 & x_{21} & & & \\ \vdots & & & & \\ 1 & x_{n1} & & \cdots & x_{np} \end{bmatrix}$$

then the model corresponding to equation (8.1) for the whole sample may be written

$$\mathbf{y} = \mathbf{X}\boldsymbol{\beta} + \boldsymbol{\varepsilon} \tag{8.2}$$

where $\boldsymbol{\varepsilon}' = [\varepsilon_1, \ldots, \varepsilon_n]$. To obtain least squares estimates one needs to minimise $\boldsymbol{\varepsilon}' \boldsymbol{\varepsilon}$ with respect to the vector $\boldsymbol{\beta}$. This leads to the so-called *normal equations* for the parameter estimates, $\hat{\boldsymbol{\beta}} = [\hat{\beta}_0, \hat{\beta}_1, \ldots, \hat{\beta}_p]$. These are:

$$\mathbf{X}'\mathbf{X}\hat{\boldsymbol{\beta}} = \mathbf{X}'\mathbf{y} \tag{8.3}$$

(Details of the derivation of (8.3) are given in Draper and Smith, 1981.)

Two situations involving the solution of the normal equations can be distinguished. The first and simplest is where the matrix $\mathbf{X}'\mathbf{X}$ is invertible, leading directly to $\hat{\boldsymbol{\beta}}$. The second is where too many parameters have been introduced by the specification of the model, and accordingly $\mathbf{X}'\mathbf{X}$ cannot be inverted to yield unique estimates. We shall consider the two cases in turn under Sections 8.3 and 8.4.

8.3 Multiple Regression Models

The investigator usually wishes to use the techniques of multiple regression in situations when the explanatory variables are quantitative, and the matrix $\mathbf{X}'\mathbf{X}$ contains the sums of squares and cross-products derived from the measurements of these variables. Here the solution of the normal equations is straightforward, and leads to

$$\hat{\boldsymbol{\beta}} = (\mathbf{X}'\mathbf{X})^{-1}\mathbf{X}'\mathbf{y} \tag{8.4}$$

A number of numerical examples are discussed in Section 8.6.

Under certain assumptions the estimates of the regression co-efficients obtained from equation (8.4) are the 'best' estimates in the sense that, of all the estimates that are unbiased (their expected values being equal to the true parameter values), they have *minimum variance*. This also applies to the estimates for the ANOVA models of the next section. In both cases the estimates are generally known as *ordinary least squares* (OLS) estimates, and the most important assumptions necessary for them to be optimal are as follows:

(a) each disturbance term has the same variance;

(b) the disturbance terms are uncorrelated with each other;

(c) the disturbances are statistically independent of the explanatory variables;

(d) the values of the explanatory variables are known without error.

It is clear that these assumptions are unlikely to be met in all data sets arising in the behavioural or social sciences. Often, however, small violations of the assumptions do not lead to major problems. Still, it is important to try to detect any departures from assumptions that do occur, and, if possible, to adjust estimation procedures accordingly. (These topics will be discussed later in this chapter.)

A further assumption that ought to be satisfied is that the values of the explanatory variables be non-stochastic; that is, their values should be fixed or selected in advance. Clearly this is very rarely the case in the social sciences, so all inferences are assumed in practice to be conditional of the values of the explanatory variables observed.

Interpretation of a multiple regression equation is very dependent on the implicit assumption that the explanatory variables are not strongly interrelated. The regression coefficients may be interpreted as a measure in the change in the response variable when the corresponding explanatory variable is increased by one unit and all other explanatory variables are held constant. Such an interpretation would no longer be valid in the presence of strong linear relationships amongst the explanatory variables, simply because in such situations it is obviously impossible to change one variable whilst holding all others constant.

When there is a complete absence of linear relationships among the explanatory variables, they are said to be *orthogonal*. In most applications this condition will not hold, but small departures from it are unlikely to affect the analysis at all seriously. However, if two or more of the explanatory variables are highly correlated then the statistical significance of these variables will be very dependent on the order in which they are added to the model, and the resulting parameter estimates will be very unstable.

The condition of severe non-orthogonality of the explanatory variables is often referred to as the problem of *collinear* data, and in practice we would first like to be able to detect collinearity and then, if possible, to cope with it. One method of detection is to apply principal components analysis to the covariance matrix of the explanatory variables (see Chapter 4). Collinearity is indicated by one or more very small eigenvalues. It is also possible to watch out for instability in parameter estimates as differing models are fitted and also, of course, visually examine the correlation matrix of the explanatory variables.

Once detected, the problem of collinearity can be dealt with in a variety of ways. One involves regressing the response variable on a number of the important principal components. These are also useful in identifying those linear combinations of the regression coefficients that can be accurately estimated (see Chatterjee and Price, 1977, Chapter 7). A further possibility, and one which has become popular over the last decade, is *ridge regression*. This involves an adaptation of least squares estimation, and gives parameter estimates which are biased, but which in general will be 'closer' to the true parameter values than those obtained by the use of OLS in circumstances of severe departures from orthogonality. The so-called ridge estimator of the regression coefficients, $\hat{\boldsymbol{\beta}}^*$, is obtained by solving the equation

$$(\mathbf{X}'\mathbf{X} + k\mathbf{I})\hat{\boldsymbol{\beta}}^* = \mathbf{X}'\mathbf{y} \tag{8.5}$$

to give

$$\hat{\boldsymbol{\beta}}^* = (\mathbf{X}'\mathbf{X} + k\mathbf{I})^{-1}\mathbf{X}'\mathbf{y} \tag{8.6}$$

where k is a constant and $\mathbf{I}$ is the identity matrix. The essential parameter that distinguishes ridge regression from OLS is k. When $k = 0$, $\hat{\boldsymbol{\beta}}^*$ is simply the usual least squares estimate. As k increases from zero, the bias of the estimates increases, and as it continues to increase without limit, the regression estimates all tend toward zero. Hoerl and Kennard (1970) have shown that there is a positive value of k for which the ridge estimate will be resistant to small changes in the data. In practice a range of values of k (between 0 and 1) are explored, and the estimates of the regression coefficients plotted against k. The resulting graph is known as a *ridge trace*, and may be used to select an appropriate value for k.

To summarise, the rationale behind ridge regression is essentially to overcome the problems involved with the inverse of the matrix $\mathbf{X}'\mathbf{X}$, which, in situations where collinearity is present, is ill-conditioned. Adding a small constant to the diagonal elements of $\mathbf{X}'\mathbf{X}$ leads to biased estimates, but improves the properties of the inverse and allows more stable estimates of the regression coefficients. Examples of the use of ridge regression are given in Chatterjee and Price (1977).

8.4   ANOVA Models

Let us reconsider the example introduced in Chapter 7, involving the effect of social class on the number of visits to a physician, and suppose that we have a single individual from each class and a corresponding record of the number of visits. If social class is indicated by the use of five dummy variables (see Table 7.1), the linear model equivalent to equation (8.2) for these five individuals is

$$\mathbf{y} = \begin{bmatrix} 1 & 1 & 0 & 0 & 0 & 0 \\ 1 & 0 & 1 & 0 & 0 & 0 \\ 1 & 0 & 0 & 1 & 0 & 0 \\ 1 & 0 & 0 & 0 & 1 & 0 \\ 1 & 0 & 0 & 0 & 0 & 1 \end{bmatrix} \begin{bmatrix} \mu \\ \alpha_1 \\ \alpha_2 \\ \alpha_3 \\ \alpha_4 \\ \alpha_5 \end{bmatrix} + \varepsilon \qquad (8.7)$$

The normal equations for the estimation of the parameters are as in equation (8.3). These normal equations, however, cannot be solved to yield unique estimates. This problem arises because the model, as formulated, requires the estimation of six parameters from only five observations, one from each social class. The problem would remain even if we were to increase the number of observations in each of the social classes; here one would be attempting to estimate the six parameters from the five class means.

To illustrate the above points, consider the following set of hypothetical records. Let the number of visits recorded for a single individual from social class one be 5. Similarly let the counts for single individuals from each of the other social classes be 7, 9, 18 and 20, respectively. The normal equations are as follows:

$$\begin{bmatrix} 5 & 1 & 1 & 1 & 1 & 1 \\ 1 & 1 & 0 & 0 & 0 & 0 \\ 1 & 0 & 1 & 0 & 0 & 0 \\ 1 & 0 & 0 & 1 & 0 & 0 \\ 1 & 0 & 0 & 0 & 1 & 0 \\ 1 & 0 & 0 & 0 & 0 & 1 \end{bmatrix} \begin{bmatrix} \mu \\ \alpha_1 \\ \alpha_2 \\ \alpha_3 \\ \alpha_4 \\ \alpha_5 \end{bmatrix} = \begin{bmatrix} 59 \\ 5 \\ 7 \\ 9 \\ 18 \\ 20 \end{bmatrix} \qquad (8.8)$$

that is,

$$5\mu + \alpha_1 + \alpha_3 + \alpha_3 + \alpha_4 + \alpha_5 = 59$$
$$\mu + \alpha_1 = 5$$
$$\mu + \alpha_2 = 7$$
$$\mu + \alpha_3 = 9 \qquad (8.9)$$
$$\mu + \alpha_4 = 18$$
$$\mu + \alpha_5 = 20$$

Since the sum of the last five rows or equations is equal to the first, there are infinitely many solutions. In other words, the matrix $\mathbf{X}$ of (8.7) does not have full column rank, and, consequently, the matrix $X'X$ in (8.8) does not have a simple inverse. Examples of possible solutions to these equations are given in Table 8.1. Clearly, as they stand, they are of very little use to the investigator. We will now introduce a number of ways in which this problem can be overcome.

Table 8.1   *Four solutions to matrix equation* (8.8)

Parameter	Solution			
	1	*2*	*3*	*4*
μ	10	5	1	1000
α_1	-5	0	4	-995
α_2	-3	2	6	-993
α_3	-1	4	8	-991
α_4	8	13	17	-982
α_5	10	15	19	-980

One approach is to arbitrarily set one of the parameters to zero. One could, for example, let $\mu = 0$, or alternatively, let $\alpha_1 = 0$. In the latter case the αs to be estimated would then be measures of deviation from the number of visits for the individual in social class 1. This type of constraint on the value of one of the parameters might appear to be rather arbitrary, but in some situations, for example when one of the groups could be considered as a control, it would be thought quite reasonable. Whatever the type of constraint introduced, however, it does enable one to obtain unique estimates for the other parameters, that is, the matrix $X'X$ is now invertible. The method of constraint adopted in most elementary treatments on the analysis of variance is to let the sum of the αs be zero (that is $\sum_i \alpha_i = 0$). In this case, equation (8.7) would be rewritten as

$$\mathbf{y} = \begin{bmatrix} 1 & 1 & 0 & 0 & 0 \\ 1 & 0 & 1 & 0 & 0 \\ 1 & 0 & 0 & 1 & 0 \\ 1 & 0 & 0 & 0 & 1 \\ 1 & -1 & -1 & -1 & -1 \end{bmatrix} \begin{bmatrix} \mu \\ \alpha_1 \\ \alpha_2 \\ \alpha_3 \\ \alpha_4 \end{bmatrix} + \varepsilon \qquad (8.10)$$

(α_5 has been replaced by $-\alpha_1 - \alpha_2 - \alpha_3 - \alpha_4$). Since $X'X$ is now invertible the normal equations may be solved directly to give estimates of μ, α_1, α_2, α_3 and α_4.

The computer package SPSS (and several others) use this method, but

GLIM sets the equivalent of α_1 to zero. In this and the following chapters we will usually present analyses that have been carried out using GLIM, and the reader should make certain that the way of specifying the models is understood.

Another approach to solving the problem of having matrices of deficient rank is to consider certain contrasts or linear functions of parameters that are invariant to whatever solution of the normal equations is considered. To illustrate this concept, consider the linear function l_1 given by

$$l_1 = \alpha_1 - \alpha_2 \tag{8.11}$$

For each of the solutions in Table 8.1, l_1 takes the value -2, and this will be so for all the infinitely many solutions of the normal equations (8.8). Again consider the function, l_2, given by

$$l_2 = \alpha_1 - \tfrac{1}{4}(\alpha_1 + \alpha_2 + \alpha_3 + \alpha_4) \tag{8.12}$$

This always takes the value -8.5.

But do such invariant linear functions provide useful information? To answer this question consider again l_1 and l_2; the first is a measure of the difference between the effects of social class 1 and social class 2, and the second is a measure of the difference between the effect of social class 1 and the average effect of the other four levels. Both of these might be of specific interest in particular situations.

The terms l_1 and l_2 are, of course, only two of many such linear functions of the parameters which have the property of being invariant to whatever solution of the normal equations is considered. Because of their invariance property they are the only functions which can be of interest, so far as the estimation of the parameters of a linear model is concerned. The question as to which particular linear functions have the invariance property is discussed by Searle (1971), Chapter 5; details of the re-parameterisation of the models in terms of these linear functions is given by Finn (1974), Chapter 7. Essentially, however, the procedure is equivalent to coding a qualitative variable with k categories (in this example, social class has 5 categories) in terms of only $k - 1$ dummy variables. This is always possible, and Table 8.2 shows such a coding for social class. The model for the effect of social class on visits to a physician can now be rewritten as

$$y = \beta_0 + \beta_1 x_1 + \beta_2 x_2 + \beta_3 x_3 + \beta_4 x_4 \tag{8.13}$$

so that equation (8.7) is replaced by

$$\mathbf{y} = \begin{bmatrix} 1 & 0 & 0 & 0 & 0 \\ 1 & 1 & 0 & 0 & 0 \\ 1 & 0 & 1 & 0 & 0 \\ 1 & 0 & 0 & 1 & 0 \\ 1 & 0 & 0 & 0 & 1 \end{bmatrix} \begin{bmatrix} \beta_0 \\ \beta_1 \\ \beta_2 \\ \beta_3 \\ \beta_4 \end{bmatrix} + \varepsilon \qquad (8.14)$$

The βs are now clearly estimable and they are, in fact, linear combinations of the parameters in (8.7): $\beta_0 = \mu + \alpha_1$, $\beta_1 = \alpha_2 - \alpha_1$, $\beta_2 = \alpha_3 - \alpha_2$, $\beta_3 = \alpha_4 - \alpha_3$, and $\beta_4 = \alpha_5 - \alpha_4$. In general, an ANOVA model such as (8.7) can always be re-specified as a straightforward multiple regression model such as (8.14). When the investigator has recorded both categorical and quantitative explanatory variables the model can be specified either in terms of the parameters of the typical ANOVA model (as in the traditional *analysis of covariance*), or dummy variables can be created so that the situation is an extension or a special case of multiple regression. It is simply a matter of taste; computer packages such as GLIM can handle either method of model specification.

Table 8.2   *Coding of social classes in terms of binary dummy variables, leading to direct solution of normal equations*

	Dummy variables			
Social class	x_1	x_2	x_3	x_4
1	0	0	0	0
2	1	0	0	0
3	1	1	0	0
4	1	1	1	0
5	1	1	1	1

8.5   Testing the Fit of a Model

After fitting a model to a set of data it is necessary to assess the adequacy of the fit. To construct a significance test for this purpose we first have to assume a particular probability distribution for the random disturbance terms. In this chapter we will suppose that they are normally distributed, with constant variance. A test of the overall fit of the model can be obtained by the decomposition of the total variation in the response variable into that corresponding to the variation accounted for by the model and the variation caused by random deviations from the model. The sums of squares involved in this exercise, along with their degrees of freedom, are defined in Table 8.3.

Table 8.3 *Analysis of variance to test the fit of the model* $\mathbf{y} = \mathbf{X}\boldsymbol{\beta} + \varepsilon$

Source of variation	d.f.	Sum of squares	Mean square
Mean	1	$n\bar{y}^2$	
Model after fitting mean (i.e. explanatory variables)	$r-1$	$\text{ESS} = \hat{\boldsymbol{\beta}}'\mathbf{X}'\mathbf{y} - n\bar{y}^2$	$\text{EMS} = \text{ESS}/(r-1)$
Residual (due to random disturbance terms)	$n-r$	$\text{RSS} = \mathbf{y}'\mathbf{y} - \hat{\boldsymbol{\beta}}\mathbf{X}'\mathbf{y}$	$\text{RMS} = \text{RSS}/n-r$
Total	n	$\text{TSS} = \mathbf{y}'\mathbf{y}$	

(See Searle, 1971, Chapters 3 and 5, for further details.) The terms in this table apply to models both of full rank and not of full rank. For the former, $r = p+1$, and for the latter the value will depend upon the number of independent parameters that can be estimated. For example, in the social class example, r takes the value 5.

If there is no relationship between the response variable and the explanatory variables, i.e. $\beta_1 = \beta_2 = \cdots = \beta_p = 0$, then

$$F = \text{EMS}/\text{RMS} \qquad (8.15)$$

will have an F distribution with $r-1$ and $n-r$ degrees of freedom. Of course, such a very general test is unlikely to be of much help in practice. More specific tests for identifying important explanatory variables appear later in this section.

From Table 8.3 we see that the proportion of variation in the response variable accounted for by the explanatory variables is

$$P = (\text{TSS} - \text{RSS})/\text{TSS} \qquad (8.16)$$

that is,

$$P = 1 - \text{RSS}/\text{TSS} \qquad (8.17)$$

It is straightforward to show that P is equal to the square of the Pearson product moment correlation coefficient between the response variable, and its value as predicted by the explanatory variables, that is, $\hat{y}_i$, given by

$$\hat{y}_i = \mathbf{x}_i \hat{\boldsymbol{\beta}} \qquad (8.18)$$

Pearson's coefficient for y_i and $\hat{y}_i$ is known as the *multiple correlation coefficient*, and usually designated by the letter R. It is a useful index of the goodness-of-fit of a regression model, but there are pitfalls in its uncritical use, as we shall illustrate later.

The F-test outlined above, for the hypothesis that none of the explanatory variables affects the response variable, is likely to be significant in most applications, leading to a rejection of this very general hypothesis. On its own this is not of great interest since the investigator is more often concerned with assessing whether a subset of the explanatory variables provides an adequate explanation for the variation in the response variable. If a small number of the explanatory variables produces a linear model which fits the data only marginally worse than a larger set, the investigator would usually be happier with the former since it would provide a more parsimonious model, easing the, at times, difficult problem of interpretation.

In part, the solution to this problem lies in computing the various sums of squares already met earlier in this section. For example, consider first the fitting of the following model to a set of data. (We shall assume here that we are dealing with a model of full rank, although the procedure to be outlined may also be applied to other models as we shall see in Section 8.6.)

$$y = \beta_0 + \beta_1 x_1 + \cdots + \beta_p x_p \tag{8.19}$$

Sums of squares due to the explanatory variables and a residual sum of squares can be calculated as outlined in Table 8.2, and from these an F statistic may be constructed to test the fit of the model. A significant F implies that we should reject the hypothesis that the regression coefficients $\beta_1, \beta_2, \ldots, \beta_p$ are all equal to zero. It does not, however, indicate whether all are non-zero, or whether all explanatory variables are needed in the model.

Now let the term $\beta_p x_p$ be deleted from the model in equation (8.19). Again the sum of squares due to the modified model can be calculated, as can the difference between this sum of squares and the regression sum of squares due to the original model. On the assumption that $\beta_p = 0$, this difference is distributed as x^2 with a single degree of freedom. Consequently an F statistic with 1 and $n - p - 1$ degrees of freedom can be obtained by dividing this difference sum of squares by the original residual sum of squares after fitting equation (8.19). This can then be used to test whether $\beta_p = 0$ or, in other words, whether explanatory variable x_p contributes significantly to the model, over and above variables $x_1, \ldots, x_{p-1}$. We could have removed any of the other $p - 1$ explanatory variables instead of x_p and tested their significance accordingly. Note that in each case the significance of the deleted term is conditional on the presence of the other $p - 1$ terms; that is, the importance of the deleted term is being assessed by a conditional significance test. An alternative approach is to add an extra variable and test its significance. This procedure can be extended in an obvious way to test whether a subset of regression coefficients is equal to zero (see Draper and Smith, 1981, for details).

Using this method of conditional significance testing, all possible combinations of explanatory variables could be tried, and the 'best' selected—with this taken to mean the simplest model (fewest explanatory variables) compatible with the data. The number of possible models to be examined is $2^p - 1$, and, if the set of possible explanatory variables is large, this method of model building becomes practically impossible to use, despite the development of a number of algorithms designed to reduce the computational difficulties (see, for example, Hand, 1981a). Consequently we are led to consider methods that do not need to take into account every possible model. The most popular of these are ones involving some kind of stepwise fitting procedure. There are basically two approaches to stepwise selection of variables, *forward selection* and *backward elimination*. We shall now consider each of these in turn.

The procedure of forward selection of variables starts by fitting just a constant term (the mean) to the observations, i.e., the parameter β_0. Then each of the possible variables is added to the model in turn, and the most significant, provided that the significance level is below some predetermined level, is selected for inclusion. Each of the remaining variables is then added in turn, and again the most significant selected for inclusion. This procedure is repeated until there is no further significant improvement in the fit of the model. The procedure can be modified in several ways, for example, by fitting pairs of variables sequentially rather than trying each separately. In addition, the variables already included in the model can be considered again in turn at each of the stages in the process to see if they still make a significant contribution to the fit of the model. If not, they can be deleted.

Backward elimination of variables starts with the most complicated of the possible models; that is, it starts with a model containing all of the possible explanatory variables. Then each variable is deleted in turn, and the least significant left out, provided that the significance level is above some predetermined level. The process is repeated until the simplest model that is compatible with the data is obtained. Often the resulting model will be identical to that found by forward selection of variables, but this is not necessarily so. It should be stressed that both of these procedures or algorithms should be used with care. They are not foolproof. They should be used as aids in the model-building process, and, wherever possible, they should be used in conjunction with more intuitive model selection procedures based on the theoreti-

cal knowledge of the investigator. We will not discuss these methods in
any detail here, but an example of the use of forward selection and
backward elimination methods is given in the next section and in
Chapter 9.

Other interesting methods which have been developed for selecting
subsets of explanatory variables are discussed by Mallows (1973) and
Allen (1971).

8.6 Numerical Examples

To illustrate some of the topics discussed in the previous sections we
shall begin by considering the hypothetical data on visits to a physician
given in Table 8.4. The results of fitting a number of models to these
data appear in Table 8.5. In part (a) the sum of squares due to the

Table 8.4 *Hypothetical data on number of visits to a physician*

Individual	Age (yr)	Weight (kg)	Number of visits in one year
1	15	45	2
2	30	80	4
3	35	70	2
4	40	90	6
5	43	75	3
6	48	130	5
7	65	75	3
8	67	120	8
9	72	90	5
10	80	75	7

Table 8.5 *Fitting linear regression models for the number of visits to a physician shown in Table 8.4*

(a) *Fitting age first*

Model	s.s (d.f.)	Residual s.s. (d.f.)
Visits $= \beta_0$	38.50 (9)	
Visits $= \beta_0 + \beta_1 \times$ Age	16.35 (1)	22.15 (8)
Visits $= \beta_0 + \beta_1 \times$ Age $+ \beta_2 \times$ Weight	23.24 (2)	15.26 (7)

(b) *Fitting weight first*

Model	s.s (d.f.)	Residual s.s. (d.f.)
Visits $= \beta_0$	38.50 (9)	
Visits $= \beta_0 + \beta_1 \times$ Weight	16.51 (1)	21.99 (8)
Visits $= \beta_0 + \beta_1 \times$ Weight $+ \beta_2 \times$ Age	23.24 (2)	15.26 (7)

addition of the variable weight to the model is $23.24 - 16.35 = 6.89$ with 1 degree of freedom. Note that this is considerably less than that due to weight in part (b), the reason being the correlation between age and weight. In part (b) the sum of squares due to the addition of age to the model is $23.24 - 16.51 = 6.73$, again with 1 degree of freedom. It will be left as an exercise for the reader (see Exercise 8.2) to construct appropriate F-tests to assess the fit of these models.

Now let us examine the model fitting procedure for examples of the analysis of variance (ANOVA) type. Consider first a design with two qualitative factors A and B, and with an equal number of observations in each cell. Suppose we fit the following series of models:

$y = $ mean,

$y = $ mean + effect of factor A,

$y = $ mean + effect of factor A + effect of factor B,

$y = $ mean + effect of factor A + effect of factor B
      $+ AB$ interaction effect.

By employing the procedure outlined in the previous examples we could find a sum of squares A given the mean, for B given A and the effect of the mean, and for AB given the effects of the mean and A and B. Here, however, the order of adding terms to the model is irrelevant since the design is orthogonal. Consequently terms such as sum of squares due to B given A and the mean, and sum of squares due to B given the mean, will be the same. The total sum of squares of the response variable may be partitioned into non-overlapping components corresponding to the effect of factor A, the effect of factor B, the AB interaction effect and a residual term. These will be the usual sums of squares in the analysis of variance table for such a design.

If we now consider the same simple design but assume that there are different numbers of observations in each cell the analysis becomes more complex, since the order of entering effects into the model now becomes of importance. We can illustrate this with the small set of data shown in Table 8.6. The results of fitting various models appear in Table 8.7.

Because of the different numbers of observations in each cell the order of entering parameters into the models is of importance. We see, for example, that the sum of squares for B given the mean, and that for B given A and the mean are not the same. The sums of squares in these tables were obtained from the 'deviance' goodness-of-fit criterion of the GLIM program, specifying an 'identity' link function and normally

Table 8.6   *Example of a non-orthogonal analysis of variance design*

	B_1	B_2
	10	15
A_1	5	20
		25
		30
	5	10
A_2	8	12
	8	

Table 8.7   *Results of fitting various models to data of Table 8.6*

(I) *Fitting A, followed by B, followed by AB interaction*		*d.f.*
Sum of squares due to A given the mean	$= 216.0$	1
Sum of squares due to B given A and the mean	$= 242.8$	1
Sum of squares due to AB given A, B and the mean	$= 76.4$	1
Residual sum of squares	$= 145.5$	7
(II) *Fitting B, followed by A, followed by AB interaction*		
Sum of squares due to B given the mean	$= 358.6$	1
Sum of squares due to A given B and the mean	$= 100.2$	1
Sum of squares due to AB given A, B and the mean	$= 76.4$	1
Residual sum of squares	$= 145.5$	7

distributed errors. For example, the deviance for a model containing only a term for the mean is 680.7, with 10 degrees of freedom. This is equivalent to the sum of squares in the response variable remaining after the mean has been included in the model. Adding a parameter for factor A results in a deviance of 464.7 with 9 degrees of freedom. This is equivalent to the residual sum of squares after fitting the mean and A. Subtracting this from the previous deviance gives the additional sum of squares for A over that due to the mean, that is, 216.0. Other sums of squares are obtained in a similar fashion.

As a further example of a non-orthogonal design we will consider the data originally discussed by Francis (1973), in which individuals categorised by religion and by sex were scored on a six-point psychological scale. The means and number of observations in each cell appear in Table 8.8. The various sums of squares associated with the fitting of various models are given in Table 8.9. These indicate that a satisfactory model for these data would contain a term for sex and a

Table 8.8   *Means and frequencies, for example from Francis (1973)*

Religion	1	2	3	4	5
Sex *1*	3.468 (299)	3.511 (131)	3.368 (38)	2.700 (60)	2.973 (37)
2	3.143 (342)	2.925 (207)	3.097 (72)	2.667 (165)	2.983 (59)

Table 8.9   *Models fitted to Francis data*

Source	s.s.	d.f.	Source	s.s.	d.f.
Sex	43.58	1	Religion	69.36	4
Religion given the effect of Sex	54.49	4	Sex given the effect of Religion	28.71	1
Sex × Religion given the main effects of Sex and Religion	10.25	4	Sex × Religion given the main effects of Sex and Religion	10.25	4
Residual sum of squares	2988.95	1300	Residual sum of squares	2988.95	1300

term for religion, but that an interaction term would be unnecessary. These data are particularly interesting since Francis used them to show that several computer packages for analysis of variance were failing to deal appropriately with non-orthogonal designs. The analysis of unbalanced cross-classifications can be a troublesome task, and the reader concerned with such designs is urged to consult the two excellent papers of Nelder (1977) and Aitken (1978).

Next, we shall consider a relatively complex analysis of data derived from a learning experiment on eye-blink conditioning. The aim of the experiment was to condition the subjects to react to an audio tone by blinking, and this was achieved by presenting the audio tone together with an electric shock. The extent of learning was assessed by the number of conditioned responses (eye-blinks) given in 50 acquisition trials. The results are shown in Table 8.10. There were a number of factors that were thought to influence the extent of conditioning, and measurements on eight of these covariates are also given in Table 8.10. They are defined in Table 8.11. Some of them are interval-scaled, others merely have ordinal or qualitative significance. In the analysis described here, the variables APR, PSY, EXTR and CAWR were treated as quantitative covariates, and Q14, Q15, Q20 and THRE were

Table 8.10 *Eye blink conditioning data (from Freka, Beyts, Martin and Levey 1982)*

TOTCR	APR	PSY	EXTR	CAWR	THRE	Q14	Q15	Q20
0	31	6	16	9	2	4	3	1
0	36	3	16	9	2	4	5	1
0	38	1	16	7	1	4	4	2
0	41	2	19	14	1	5	6	2
0	24	1	21	−16	1	5	4	1
0	32	0	15	14	1	4	4	1
0	31	7	14	4	2	4	3	2
1	30	8	15	14	1	5	3	1
1	35	5	4	14	2	3	4	1
1	37	8	17	9	1	6	2	1
1	31	8	7	9	2	5	2	1
1	42	5	19	14	1	4	3	1
1	23	1	19	14	2	4	3	1
1	41	5	8	−2	2	6	4	3
1	33	2	19	11	2	4	2	1
1	47	3	9	9	2	6	3	2
2	32	4	18	−18	2	4	4	3
2	35	1	11	−1	1	5	5	1
2	41	5	19	13	1	4	5	3
2	49	4	6	−18	2	4	2	1
2	31	5	5	9	1	4	5	1
3	43	9	17	9	2	4	4	3
3	21	1	16	−2	2	6	6	1
3	37	4	2	14	2	5	6	3
3	33	2	14	14	2	4	2	1
4	49	8	20	14	1	1	4	1
4	35	9	14	−19	1	5	4	1
5	23	6	16	−11	2	4	5	1
5	45	4	15	−1	1	7	6	1
5	37	1	11	9	2	4	4	7
5	41	2	7	14	2	5	6	7
6	49	4	15	14	1	4	6	3
6	43	6	18	14	2	4	4	3
6	39	8	12	9	2	5	4	3
7	30	7	19	−19	1	4	5	2
8	26	1	16	4	1	5	5	3
9	27	3	16	−1	2	5	4	1
9	32	3	11	9	2	6	5	3
9	32	9	13	14	2	4	4	1
9	30	2	15	14	2	4	3	1
9	33	3	10	14	1	4	4	1
9	30	2	3	9	1	5	5	1
9	33	6	18	9	1	4	4	3
10	34	7	15	14	2	5	3	5
10	33	4	12	4	1	5	6	6

Table 8.10 *Continued*

TOTCR	APR	PSY	EXTR	CAWR	THRE	Q14	Q15	Q20
11	40	10	7	−18	2	5	5	1
11	34	6	16	9	1	6	5	6
11	56	5	5	9	2	4	4	4
12	25	4	14	14	1	4	3	2
12	36	1	19	−24	1	6	5	2
12	31	1	8	−1	1	4	4	1
12	30	12	9	9	2	5	3	3
13	28	2	13	−6	2	4	2	1
13	21	8	18	4	2	4	6	1
13	50	5	12	14	1	7	7	1
14	37	5	15	9	2	7	6	7
14	32	1	10	14	2	5	5	1
14	40	7	19	−13	1	7	5	6
14	46	4	7	2	2	4	4	4
15	30	4	8	4	2	6	6	1
15	24	13	10	9	2	5	2	4
15	44	6	11	−2	2	6	5	7
15	39	5	20	−10	1	5	4	2
17	32	4	19	2	1	4	4	1
18	30	2	11	11	2	4	2	2
19	42	4	11	9	2	5	5	4
19	41	3	20	14	1	5	4	1
21	26	2	18	14	1	4	4	6
21	34	4	2	14	2	6	2	1
22	35	0	19	14	2	5	5	3
22	29	1	11	9	1	4	4	6
23	26	7	11	14	1	5	4	6
24	39	1	16	7	1	6	6	1
25	45	0	9	8	1	6	5	3
25	31	3	19	−8	2	4	4	5
26	35	4	10	9	1	6	5	3
27	45	3	15	4	1	4	5	1
29	26	1	12	−19	1	4	4	6
30	38	5	14	14	1	6	5	5
30	35	3	20	−14	1	4	4	3
32	40	4	8	−8	1	5	6	1
33	35	3	21	−1	1	4	6	6
34	48	1	3	−25	1	5	4	1
35	31	5	14	9	1	6	5	3
35	24	0	20	14	1	6	5	1
43	37	1	15	−18	1	6	5	4

treated as qualitative factors. This treatment may not have been the
best or the most appropriate (see Exercise 8.8) but the data have been
analysed in this way to illustrate how to construct multiple regression

Table 8.11   *Definitions of variables listed in Table 8.10**

TOTCR	The total number of conditioned responses given in 50 acquisition trials
APR	Score for Anxiety
PSY	Score for Psychoticism
EXTR	Score for Extraversion
CAWR	Contingency awareness assessment
THRE	Binary variable indicating whether the subject's threshold for a blink reflex is over a given shock level
Q14	Ordinal scale for subject's rating of the pleasantness of the shock
Q15	Ordinal scale for the subject's rating of the strength of the shock
Q20	Ordinal scale indicating frequency in which subject blinked purposely to avoid the shock

* Details of the experiment are given in the text.

Table 8.12   *Analysis of variance for data in Table 8.10*

(a) TOTCR BY Q14, Q15, Q20, THRE WITH APR, PSY, EXTR, CAWR

Source of variation	Sum of squares	d.f.	Mean square	F	Significance of F
Q14	313.098	5	62.620	0.745	0.593
Q15	89.104	5	17.821	0.212	0.956
Q20	1522.960	6	253.827	3.018	0.012
THRE	472.565	1	472.565	5.618	0.021
APR	68.471	1	68.471	0.814	0.370
PSY	204.652	1	204.652	2.433	0.124
EXTR	48.366	1	48.366	0.575	0.451
CAWR	171.125	1	171.125	2.035	0.159
EXPLAINED	3964.595	21			
RESIDUAL	5382.998	64			
TOTAL	9347.593	85			

(b) TOTCR BY Q14, Q20, THRE WITH APR, PSY, EXTR, CAWR

Source of variation	Sum of squares	d.f.	Mean square	F	Significance of F
Q14	442.875	5	88.575	1.117	0.360
Q20	1691.270	6	281.878	3.554	0.004
THRE	569.655	1	569.655	7.183	0.009
APR	58.888	1	58.888	0.743	0.392
PSY	273.907	1	273.907	3.454	0.067
EXTR	58.765	1	58.765	0.741	0.392
CAWR	212.572	1	212.572	2.680	0.106
EXPLAINED	3875.491	16			
RESIDUAL	5472.102	69			

Table 8.12   *Continued*

(c) TOTCR BY Q14, Q20, THRE WITH PSY, EXTR, CAWR

Source of variation	Sum or squares	d.f.	Mean square	F	Significance of F
Q14	469.857	5	93.971	1.189	0.323
Q20	1651.276	6	275.213	3.483	0.005
THRE	514.740	1	514.740	6.515	0.013
PSY	269.343	1	269.343	3.409	0.069
EXTR	30.689	1	30.689	0.388	0.535
CAWR	205.729	1	205.729	2.604	0.111
EXPLAINED	3816.602	15			
RESIDUAL	5530.991				

(d) TOTCR BY Q14, Q20, THRE WITH PSY, CAWR

Source of variation	Sum of squares	d.f.	Mean square	F	Significance of F
Q14	525.870	5	105.174	1.343	0.256
Q20	1681.338	6	280.223	3.577	0.004
THRE	484.058	1	484.058	6.179	0.015
PSY	268.416	1	268.416	3.427	0.068
CAWR	200.557	1	200.557	2.560	0.114
EXPLAINED	3785.913	14			
RESIDUAL	5561.680	71			

(e) TOTCR BY Q20, THRE WITH PSY, CAWR

Source of variation	Sum of squares	d.f.	Mean square	F	Significance of F
Q20	1861.589	6	310.265	3.874	0.002
THRE	608.996	1	608.996	7.603	0.007
PSY	415.238	1	415.238	5.184	0.026
CAWR	237.815	1	237.815	2.969	0.089
EXPLAINED	3260.043	9			
RESIDUAL	6087.550	76			

(f) TOTR BY Q20, THRE WITH PSY

Source of variation	Sum of squares	d.f.	Mean square	F	Significance of F
Q20	1835.668	6	305.945	3.724	0.003
THRE	701.386	1	701.386	8.538	0.005
PSY	421.571	1	421.571	5.132	0.026
EXPLAINED	3022.228	8			
RESIDUAL	6325.365	77			

models when the explanatory variables are a mixture of quantitative measurements and qualitative factors.

Consider now Table 8.12(a). This shows an analysis of variance for a multiple regression model incorporating all eight of the explanatory variables. The words 'by' and 'with' in the heading are used to distinguish the qualitative and quantitative variables. It has been assumed that there are no interaction terms required in the model. The significance of end of the model terms is assessed from an F-statistic derived from the decrease in the sum of squares explained by the model, on deletion of the appropriate term from the full model (containing all eight explanatory variables). That is, the statistical significance of these terms is assessed from a conditional F-test.

By inspecting the last column of Table 8.12(a) it can be seen that very few of the F-statistics derived in this way are statistically significant (using 0.05 as the level of significance), and that that for Q15 is the least significant. Table 8.12(b) shows the repeat of the analysis of variance after removing the effect of Q15 from the model. In this analysis, the conditional F-statistics are obtained in a similar way to those in Table 8.12(a), but here the full model only contains the effects of seven explanatory variables. Note that the sum of squares explained by the model in Table 8.12(b) is less than that in Table 8.12(a)—the difference being that due to Q15 in Table 8.12(a). Similarly the residual sum of squares in Table 8.12(b) has increased by the same amount. In this table the least significant F-statistics are those due to the effects of APR and EXTR. The effect of APR was deleted from the model and the analysis of variance repeated (Table 8.12(c)). By continuing this procedure one eventually arrives at a fairly simple linear model containing the effects of only three explanatory variables, Q20, THRE and PSY—see Table 8.12(f).

The above analyses illustrate the method of backward elimination. The data could also have been analysed using a forward selection procedure (see Exercise 8.6). The use of either, or both, of these methods on their own, however, might lead to unjustified conclusions about the data. Before plunging into a complicated statistical analysis of this sort we should always ask whether it is reasonable to assume that the response variable can be modelled by a linear combination of the explanatory variables. And, if so, whether the assumptions required for an analysis of variance are also justified. To answer these questions a graphical analysis of the data (including the plotting of residuals) is necessary. This is the subject of the next section (but see also Exercise 8.7).

8.7   Checking Assumptions by Graphical Analysis and Examination of Residuals

Consider the hypothetical data given in Table 8.13 (from Anscombe, 1973). These are four sets of results, each comprising 11 (x, y) pairs. The variable x is taken to be the explanatory variable, and we wish to examine the dependence of the response variable y on x. What can be learnt from Table 8.13? Many people, when presented with observations of this type, are inclined immediately to reach for their electronic calculator or computer terminal to determine values of correlation or regression coefficients. But often, much more can be learnt from a preliminary graphical exploration of the data. It is possible to judge from graphs which statistical model is likely to be applicable to the observations, and to assess the extent of departures of the data from any initial assumptions that are likely to be made in a formal analysis of the results.

Table 8.13   *Four hypothetical data sets, each comprising 11* (x, y) *pairs* (*from Anscombe, 1973*)

Data set		1–3	1	2	3	4	4
Variable		x	y	y	y	x	y
Obs. no.	1	10.0	8.04	9.14	7.46	8.0	6.58
	2	8.0	6.95	8.14	6.77	8.0	5.76
	3	13.0	7.58	8.74	12.74	8.0	7.71
	4	9.0	8.81	8.77	7.11	8.0	8.84
	5	11.0	8.33	9.26	7.81	8.0	8.47
	6	14.0	9.96	8.10	8.84	8.0	7.04
	7	6.0	7.24	6.13	6.08	8.0	5.25
	8	4.0	4.26	3.10	5.39	19.0	12.50
	9	12.0	10.84	9.13	8.15	8.0	5.56
	10	7.0	4.82	7.26	6.42	8.0	7.91
	11	5.0	5.68	4.74	5.73	8.0	6.89

Blindly fitting a simple regression model ($y = \beta_0 + \beta_1 x$) to the four sets of data in Table 8.13 yields 3.0 and 0.5 as the estimates of β_0 and β_1, respectively, in all cases. In each case, R^2 is found to be 0.667. If presented with these statistics, most people would visualise a graph like Figure 8.1. This, in fact, is a graphical representation of data set 1. Here the linear regression models seems to be justified. But now look at Figure 8.2. This is a similar graphical representation of data set 2. Here the simple regression model is clearly inapplicable. Instead, y has a smooth curved relation with x, possibly quadratic, and there is little residual variability. Here an R^2 of 0.667 is an underestimate of the amount of variation in the values of y that can be explained by x. Figure 8.3 which illustrates data set 3, shows another potential pitfall of fitting straight lines by least squares methods before plotting simple graphs. Here, all but one of the data points lie on a straight line (but not the one yielded by ordinary least squares estimation), and the other observation lies far from this line. Deleting the atypical or outlying observation, β_0 and β_1 are estimated to be 4.0 and 0.346 respectively.

Finally, look at the scatterplot for data set 4 (Figure 8.4). Our linear model may be justified, but this depends very much on the reliability of one of the measurements. All the information about the slope of the fitted line comes from one observation, and if that observation were to be deleted from the data set the slope could not be estimated. In both data sets 3 and 4 it is one, possibly unreliable, observation that has a crucial influence on the estimation of the parameters of the regression model.

The most common way of checking the assumptions of the linear models considered in this chapter is by an examination of *residual values*, which are defined as (observed response less response predicted by the model), i.e. $y_i - \hat{y}_i$.

Figures 8.1–8.4   *Graphical representations of data sets 1–4 of Table 8.13*

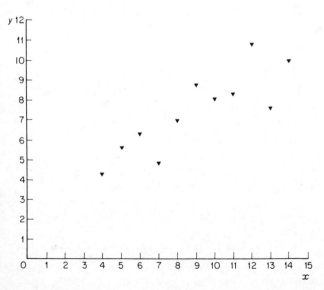

Figure 8.1   *Graph of data set 1*

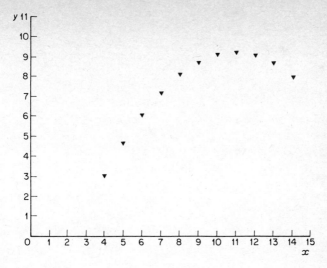

Figure 8.2 *Graph of data set 2*

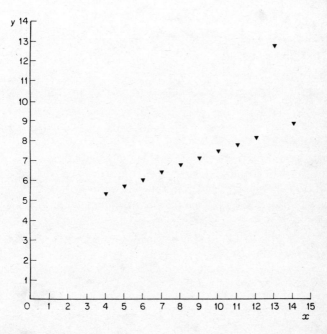

Figure 8.3 *Graph of data set 3*

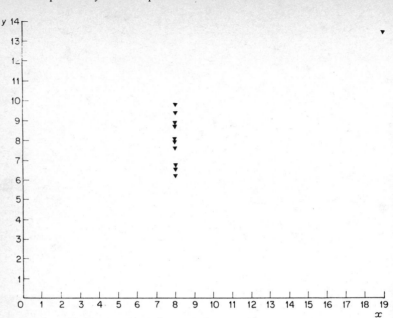

Figure 8.4   *Graph of data set 4*

The plotting of residuals is of considerable importance when assessing the applicability of a given model to a set of data, and the most useful types of plot are as follows:

(a) Plot a frequency distribution of the residuals to check for symmetry and, in particular, approximate normality.

(b) Plot the residuals as a time sequence if the order of obtaining the values of the response variable is known. This is useful for indicating whether or not the variance of the measurements is constant, and in assessing whether a term allowing for the effects of time should be included in the model.

(c) Plot the residuals against the fitted values of the response variable.

(d) Plot the residuals against any of the possible explanatory variables whether or not they have already been included in the model.

Consider Figure 8.5. These plots are typical of what one might observe when investigating the association between residual values and time, the response variable, or one of the explanatory variables. Plot (a) is what one might expect if the fitted model were adequate. Plot (b) indicates that the assumption of constant variance is not justified and

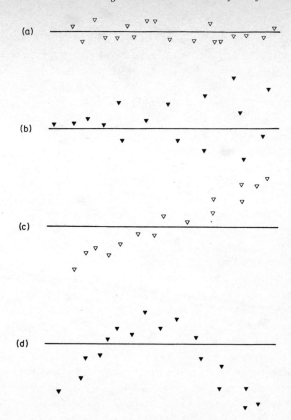

Figure 8.5 *Examples of residual plots*

that a weighted least squares analysis is more appropriate (see Section 8.8); or that the response variable should be transformed to stabilise the variance of the measurements. Plots (c) and (d) indicate that appropriate linear or quadratic terms need to be added, respectively, to the model.

Other useful ways of using residuals to check the adequacy of the linear model are discussed in Mosteller and Tukey (1977).

8.8 Weighted Least Squares

When an ordinary least squares (OLS) estimation is carried out all the measurements of the response variable are given equal weight; that is, they are assumed to be of equal importance in the estimation of the parameters of the required regression model. If the assumptions for linear regression hold (see Section 8.3), the resulting estimates are also the best of the possible unbiased estimates of the true parameter values. What should be done, however, if it is assumed that some of the measurements are probably less reliable or less trustworthy than the others? If this were true the OLS estimates would then not be the best. Here, we will briefly discuss methods that have been investigated to get around this problem. The emphasis of the discussion will be on methods of data exploration, mainly to give the student a better feel for the analysis of data using multiple regression; little or no mention of statistical significance testing will be made.

In the discussion of graphical exploration of data and analysis of residuals (Section 8.7) it was pointed out that possible unreliable measurements, in the form of extreme values, or outliers, are often detected. They are characterised, after OLS fitting of the required model, by correspondingly extreme residuals. They might be abnormal merely by chance, or they might be the result of mistakes in the measurement or coding of the data; it is usually impossible to tell which. From the derivation of the OLS method of model-fitting it is clear that these outliers have an inordinate effect on the estimated parameter values. OLS estimation is extremely sensitive to the presence of outliers, and one method of overcoming this sensitivity, that is, to produce a more robust method, is to give the more abnormal measurements less weight or importance. One could argue, however, that it is the outliers that are potentially more illuminating in the analysis of a set of results. For this reason it is still wise to try OLS estimation after a preliminary graphical analysis, and then, after careful examination of the residuals, proceed to a weighted analysis of the results.

Consider the deviation of an observed measurement of the response variable, y_i, from its predicted or estimated value $\hat{y}_i$. OLS minimises the sum of the squares of these deviations; that is, it minimises

$$\sum_{i=1}^{n} (y_i - \hat{y}_i)^2 \qquad (8.20)$$

Weighted least squares gives to each deviation a weight, w_i, so that it is the following expression that is minimised:

$$\sum_{i=1}^{n} w_i(y_i - \hat{y}_i)^2 \qquad (8.21)$$

That is, each measurement, y_i, is given a corresponding weight, w_i. All we need now is a sensible choice of the w_is. If we knew the variance of each of the y_is (assuming that it might vary from one measurement to another), an obvious method of weighting would be to make the w_is inversely proportional to the corresponding variance. Here each weighted deviation can be thought of as having equal reliability or precision. Usually, however, the variances will not be known.

Weighted least squares can be used in situations other than where there are suspect measurements. Sometimes it is clear from a pre-liminary graphical or OLS analysis that the variance of the response variable is not constant. The variance, for example, could be pro-portional to the fitted values of the response variable, or proportional to the square of the fitted value, and so on. An obvious way to proceed with the analysis would be to re-fit the model by minimising a function proportional, respectively, either to

$$\sum_{i=1}^{n} \frac{(y_i - \hat{y}_i)^2}{y_i} \tag{8.22}$$

or to

$$\sum_{i=1}^{n} \frac{(y_i - \hat{y}_i)^2}{y_i^2} \tag{8.23}$$

Allocation of the prior weights to the observations can easily be undertaken when using a model-fitting package such as GLIM.

Consider a further example, where the linear model is to be fitted to the means of grouped observations. Suppose that the individual observations making up the groups have a common variance, say σ^2, but that the groups comprise different numbers of observations. For group i, containing n_i observations, the variance of the mean is σ^2/n_i. An obvious candidate for the weight, w_i, for this mean is proportional to n_i. That is, we attempt to minimise a function proportional to

$$\sum_{i=1}^{n} n_i(y_i - \hat{y}_i)^2 \tag{8.24}$$

Finally, we return to the problem of coping with outliers. Consider data set 3 of Table 8.13. We have shown that the OLS estimates of β_0 and β_1 in the equation $y = \beta_0 + \beta_1 x$ are 3.0 and 0.5, respectively. If the outlying observation is discarded (that is, it is given a prior weight of zero) these estimates change to 4.0 and 0.346 respectively. These are the two extreme pairs of estimates. In the first, all of the weights are equal to 1; in the second all except the outlier are set to 1. Another possible alternative is first to find the OLS estimates, and then re-estimate the parameter values using weights that are inversely proportional to the absolute values of the corresponding residuals. But is this the best that can be done? Not necessarily since new residuals can be calculated using these weighted least squares estimates, and a second weighted analysis carried out using weights inversely proportional to the absolute values of the second set of residuals. This cycle of estimation can be repeated indefinitely until no further change in the estimates takes place.

In an analysis of data set 3 of Table 8.13 the final estimates are practically identical to those obtained by OLS estimation after deleting the outlying observation (see Table 8.14), but with more realistic data this is unlikely to be the case. A similar iterative analysis of data set 1 of Table 8.13 is shown in Table 8.15. The method is called *iterative*

Table 8.14   *Iterative weighted least squares estimation for data set 3 of Table 8.13*

Cycle	Estimate of β_0	Estimate of β_1
1 (OLS)	3.00	0.50
2	3.75	0.39
3	3.95	0.35
4	3.99	0.35
5	4.00	0.35

Table 8.15   *Iterative weighted least squares estimation for data set 1 of Table 8.13*

Cycle	Estimate of β_0	Estimate of β_1
1 (OLS)	3.00	0.50
2	3.06	0.49
3	3.07	0.49
4	3.08	0.49
5	3.09	0.49

weighted least squares estimation. Note that the weights could have been given a value proportional to the absolute value of any function of the residuals. The ones used in the present analyses are not necessarily the best or the most useful. They were introduced merely to give the student a feel for the method. Other approaches to weighting, and a much more detailed discussion of robust estimation procedures, are given in Mosteller and Tukey (1977). Suitable algorithms for an iterative weighted analysis are available within GLIM.

8.9   Summary
Regression is one of the most commonly used statistical techniques in the social and behavioural sciences. However, the technique is often

misused. The models described in this chapter are not usually appropriate for the analysis of variation in nominal (categorical) or ordinal response variables, but because there are several easily-used computer packages that include methods of fitting them, they are often used for data of this type. Social scientists are also prone to investigate the joint effects of too many explanatory variables. Forward selection or backward elimination algorithms (Section 8.5) should not be used to replace carefully thought and disciplined research designs. A serious weakness of multiple regression and, indeed, of other modelling techniques, is the possible unreliability of parameter estimates. If one carries out identical analyses on two or more sets of independent data the results are, at times, inconsistent. Methods of tackling this problem are beyond the scope of this text, and the interested reader is referred to Mosteller and Tukey (1977) for a discussion of cross-validation and the use of techniques such as the 'jacknife'.

In this chapter we have only considered the analysis of data for which there is a single response variable. However, the models are easily extended to deal with multivariate responses, leading to methods such as canonical correlation analysis and multivariate analysis of variance (MANOVA). These methods are clearly described in Finn (1974).

EXERCISES

8.1 From the data given in Table 8.4 fit the following three models, using ordinary least squares estimation:

(a) $\text{Visits} = \beta_0 + \beta_1 \times \text{Age}$
(b) $\text{Visits} = \beta_0 + \beta_2 \times \text{Weight}$
(c) $\text{Visits} = \beta_0 + \beta_1 \times \text{Age} + \beta_2 \times \text{Weight}$

In each case estimate the appropriate parameters (with their standard errors) and note how their value depends on the presence of the other terms in the models.

8.2 Construct appropriate F-statistics to test the fit of the three models in Exercise 8.1. From the regression and residual sums of squares given in Table 8.5, assess the statistical significance of the effects of age and weight on visits to a physician. Should an interaction term be added?

8.3 Use weighted least squares estimation to determine the effect of age and sex on the means of number of symptoms given in Table 8.4.

8.4 Use iterative weighted least squares estimation to fit model (c) of Exercise 8.1. Discuss how you would choose appropriate iterative weights, and compare the results of a few of your alternative choices.

Table 8.16 *Relationship between sex, age and number of symptoms in a sample from West London (Tarnopolsky and Morton-Williams, 1980)*

Men: Number of symptoms	Age group				
	1	2	3	4	5
0	121	147	143	49	21
1	117	106	126	57	12
2	117	78	104	43	16
3	79	73	86	43	10
4	70	51	70	34	14
5	72	44	60	27	10
6	32	39	47	26	5
7	32	28	32	12	6
8	17	18	24	10	6
9	9	18	15	8	6
10	9	14	18	7	1
11	10	3	18	7	5
12	9	2	11	3	2
13	3	2	1	4	1
14	3	1	9	0	0
15	2	1	6	3	2
16	0	2	3	1	0
17	1	0	1	3	0
18	1	0	2	0	0
19	0	0	0	0	1
20	0	1	0	1	0
21	0	0	0	0	0

Women: Number of symptoms	Age group				
	1	2	3	4	5
0	105	115	101	41	22
1	89	86	111	43	25
2	84	93	111	41	27
3	93	95	98	43	29
4	77	90	110	45	20
5	76	59	67	45	19
6	60	62	90	37	17
7	47	55	65	25	16
8	38	31	54	30	21
9	25	24	61	15	11
10	36	22	32	18	13
11	13	19	30	13	5
12	12	8	25	10	7
13	13	14	19	13	7
14	7	6	15	6	2
15	2	6	12	1	3
16	1	1	9	2	1
17	3	0	3	2	0
18	2	3	1	1	0
19	1	0	0	1	1
20	0	0	1	0	1
21	0	0	1	1	0

8.5   In Table 9.3 is given the proportions of men and women in five age-groups who admit to being prescribed psychotropic drugs in a given fortnight. If the proportions, say p_i, are transformed to $\log(p_i/1-p)$, it can be shown that the resulting measure has a variance of

$$\frac{1}{n_i p_i (1 - p_i)}$$

where n_i is the total number in the appropriate category (see Cox, 1970). Use weighted least squares to estimate the effects of age and sex on psychotropic drug prescription, and compare the results with those given in Chapter 9.

8.6   Consider Table 8.16. Using weighted least squares estimation, fit a regression model to the effects of sex and age on the mean number of symptoms.

8.7   Re-analyse the data in Table 8.10 using forward selection procedures rather than backward elimination (see Table 8.12).

8.8   Consider Table 8.10. Plot TOTCR against each of the eight dependent variables. Suggest ways in which the analysis of these data in Table 8.12 might be improved.

8.9   Repeat Exercise 8.7 after first transforming TOTCR by taking its square root.

9. Regression Models for Categorical Data

9.1 Introduction

The techniques described in the last chapter involved linear models for continuous response variables with normally distributed random disturbance terms. In this chapter we shall consider linear models suitable for categorical and ordinal response variables, which, as we have seen briefly in Chapter 7, involve logarithmic or logistic link functions and Poisson or binomial random disturbance terms.

In order to examine the relationships between categorical variables the data are usually arranged in the form of a *contingency table*. Table 9.1, for example, is a simple two-dimensional contingency table arising from the cross-classification of a sample of 5883 West Londoners with respect to their age-group and sex. Tables 9.5 and 9.6 are examples of contingency tables with more than two dimensions. We shall assume here that readers are familiar with the simple analysis of such tables by means of the chi-square statistic, and with the more common measures of association such as the odds-ratio. (Details of both topics are available in Everitt, 1977.)

Table 9.1 *A sample of West Londoners cross-classified by age and sex (taken from Murray, Dunn, Williams and Tarnopolsky, 1981)*

Age	16–29	30–44	45–64	65–74	Over 75	Total
Male	704	628	775	338	118	2563
Female	784	789	1016	434	247	3270
Total	1488	1417	1791	772	365	5833

9.2 Maximum Likelihood Estimation for Log-Linear and Logistic Models

To obtain the maximum likelihood estimates for a particular model we need to consider the sampling distribution of the observations. Three commonly encountered sampling plans lead to different distributions.

(a) Independent Poisson sampling
With no restrictions on the sample size N, each count y_i in a contingency table has an independent Poisson distribution with mean m_i, and the likelihood is given by

$$\mathscr{L} = \prod_i \frac{m_i^{y_i} e^{-m_i}}{y_i!} \tag{9.1}$$

Such a situation arises if observations are made over a period of time with no *a priori* knowledge of the total number of observations.

As we have seen in Chapter 7, the mean count m_i is related to the explanatory variables by a relationship of the form

$$m_i = \exp\left(\sum_j \beta_j x_{ij}\right) \tag{9.2}$$

where the x_{ij} are appropriate dummy variables, and the β_j are the parameters we wish to estimate. Substitution of equation (9.2) into (9.1) followed by the usual maximum likelihood process leads to the required estimates, although details are outside the scope of this text. Interested readers are referred to Birch (1963) and Bishop, Fienberg and Holland (1975).

(b) Simple multinomial sampling

Sometimes the total sample size N is fixed. This restriction imposed on a series of independent Poisson distributions leads to a multinomial distribution and a likelihood function

$$\mathscr{L} = \frac{N!}{\pi_i y_i!} \prod_i \left(\frac{m_i}{N}\right)^{y_i} \tag{9.3}$$

Again, equation (9.2) would be substituted into this function, to get the maximum likelihood estimates of the β_js.

(c) Product multinomial sampling

Although in observational studies only a single sample may be examined, in experimental situations it is more usual to have several groups, with the total number of individuals in each group determined by the sampling plan. If the total count in the j-th group is fixed at N_j, the likelihood is then given by

$$\mathscr{L} = \prod_j \left\{ \frac{N_j!}{\prod_i y_{ij}!} \prod_i \left(\frac{m_{ij}}{N_j}\right)^{y_{ij}} \right\} \tag{9.4}$$

where m_{ij} and y_{ij} are the population means and observed counts in the i-th cell of the j-th stratum, respectively. Here, the likelihood is seen to be the product of several multinomial density functions of the form of equation (9.3). Again, the substitution of an appropriate form of (9.2) for the m_{ij} followed by differentiation, and so on, will lead to estimates of the β_j.

(d)   Likelihood function for logistic models

Here we assume that the i-th cell of the contingency table contains counts for two types of individual, a total of r_i being positive for some criterion and $n_i - r_i$ negative. In the population, we assume that the probability of an individual in the i-th cell being scored as positive is p_i, and accordingly the probability of being negative is $1 - p_i$. The likelihood for this situation is simply the product of the binomial distributions appropriate for each cell,

$$\mathscr{L} = \prod_i \frac{n_i!}{r_i!\,(n_i - r_i)!}\; p_i^{r_i}(1 - p_i)^{n_i - r_i} \qquad (9.5)$$

with, as we have seen in Chapter 7, the probabilities p_i being related to the explanatory variables as follows:

$$p_i = \frac{\exp\left(\sum_j \beta_j x_{ij}\right)}{1 + \exp\left(\sum_j \beta_j x_{ij}\right)} \qquad (9.6)$$

9.3   Goodness-of-Fit Measures and the Exploration of Alternative Models

Maximum likelihood estimation for log-linear and logistic models leads, in addition to estimates for the parameters β_j, to a set of estimated cell counts to be expected under the model currently being entertained. The goodness-of-fit of the model is then assessed by comparing these to the observed counts by means of either of two statistics, namely

$$\chi^2 = \sum \frac{(\text{observed} - \text{expected})^2}{\text{expected}} \qquad (9.7)$$

or

$$G^2 = 2 \sum \text{observed} \times \log\left(\frac{\text{observed}}{\text{expected}}\right) \qquad (9.8)$$

where the summation in both cases is over all cells in the table. X^2 is the familiar chi-square statistic; G^2 is a likelihood ratio criterion. If the current model is adequate and the sample size is relatively large, both statistics are approximately distributed as χ^2 with degrees of freedom given by d.f. = number of cells in table − number of parameters fitted   (9.9)

In general we shall use the less familiar G^2 criterion, which enables us to compare models. Thus, if $G^2(a)$ if the value for a model with n_a d.f. and $G^2(b)$ is the value for a more complex model derived from the first by the addition of extra parameters, then the quantity

$$G^2(b \mid a) = G^2(a) - G^2(b) \qquad (9.10)$$

can be used to assess whether the second model has improved the fit, by testing it by means of a comparison with χ^2 with $n_a - n_b$ d.f. This procedure is analogous to the use of the regression sum-of-squares and F-tests of the previous chapter, and the forward and backward selection procedures described there may also be used in attempting to find an adequate model. Examples of this will be given in the next section.

9.4   Some Numerical Examples

Let us begin by examining the application of log-linear and logistic models to the simple 2×2 table shown in Table 9.2(a). Here, we are interested in the possible association between age and heavy smoking (over 20 cigarettes per day). First consider fitting the log-linear model

$$\log m_{ij} = \beta_0 + \text{Age}(i) + \text{Smoke}(j) + \text{AS}(ij) \qquad (9.11)$$

where Age (i), Smoke (j) and AS (ij) are parameters representing main effects and interactions respectively. (This model could, of course, be rewritten in terms of suitable dummy variables as indicated in the previous chapter.) As written the model has nine parameters, but since the table only has four cells, some will not have unique estimates. The model could be re-parameterised in terms of four estimatable contrasts, or constraints on the parameters introduced. As mentioned in the previous two chapters, GLIM uses the latter approach and sets a number of the parameters at zero. For the model of (9.11) the GLIM estimates of the non-zero parameters are given in Table 9.2(b). Since the estimated expected values under this model are equal to the observed values, G^2 takes the value zero; a model with the same number of free parameters as number of cells is known as a *saturated model*. If we now fit a model which sets all the interaction parameters to zero, that is

$$\log m_{ij} = \beta_0 + \text{Age}(i) + \text{Smoke}(j) \qquad (9.12)$$

we obtain estimates as shown in Table 9.2(c) and a G^2 value of 22.5, with a single degree of freedom. This model clearly does not describe the data very well and we conclude that there is a significant interaction between age and smoking.

If we now reformulate our interest in these data as that of investigating the effect of age-group on heavy smoking, we might consider fitting a logistic model of the form

$$\log \frac{p_i}{1 - p_i} = \beta_0 + \text{Age}\,(i) \tag{9.13}$$

(The parameters β_0 and Age (i) will not be the same as in equation (9.11) or (9.12).) In equation (9.13), p_i is the probability that an individual is a heavy smoker when he comes from age-group i, $i = 1, 2$. Fitting this model using GLIM results in the parameter estimates given in Table 9.2(d). Again G^2 is zero since this model fits the data perfectly. If we fit a model assuming that age has no effect, that is

$$\log \frac{p_i}{1 - p_i} = \beta_0 \tag{9.14}$$

then we obtain the results shown in Table 9.2(e). G^2 now takes the value 22.5. Consequently, we are led to exactly the same conclusion as in the previous analysis. The equivalence of some of the parameter estimates is easily explained if we return to examining the log-linear models for heavy smokers, that is

$$\log m_{i2} = \beta_0 + \text{Age}\,(i) + \text{Smoke}\,(2) + \text{AS}\,(i2) \tag{9.15}$$

and for light smokers

$$\log m_{i1} = \beta_0 + \text{Age}\,(i) \tag{9.16}$$

(remembering that some parameters are *a priori* set to zero).

Subtracting equation (9.16) from (9.15) gives

$$\log m_{i2}/m_{i1} = \text{Smoke}\,(2) + \text{AS}\,(i2) \tag{9.17}$$

which, since $m_{i2}/m_{i1} = p_i/(1 - p_i)$, is equivalent to equation (9.13). Hence the parameter Smoke (2) in the log-linear model takes the same value as β_0 in the logistic model, and AS $(i2)$ in the former model, the same value as Age (2) in the latter.

As a further example we will consider the data shown in Table 9.3. This gives the number of people who admit to have been prescribed psychotropic drugs in the fortnight prior to interview as a function of their sex and age-group. We could explore the relationships between the three variables through the construction of appropriate log-linear models. Alternatively we can explore one aspect of the data, that is, the

Table 9.2 *Association of age with heavy smoking*

(a) Observed counts

		Age		
		1	*2*	(*2* = over 40)
Smoking habits (2 = over 20 per day)	1	50	15	
	2	10	25	

(b) Log-linear model: $\log m_{ij} = \beta_0 + \text{Age}\,(i) + \text{Smoke}\,(j) + \text{AS}\,(ij)$

Parameter	Estimate	Standard Error
β_0	3.91	0.14
Age (2)	−1.20	0.29
Smoke (2)	−1.61	0.35
AS (22)	2.12	0.48

$$G^2 = 0 \text{ with 0 d.f.}$$

(c) Log-linear model: $\log m_{ij} = \beta_0 + \text{Age}\,(i) + \text{Smoke}\,(j)$

Parameter	Estimate	Standard Error
β_0	3.66	0.15
Age (2)	−0.41	0.20
Smoke (2)	−0.62	0.21

$$G^2 = 22.50 \text{ with 1 d.f.}$$

(d) Linear-logistic model: $\log\,(\text{true odds}) = \beta_0 + \text{Age}\,(i)$

Parameter	Estimate	Standard Error
β_0	−1.61	0.35
Age (2)	2.12	0.48

$$G^2 = 0 \text{ with 0 d.f.}$$

(e) Linear-logistic model: $\log\,(\text{true odds}) = \beta_0$

Parameter	Estimate	Standard Error
β_0	−0.62	0.21

$$G^2 = 22.50 \text{ with 1 d.f.}$$

dependence on psychotropic drug usage on age and sex, by construct-ing a logistic model for the proportion of people in each category who admit to having been prescribed a psychotropic drug. Here we shall consider this latter alternative. (See Exercise 9.1 for the analysis of these data using log-linear models.)

If we begin by looking at the log (odds) in the last column of Table 9.3. it can be seen that for any particular age range the women are more likely to take drugs than their male counterparts. Considering men and women separately, it is clear that the risk of taking psychotropic drugs increases with age. To get a clear picture of how the proportion is changing over these ten categories, we need to draw two graphs, one for men, and the other for women. The variable to be predicted, log (odds), plotted on the vertical axis against mean age on the horizontal axis, is shown in Figure 9.1. The data can be represented by two parallel straight lines, whose slope is about 0.03, and distance apart about 0.7. The algebraic equation describing these lines has the following form:

$$\log(\text{odds}) = -4.1 + 0.7 \times \text{Sex} + 0.03 \times \text{Age} \qquad (9.18)$$

where Sex is a dummy variable taking the value 0 for men and 1 for women, and Age is the person's age.

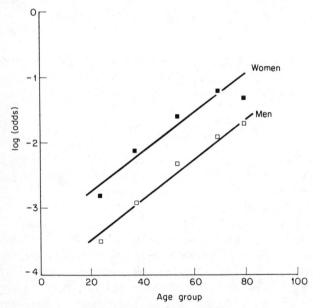

Figure 9.1   *Graphical representation of data in Table 9.3*

One can draw two conclusions from this simple analysis (in fact, they are logically or mathematically equivalent):

(1) When comparing drugs taken by men and women, the ratio of odds remains constant over all age-groups.

(2) The effect of ageing on drug taking is the same for men and women.

However, close examination of Figure 9.1 shows that the effect of

Table 9.3   *Patterns of psychotropic drug consumption in a sample from West London (taken from Dunn, 1981)*

Sex	Age group	Mean age	No. taking drugs	No. not on drugs	Odds	log (odds)
Male	16–29	23.2	21	683	0.03	− 3.5
Male	30–44	36.5	32	596	0.05	− 2.9
Male	45–64	54.3	70	705	0.10	− 2.3
Male	65–74	69.2	43	295	0.15	− 1.9
Male	over 74	79.5	19	99	0.19	− 1.7
Female	16–29	23.2	46	738	0.06	− 2.8
Female	30–44	36.5	89	700	0.13	− 2.1
Female	45–64	54.3	169	847	0.20	− 1.6
Female	65–74	69.2	98	336	0.29	− 1.2
Female	over 74	79.5	51	196	0.26	− 1.3

ageing might be quadratic (the curve being slightly convex) rather than linear, and so a rather more formal analysis of the data could lead to additional insights. Consequently a logistic model of the form

$$\log \frac{p_i}{1 - p_i} = \beta_0 + \beta_1 \times \text{Sex} + \beta_2 \times \text{Age} \qquad (9.19)$$

was fitted to the data, producing the results shown in Table 9.4(a). The parameter estimates are quite close to the values in equation (9.18), as we would expect. The model fits reasonably well since a G^2 of 12.21 with 7 d.f. is not significant at the 5 % level. However, since Figure 9.1 indicates that a pair of quadratic curves might provide a better description of the data, residuals from fitting (9.19) deserve examination. As expected, these tend to be negative for both ends of the age range considered. Table 9.4(b) gives the estimates of parameters and the value of G^2 after the introduction of a quadratic term for age into equation (9.19). The reduction in G^2 is significant so that the more complex model is needed to provide an adequate description of the data.

As a final example we shall consider the data shown in Table 9.5 taken from Ries and Smith (1963). These data arise from a study in which a sample of 1008 people was asked to compare two detergents, brand M and brand X. In addition to stating their brand preference the sample members provided information on previous use of brand M (yes or no), the degree of softness of the water they used (soft, medium, hard), and the temperature of the water (high, low). The main topic of interest here is the effect of the variables—previous usage, degree of

Table 9.4　*Models for psychotropic drug consumption*

(a) Linear-logistic model:　$\log(\text{true odds}) = \beta_0 + \beta_1 \times \text{Sex} + \beta_2 \times \text{Age}$

Parameter	Estimate	Standard Error
β_0	-4.04	0.15
β_1	0.80	0.09
β_2	0.03	0.002

$$G^2 = 12.21 \text{ with } 7 \text{ d.f.}$$

Sex	Mean age	Observed count	Total count	Fitted count	Residual
0	23.2	21	683	24.75	-0.77
0	36.5	32	596	32.68	-0.12
0	54.3	70	705	66.19	0.49
0	69.2	43	295	42.51	0.08
0	79.5	19	99	18.87	0.03
1	23.2	46	738	56.74	-1.49
1	36.5	89	700	79.70	1.11
1	54.3	169	847	158.10	0.96
1	69.2	98	336	91.27	0.83
1	79.5	51	196	67.20	-2.44

(b) Linear-logistic model:　$\log(\text{true odds}) = \beta_0 + \beta_1 \times \text{Sex} + \beta_2 \times \text{Age} + \beta_3 \times \text{Age}^2$

Parameter	Estimate	Standard Error
β_0	-4.99	0.37
β_1	0.80	0.09
β_2	0.08	0.02
β_3	0.0003	0.0001

$$G^2 = 4.02 \text{ with } 6 \text{ d.f.}$$

---

softness and temperature—on brand preference (M as opposed to X). Initially, however, we will use log-linear models to explore associations between the four variables and to demonstrate the use of forward and backward selection procedures for this type of data.

We start by choosing an arbitrary significance level of, say, 0.05 and use it to assess the fit of the following three log-linear models

(A)　Brand + Prev + Soft + Temp　　　　　　　　　　　　　(9.20)

(B)　(A) + Brand × Prev + Brand × Soft + Brand × Temp
　　　+ Prev × Soft + Prev × Temp + Soft × Temp　　　　(9.21)

(C)　(B) + Brand × Prev × Soft + Brand × Prev × Temp
　　　+ Brand × Soft × Temp + Prev × Soft × Temp　　　(9.22)

where the variable names have a meaning that is obvious within the

Table 9.5   *Cross-classification of a sample of 1008 consumers in a blind trial according to (1) water softness, (2) previous use of detergent brand M, (3) water temperature, and (4) preference for brand M (Ries and Smith, 1963)*

| Water softness | Brand preferemce | Previous user of M (Prev=1) | | Not previous user of M (Prev=2) | |
		High temp. (Temp=2)	Low temp. (Temp=1)	High temp.	Low temp.
Soft (Soft=1)	X (Brand=1)	19	57	29	63
	M (Brand=2)	29	49	27	53
Medium (Soft=2)	X	23	47	33	66
	M	47	55	23	50
Hard (Soft=3)	X	24	37	42	68
	M	43	52	30	42

context of this example, and suffices indicating variable categories have been dropped to simplify the nomenclature. Terms such as Brand × Prev are used for first-order interaction parameters, and Brand × Prev × Soft for second-order interactions. Model (A) contains only main effects, Model (B) main effects and first-order interactions, and Model (C) contains main effects and both first- and second-order interactions. The results of fitting each of these models is shown at the top of Table 9.6. Model (A) does not describe the data adequately, but (B) and (C) do. Clearly a model more complex than (A) but less complex than (B) is going to be the simplest model that provides an adequate description of the data. Consequently, we can proceed by either forward selection of interaction terms to add to (A) or backwards elimination of terms from (B) to search for the 'best' model.

For forward selection we add each two-factor interaction term in turn and choose the one for which the change in the conditional goodness-of-fit criterion of equation (9.10) is most significant. From Table 9.6 this is Brand × Prev. Next, having included Brand × Prev in the model, we add the remaining two-factor interaction terms in turn, and again choose the one for which the change in the conditional goodness-of-fit statistic is most significant. This leads to the addition of the term Brand × Temp. Repeating this procedure we find that we must add Soft × Temp, but that addition of further terms causes no significant improvement of fit. Hence we are led to the following model as the simplest that adequately describes the data

$$(A) + Brand \times Prev + Brand \times Temp + Soft \times Temp \qquad (9.23)$$

As an optional step, after the addition of each of the two-factor interaction terms, we might have considered deleting any of the terms currently included that no longer contributed significantly to the fit. However, in this example no terms could be deleted.

Backwards elimination is a very similar procedure, but here we start with model (B) and delete each two-factor interaction in turn. First, the least significant term is deleted, and so on. At each step we add back two-factor interaction terms that now significantly improve the fit of the current model. The results of applying this procedure to the Ries–Smith data are also shown in Table 9.6. The 'best' model is:

$$(B) - Soft \times Brand - Soft \times Prev - Prev \times Temp \qquad (9.24)$$

In this case, it is the same model as the one found by forward selection, but this is not always so. The estimated parameters of the model are given in Table 9.7. Other authors have analysed these data, and the reader is referred to Fienberg (1980) and Aitken (1979) for detailed discussions of their results.

9.5   Linear Models for Ordinal Response Variables

Consider the data shown in Table 9.8, which comprises counts of people in the West London sample, first considered in Table 9.1, now cross-classified with respect to the same five age-groups and their perceptions of their own health over the two weeks prior to being interviewed. This assessment is made on an ordinal five-point scale ranging from 'very good' (coded as 1) to 'very poor' (coded as 5). Of interest is the manner in which the age of the respondent influences self-assessment of health.

If one fits simple log-linear models to these data, the results in Table 9.9 are obtained. These show that there is a significant association between age and self-assessment of health, but convey little about the detailed structure of the relationship. Some consideration might be given to fitting linear and quadratic effects but this might still only be of limited value.

Table 9.6 *Log-linear models: analysis of G^2 for Ries–Smith data*

Model	G^2	d.f.
(A)	42.93	18
(B)	9.85	9
(C)	0.74	2
1 Forward selection		
(A) + Soft × Brand	42.53	16
(A) + Soft × Prev	41.85	16
(A) + Soft × Temp	36.83	16
(A) + Brand × Prev	22.35	17
(A) + Brand × Temp	38.57	17
(A) + Prev × Temp	41.68	17
(A) + Brand × Prev + Soft × Brand	21.95	15
(A) + Brand × Prev + Soft × Prev	21.27	15
(A) + Brand × Prev + Soft × Temp	16.25	15
(A) + Brand × Prev + Brand × Temp	17.99	16
(A) + Brand × Prev + Prev × Temp	21.09	16
(A) + Brand × Prev + Brand × Temp + Soft × Brand	17.59	14
(A) + Brand × Prev + Brand × Temp + Soft × Prev	16.91	14
(A) + Brand × Prev + Brand × Temp + Soft × Temp	11.89	14
(A) + Brand × Prev + Brand × Temp + Prev × Temp	17.29	15
⋮		
etc.		
2 Backward elimination		
(B) − Soft × Brand	10.06	11
(B) − Soft × Prev	10.85	11
(B) − Soft × Temp	15.94	11
(B) − Brand × Prev	29.74	10
(B) − Brand × Temp	13.58	10
(B) − Prev × Temp	10.59	10
(B) − Soft × Brand − Soft × Prev	11.19	13
(B) − Soft × Brand − Soft × Temp	16.22	13
(B) − Soft × Brand − Brand × Prev	30.08	12
(B) − Soft × Brand − Brand × Temp	13.86	12
(B) − Soft × Brand − Prev × Temp	10.80	12
(B) − Soft × Brand − Soft × Prev − Soft × Temp	17.29	15
(B) − Soft × Brand − Soft × Prev − Brand × Prev	31.21	14
(B) − Soft × Brand − Soft × Prev − Brand × Temp	14.99	14
(B) − Soft × Brand − Soft × Prev − Prev × Temp	11.89	14
⋮		
etc.		

Now let us consider linear-logistic models for the effects of age on self-assessment of health. Initially we might think in terms of a model for the dichotomous variable produced by dividing the table between assessments of 2 and 3. Plotting log (odds) for an assessment of 3 or

Table 9.7 *Parameter estimates for Ries–Smith data*

(i) Log-linear model: Brand + Prev + Soft + Temp + Brand × Prev + Brand × Temp + Soft × Temp

Parameter	Estimate	Standard Error
β_0	3.87	0.09
Soft (2)	−0.02	0.10
Soft (3)	−0.11	0.10
Brand (2)	0.18	0.10
Prev (2)	0.37	0.09
Temp (2)	−0.90	0.14
BP (22)	−0.56	0.13
ST (22)	0.21	0.16
ST (32)	0.40	0.16
BT (22)	0.27	0.13

$$G^2 = 11.89 \text{ with } 14 \text{ d.f.}$$

(ii) Linear-logistic model: Prev + Temp

Parameter	Estimate	Standard Error
β_0	0.19	0.10
Prev (2)	−0.57	0.13
Temp (2)	0.26	0.13

$$G^2 = 8.44 \text{ with } 9 \text{ d.f.}$$

(iii) Linear-logistic model: Prev

Parameter	Estimate	Standard Error
β_0	+0.29	0.09
Prev (2)	−0.58	0.13

$$G^2 = 12.24 \text{ with } 10 \text{ d.f.}$$

---

higher against age-group leads to Figure 9.2. We can also consider other places in the table at which to make these 'cuts' (there being four in all), and again plot the log (odds) for assessing our own health above the cut against age-group. Figure 9.3 shows such a plot for a cut between 3 and 4.

If we now rearrange the data in Table 9.8 in terms of age-group and the cutting point of self-assessment of health we obtain Table 9.10. This table may now be investigated by fitting linear-logistic models with explanatory variables, Age and Cut. For example, a model such as

$$\log (\text{true odds}) = \beta_0 + \text{Cut } (i) + \text{Age } (j) + \text{CA } (ij) \qquad (9.25)$$

would merely provide an alternative to the saturated log-linear model in Table 9.9. (The term 'true odds' refers, of course, to the population value of this function.) However, if in the plots of log (odds) for different

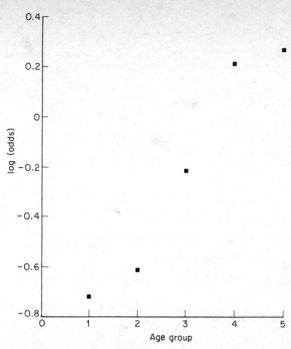

Figure 9.2 *Graphical representation of data in Table 9.8: log (odds) for an assessment of 3 or higher against age*

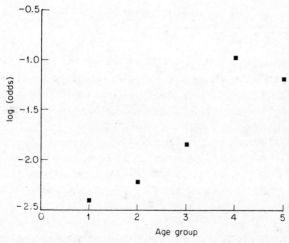

Figure 9.3 *Graphical representation of data in Table 9.8: log (odds) for an assessment of 4 or higher against age*

Table 9.8   *Self-assessment of health in a West London sample (from Murray, Dunn and Tarnopolsky, 1982)*

		Health				
		1	2	3	4	5
	1	517	475	362	113	10
	2	485	422	356	122	15
Age-group:	3	466	515	551	205	38
	3	466	515	551	205	38
	4	196	188	241	209	27
	5	64	91	118	59	27
		Cut 1	Cut 2	Cut 3	Cut 4	

cutting points the mean value of log (odds) altered, but the shape of the plot did not, then an appropriate model would be

$$\log (\text{true odds}) = \beta_0 + \text{Cut } (i) + \text{Age } (j) \qquad (9.26)$$

This model would, if it fitted the data, give a much simpler description. Finally, if one were to postulate that there was no effect of age-group on self-assessment of health, the appropriate model would be

$$\log (\text{true odds}) = \beta_0 + \text{Cut } (i) \qquad (9.27)$$

This class of models has been described by McCullagh (1980), and we shall refer to them as *cumulative odds models*.

Returning to Table 9.8, we could decide to plot the data in a slightly different way. We could, for instance, select those subjects with a self-assessment of health over 2 (that is, above cut 2), and calculate the log (odds) for assessing our own health as 4 or 5. This is the log (odds) for an assessment over 3, given that the assessment is over 2. A plot of this statistic against age-group is shown in Figure 9.4. Again, we could consider fitting models of the form of (9.25), (9.26) and (9.27). We will refer to these models as *conditional odds models* to distinguish them from the cumulative odds models. The parameters involving the 'cut' variable will now have a slightly different interpretation, but in both cases can be regarded as 'nuisance' parameters since it is the effect of age-group which is of real interest.

The two model systems have slightly different statistical properties, but whichever one the behavioural scientist chooses to use would seem to be merely a matter of taste. Here, we shall concentrate on the

Table 9.9 *Log-linear models for self-assessment of health*

(a) Model: $\log m_{ij} = \beta_0 + \text{Age}(i) + \text{Health}(j) + \text{AH}(ij)$

Parameter	Estimate	Standard Error
β_0	6.25	0.04
Health (2)	−0.08	0.06
Health (3)	−0.36	0.07
Health (4)	−1.52	0.10
Health (5)	−3.95	0.32
Age (2)	−0.06	0.06
Age (3)	−0.10	0.06
Age (4)	−0.97	0.08
Age (5)	−2.09	0.13
AH (22)	−0.05	0.09
AH (32)	0.18	0.09
AH (42)	0.04	0.12
AH (52)	0.44	0.18
AH (23)	0.05	0.10
AH (33)	0.52	0.09
AH (43)	0.56	0.12
AH (53)	0.97	0.17
AH (24)	0.14	0.15
AH (34)	0.70	0.13
AH (44)	0.93	0.16
AH (54)	1.44	0.21
AH (25)	0.47	0.41
AH (35)	1.44	0.36
AH (45)	1.96	0.38
AH (55)	3.08	0.39

$G^2 = 0$ with 0 d.f.

(b) Model: $\log m_{ij} = \beta_0 + \text{Age}(i) + \text{Health}(j)$

$G^2 = 192.6$ with 16 d.f.

conditional models since they can be readily fitted using current versions of GLIM. The reader is referred to Fienberg and Mason (1978) or Fienberg (1980) for further discussion of their theoretical properties.

Table 9.11 shows the results of fitting conditional odds models for self-assessment of health to the counts in Table 9.8. Model (a) provides an alternative to log-linear model (a) in Table 9.9. It has fewer estimated parameters than the latter, and is also more easily interpreted. The interaction terms in this model are not very large when compared to their respective standard errors (the estimate divided by its standard error provides a standardised value that is suitable for comparison with other standardised values), suggesting that a simpler model could easily be fitted to the data. Model (b) in Table 9.11 has all the

Table 9.10   *Self-assessment of health in a West London sample: data rearranged from Table 9.8*

		Cut 1		Cut 2		Cut 3		Cut 4	
		No. less	*No. above*	*No. less*	*No. above*	*No. less*	*No. above*	*No. less*	*No. above*
	1	517	960	992	485	1354	123	1467	10
	2	485	915	907	493	1263	137	1385	15
Age-group:	*3*	466	1309	981	794	1532	243	1737	38
	4	196	665	384	477	625	236	834	27
	5	64	295	155	204	273	86	332	27

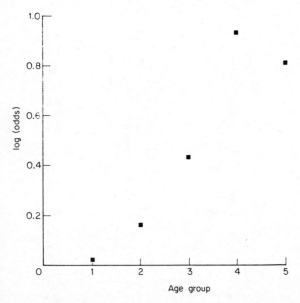

Figure 9.4   *Graphical representation of data in Table 9.8: log (odds) for an assessment over 3, given that the assessment is over 2, against age*

interaction terms constrained to be zero, and fits the data quite well. Now we have a relatively simple, parsimonious description of the results which shows quite clearly how the age-group of the subjects affects their self-assessment of health. Model (c) in Table 9.11, which would be appropriate if age-group and self-assessment of health were independent, is equivalent to (b) in Table 9.9.

Table 9.11 *Conditional odds models for self-assessment of health*

(a) Model: $\log(\text{true odds}) = \beta_0 + \text{Cut}(i) + \text{Age}(j) + \text{CA}(ij)$

Parameter	Estimate	Standard Error
β_0	0.62	0.05
Cut (2)	−0.60	0.08
Cut (3)	−1.70	0.12
Cut (4)	−3.04	0.33
Age (2)	0.02	0.08
Age (3)	0.41	0.08
Age (4)	0.44	0.10
Age (5)	0.91	0.15
CA (22)	0.12	0.12
CA (23)	−0.002	0.12
CA (24)	0.24	0.15
CA (25)	−0.12	0.21
CA (32)	0.11	0.16
CA (33)	−0.15	0.15
CA (34)	0.07	0.18
CA (35)	−0.15	0.23
CA (42)	0.31	0.44
CA (44)	1.00	0.39
CA (45)	0.73	0.43

$G^2 = 0$ with 0 d.f.

(b) Model: $\log(\text{true odds}) = \beta_0 + \text{Cut}(i) + \text{Age}(j)$

Parameter	Estimate	Standard Error
β_0	0.60	0.04
Cut (2)	−0.55	0.04
Cut (3)	−1.73	0.05
Cut (4)	−2.53	0.10
Age (2)	0.08	0.05
Age (3)	0.39	0.05
Age (4)	0.58	0.06
Age (5)	0.86	0.08

$G^2 = 16.58$ with 12 d.f.

(c) Model: $\log(\text{true odds}) = \beta_0 + \text{Cut}(i)$

Parameter	Estimate	Standard Error
β_0	0.85	0.03
Cut (2)	−0.52	0.04
Cut (3)	−1.66	0.05
Cut (4)	−2.40	0.10

$G^2 = 200.9$ with 16 d.f.

Now consider the counts in Table 9.12, in which a further variable, sex, has been introduced into the self-assessment of health investigation. Log-linear models for this three-dimensional table are considered in Table 9.13. The only unsaturated model that fits the data at all reasonably is (d), involving thirty-four free parameters! Clearly this does not provide a simple description of the structure in the table. If, on the other hand, we consider conditional odds models for health assessment, model (e) is found to describe the data adequately. This has only nine free parameters, one more than the equivalent model for the counts in Table 9.8, and provides easily interpreted measures of the effects of both sex and age on self-assessment of health. By choosing a regression model particularly appropriate for an ordinal response variable we have simplified our analysis considerably. When one comes to investigate categorical data from contingency tables with four or more variables, the choice of model types with which to describe the data might be of utmost importance in terms of the amount of effort expended in finding a simple interpretable solution. Model (e) of Table

Table 9.12   *Effect of sex and age on self-assessment of health (from Murray, Dunn and Tarnopolsky, 1982)*

		Health (Men)				
		1	2	3	4	5
	1	271	233	151	43	4
	2	243	185	140	44	6
Age-group:	3	243	235	218	60	14
	4	104	87	94	38	11
	5	21	38	35	17	3
		Health (Women)				
		1	2	3	4	5
	1	246	242	211	70	6
	2	242	237	216	78	9
Age-group:	3	223	280	333	145	24
	4	92	101	147	71	16
	5	43	53	83	42	24

Table 9.13 *Models showing interaction of sex, age and self-assessment of health*

(a) Log-linear model: $\log m_{ij} = \beta_0 + \text{Sex }(i) + \text{Age }(j) + \text{Health }(k)$

$G^2 = 312.2$ with 40 d.f.

(b) Log-linear model: $\log m_{ij} = \beta_0 + \text{Sex }(i) + \text{Age }(j) + \text{Health }(k) + \text{SA }(ij)$

$G^2 = 281.9$ with 36 d.f.

(c) Log-linear model: $\log m_{ij} = \beta_0 + \text{Sex }(i) + \text{Age }(j) + \text{Health }(k) + \text{SA }(ij) +$

$+ \text{AH }(jk)$

$G^2 = 89.30$ with 20 d.f.

(d) Log-linear model: $\log m_{ij} = \beta_0 + \text{Sex }(i) + \text{Age }(j) + \text{Health }(k) + \text{SA }(ij)$

$+ \text{AH }(jk) + \text{SH }(ik)$

$G^2 = 11.49$ with 16 d.f.

(c) Conditional odds model: $\log(\text{true odds}) = \beta_0 + \text{Sex }(i) + \text{Age }(j) + \text{Cut }(k)$

Parameter	Estimate	Standard Error
β_0	0.44	0.05
Sex (2)	0.83	0.04
Age (2)	0.04	0.06
Age (3)	0.38	0.05
Age (4)	0.55	0.07
Age (5)	0.83	0.09
Cut (2)	−0.56	0.04
Cut (3)	−1.81	0.05
Cut (4)	−2.67	0.11

$G^2 = 33.22$ with 31 d.f.

(d) Conditional odds model:
$\log(\text{true odds}) = \beta_0 + \text{Sex }(i) + \text{Age }(j) + \text{Cut }(k) + \text{SC }(ik)$

$G^2 = 27.14$ with 28 d.f.

(e) Conditional odds model:
$\log(\text{true odds}) = \beta_0 + \text{Sex }(i) + \text{Age }(j) + \text{Cut }(k) + \text{AC }(jk)$

$G^2 = 22.47$ with 19 d.f.

(f) Conditional odds model:
$\log(\text{true odds}) = \beta_0 + \text{Sex }(i) + \text{Age }(j) + \text{Cut }(k) + \text{SA }(ij)$

$G^2 = 30.04$ with 27 d.f.

9.13 simply implies that being female and ageing increase the possibility of assessing one's health as being poorer than a given threshold (conditional on the previous threshold having been passed), and that the effects of age and sex act independently.

EXERCISES

9.1   Explore the structure of the data in Table 9.3 using log-linear models. Compare your results with the analysis given in Section 9.4.

9.2   Analyse the counts in Table 7.2 using log-linear models. Then, taking 'suicide intent' as a response variable, re-analyse the data using an ordinal regression model. Compare your results.

9.3   After appropriate grouping of the counts, analyse the data given in Table 8.16 using log-linear models. These data were analysed using linear regression in Exercise 8.6, but the variable 'number of symptoms' can also be treated as if it were an ordinal response. Re-analyse these counts using a regression model for ordinal data. How does this analysis improve your understanding of counted data of this type?

9.4   Analyse and interpret the data given in Table 9.14.

Table 9.14   *Patterns of psychotropic drug consumption in a sample from West London (from Murray, Dunn, Williams and Tarnopolsky, 1981)*

Sex	Mean age	Probable psychiatric case*	No. taking drugs	Total
Male	23.2	No	9	531
Male	36.5	No	16	500
Male	54.3	No	38	644
Male	69.2	No	26	275
Male	79.5	No	9	90
Male	23.2	Yes	12	171
Male	36.5	Yes	16	125
Male	54.3	Yes	31	121
Male	69.2	Yes	16	56
Male	79.5	Yes	10	26
Female	23.2	No	12	568
Female	36.5	No	42	596
Female	54.3	No	96	765
Female	69.2	No	52	327
Female	79.5	No	30	179
Female	23.2	Yes	33	210
Female	36.5	Yes	47	189
Female	54.3	Yes	71	242
Female	69.2	Yes	45	98
Female	79.2	Yes	21	60

* High or low score on completion of the General Health Questionnaire (Goldberg, 1972)

9.5   Discuss the relative merits of the use of log-linear and linear-logistic models in the analysis of contingency tables.

9.6   Table 9.15 gives the results of a study of the relationship between car size and car accident injuries (Kihlberg, Narragon and Campbell, 1964). Accidents were classified according to type of accident, severity of accident, and whether or not the driver was ejected. Using 'severity' as the response variable, fit and interpret a linear-logistic model to these counts.

9.7   Analyse and interpret the counts given in Table 9.16.

Table 9.15   *The effect of car weight, accident type and ejection of driver on the severity of accidents (Kihlberg, Narragon and Campbell, 1964)*

Car weight	Driver ejected	Accident type	No. severe	No. not severe
Small	No	Collision	150	350
Small	No	Rollover	112	60
Small	Yes	Collision	23	26
Small	Yes	Rollover	80	19
Standard	No	Collision	1022	1878
Standard	No	Rollover	404	148
Standard	Yes	Collision	161	111
Standard	Yes	Rollover	265	22

Table 9.16   *Association between state of mental health and parental socioeconomic status (from Srole et al., 1962)*

| Mental state | Parental socioeconomic status | | | | | |
	A	B	C	D	E	F
Well	64	57	57	72	36	21
Mild symptom formation	94	94	105	141	97	71
Moderate symptom formation	58	54	65	77	54	54
Impaired	46	40	60	94	78	71

10. Models for Time-Dependent Data

10.1 Introduction

In Chapters 7 to 9 linear models for the descriptions of categorical, ordinal and interval-scaled response variables were described in some detail. In this chapter we shall concentrate on the use of the generalised linear model for investigating the results of experiments or surveys in which the behaviour of an individual, or a group of individuals, is monitored over time. Such data arise in many areas of psychology and sociology. For example, Table 10.1 shows a set of data arising in the investigation of the approach-avoidance nature of an autistic child's social behaviour. The child's behavioural state was recorded after consecutive intervals of about two seconds during a period of time in which he was engaged in a continuous one-to-one activity with his teacher. The child's behavioural repertoire was grouped into three exhaustive and mutually exclusive states which were:

(a) activities indicating a positive approach to his teacher (coded as 1),

(b) activities indicating resistance or avoidance of the teacher (coded as 3),

(c) inactivity or solitary preoccupation that gave no indication that the child might be aware of the other person (coded as 2).

(Note that the three coded behavioural states can be regarded as ordinal measures of the child's interpersonal responsiveness.)

In this chapter, we shall be interested not only in models for such behavioural sequences but also in models for measurements of response time or latencies; for example, times to failure or death, as in the analysis of life-tables, or the time taken for a subject to carry out some specified task such as learning how to tackle a particular problem or recall a memory. An example of this type of data is shown in Table 10.2, which gives the remission times, in weeks, of two groups of leukaemia patients, one of which had been treated with a drug and the other with a placebo. These data illustrate the *censoring* of the observations which frequently occurs with data of this type.

10.2 Markov Chain Models for Behavioural Sequences

Initially, let us consider a hypothetical investigation in which a patient

Table 10.1   *An autistic child's behavioural sequence (from Dunn and Clark, 1982)*

11132311123223322323222222221112121121 22

22332222221222222233222223222211 22111211

1232222222221222222231121111111221321111

1111212111122212222113111122222222222111

1212222222222222333111111111111222222212

221111111111112222111133222222222222222222

Table 10.2   *Times of remission (in weeks) of leukaemia patients (taken with permission from Freireich et al., 1963)*

Sample 1 (Drug)	6+	6	6	6	7	9	10+
	10	11+	13	16	17+	19	20
	22	23	25+	32+	32+	34+	35+
Sample 2 (Placebo)	1	1	2	2	3	4	4
	5	5	8	8	8	8	11
	11	12	12	15	17	22	23

+ Censored; that is, the remission time is known to be longer than that recorded, but the exact time of remission, or whether there was subsequent remission, is not known.

is categorised as depressed (D) or well (W) at each of a number of equally spaced points in time, say yearly. If there are many patients being observed in this longitudinal study then the pattern of diagnosis for two consecutive years can be summarised as in Table 10.3(a). This is a table of *transition counts*, the transition of interest being that from the diagnosis in the $(i-1)$th year to that in the i-th year, the previous states being ignored. Table 10.3(b) shows a similar table for the pattern of diagnoses for three consecutive years.

Concentrating for the moment on Table 10.3(a), we may use the entries in this table to estimate the probability of being depressed at the i-th diagnosis, given a diagnosis of depression at the immediately preceding diagnosis. This estimate is given simply by n_{DD}/n_{D+}. Similarly, the probability of being diagnosed as depressed at the i-th examination, given that the subject is well at the previous examination, is estimated by n_{DW}/n_{W+}. Four such *transition probabilities* can be estimated from Table 10.3(a), and these are shown in Table 10.4(a). Note that the sum of P_{DD} and P_{WW} is unity, as is that of P_{WD} and P_{WW}.

Table 10.3   *Transition counts for Markov chains*

(a) *1st-order*

		Diagnosis in i-th year		Total
		D	W	
	Diagnosis in $(i-1)$th year			
	D	n_{DD}	n_{DW}	n_{D+}
	W	n_{WD}	n_{WW}	n_{W+}

(b) *2nd-order*

		Diagnosis in i-th year		Total
Diagnosis in $(i-2)$th year	Diagnosis in $(i-1)$th year	D	W	
D	D	n_{DDD}	n_{DDW}	n_{DD+}
	W	n_{DWD}	n_{DWW}	n_{DW+}
W	D	n_{WDD}	n_{WDW}	n_{WD+}
	W	n_{WWD}	n_{WWW}	n_{WW+}

There are therefore only two independent transition probabilities to be estimated. Here we shall consider P_{WD}, the probability of becoming depressed between consecutive diagnoses, and P_{DD}, the probability of remaining depressed. (The transition probabilities corresponding to the frequencies in Table 10.3(b) are shown in Table 10.4(b). Note that here there are four independent transition probabilities that can be estimated.)

The estimates of the transition probabilities given above assume that these probabilities do not change over time, that is, that the process is stationary. For such a sequence, if the outcome of a particular diagnosis is dependent only on the immediately prior diagnosis, the process of change in patterns of diagnoses is called a *1st-order autoregressive process* or *1st-order Markov chain* (or simply Markov chain). If a diagnosis is dependent on the *two* preceding diagnoses, the process is known as a *2nd-order Markov chain*, and so on.

In general, a 1st-order Markov chain for, for example depression, can be defined in terms of the proportion of depressed subjects at the beginning of the study, and the two transition probabilities, P_{WD} and P_{DD}. If one considers, instead of probabilities, the estimated odds on being depressed, that is

Table 10.4   *Transition probabilities for Markov chains*

(a) *1st-order*

		Diagnosis in i-th year		Total
		D	W	
	Diagnosis in $(i-1)$th year	D P_{DD}	P_{DW}	1
		W P_{WD}	P_{WW}	1

(b) *2nd-order*

Diagnosis in $(i-2)$th year	Diagnosis in $(i-1)$th year	Diagnosis in i-th year		Total
		D	W	
D	D	P_{DDD}	P_{DDW}	1
	W	P_{DWD}	P_{DWW}	1
W	D	P_{WDD}	P_{WDW}	1
	W	P_{WWD}	P_{WWW}	1

$$\text{odds}_{DW} = \text{odds on being depressed in year } i \text{ given that the patient was well in year } i-1.$$

$$= n_{WD}/n_{WW} \tag{10.1}$$

and, similarly

$$\text{odds}_{DD} = n_{DD}/n_{DW} \tag{10.2}$$

then the two independent transition probabilities can be replaced by their corresponding odds, and these can then be modelled in terms of a simple linear-logistic model (see Chapter 9). A 1st-order Markov chain is characterised by stationary odds and can be illustrated graphically by two horizontal lines of points. Algebraically the model can be described by

$$\log (\text{true odds}) = \beta_0 + \beta_1 \times \text{Dep} \tag{10.3}$$

where β_0 and β_1 are the parameters of the model, and Dep is a dummy variable taking the value 0 if the patient was well at the time of the previous diagnosis, and 1 if the patient was depressed. If, in a given situation, the value of β_1 was found to be zero, then the consecutive diagnoses would be independent, and the pattern of transitions between diagnoses would be characterised by a *Bernoulli process*, rather than a Markov chain, that is, consecutive diagnoses would be independent.

Simple Markov chains have rarely been found to be sufficient to describe social and behavioural processes, although they are usually considered to be a good starting point in an analysis. How then might we improve on these models? One way is to consider the possibility that the structure of the time sequences is different for different groups of people. For example, in the depression study we might introduce differences between males and females and also between different age-groups. A possible model would now be

$$\log(\text{true odds}) = \beta_0 + \beta_1 \times \text{Dep} + \beta_2 \times \text{Sex} + \beta_3 \times \text{Age} \quad (10.4)$$

Such a model implies that age and sex have the same effect on both the transition odds of interest. If they both have different effects, the following would be more appropriate

$$\log(\text{true odds}) = \beta_0 + \beta_1 \times \text{Dep} + \beta_2 \times \text{Sex} + \beta_3 \times \text{Age} + \beta_4 \\ \times \text{Dep} \times \text{Sex} + \beta_5 \times \text{Dep} \times \text{Age} \quad (10.5)$$

where the variables and parameters are defined similarly to those in previous chapters. (Readers are reminded that although we use the same symbols for some parameters in equations (10.4) and (10.5) they will not necessarily take the same numerical values when these models are fitted to data.)

A further possible addition to a simple 1st-order Markov chain model would be to increase its order, that is to allow for more 'memory' in the model. Second-order chains would be described by a model such as

$$\log(\text{true odds}) = \beta_0 + \beta_1 \times \text{Dep 1} + \beta_2 \times \text{Dep 2} \quad (10.6)$$

or, more realistically,

$$\log(\text{true odds}) = \beta_0 + \beta_1 \times \text{Dep 1} + \beta_2 \times \text{Dep 2} + \beta_3 \times \text{Dep 1} \times \text{Dep 2} \quad (10.7)$$

where Dep 1 and Dep 2 are both dummy variables indicating the state of the subject at times $i-1$ and $i-2$ respectively.

To illustrate the use of the models described above we shall return to the data of Table 10.1. Firstly, these data can be summarised as a table of transition counts and corresponding estimates of transition probabilities. These appear in Table 10.5.

It was noted earlier that the three coded behavioural states could be

Table 10.5   *First-order transitions for the autistic child's behavioural sequence (from Dunn and Clark, 1982)*

(a) *Frequencies*

		State at time t			
		1	2	3	Total
	1	60	22	4	86
State at time $t-1$	2	21	100	11	132
	3	4	11	6	21
	Total	85	133	21	

(b) *Probabilities*

		State at time t			
		1	2	3	Total
	1	0.70	0.26	0.04	1
State at time $t-1$	2	0.16	0.76	0.08	1
	3	0.19	0.52	0.29	1

considered as ordinal measures of an autistic child's interpersonal responsiveness. Following this, the boundaries between states 1 and 2, and between states 2 and 3, may be considered as thresholds in this scale of responsiveness. If we consider the counts in Table 10.5(a) we can estimate the odds on being in state 2 or 3 at time i for each of the three rows, and also the conditional odds on being in state 3 at time i, given that that state is greater than 1, again for each of the three rows. This yields estimates of six transition odds that can replace the nine transition probabilities of Table 10.5(b). These six odds can be modelled by the ordinal regression models introduced in Section 9.5. One possible linear-logistic model for the data in Table 10.5 using the conditional odds model of Fienberg and Mason (1978) has the form,

$$\log (\text{true odds}) = C + \text{State }(j) + \text{Cut }(k) + \text{SC }(jk) \qquad (10.8)$$

where State (j) is the effect of being in state j ($j = 1$, 2 or 3) at the immediately preceding observation, Cut (k) is the effect of the passing of threshold or cut k ($k = 1, 2$), and finally SC (jk) is the corresponding interaction term. As in previous examples (see Chapter 9), the parameters are constrained to be zero when the corresponding indicators j or k are unity. Note that we have assumed that the chain is stationary (see Exercise 10.2), and is 1st-order. The likelihood ratio criterion, G^2, for this model is 39.75 with 28 degrees of freedom, indicating an adequate fit. (Note that these data could have been analysed by fitting log-linear models, but that such an approach would have been considerably more complex; see Bishop, Fienberg and Holland, 1975.)

Realistic models of social processes in groups of individuals, such as episodes of depression, patterns of voting transitions in political elections, or of movement of workers between industrial organisations, can soon become very complicated; see, for example, Blumen, Kogan and McCarthy (1955), Butler and Stokes (1975) and Dunn and Skuse (1981). We do not recommend beginners to try to find the 'correct' model for any set of complex longitudinal data (even if this were possible). They should, instead, use simple models for Markov chains to explore the observations and to generate simple testable hypotheses on new data sets. The exercises at the end of this chapter should help the reader to become more familiar with handling data of this type.

10.3   Latency or Survival Models

Measurements of response times or latencies occur in many investigations in the social and behavioural sciences, and a number of examples have already been described in Section 10.1. In analysing data of this kind it is the probability of a response in a given time interval that is of primary interest. In the analysis of life-tables, for example, we investigate the probability of death at a particular age given that the individual has survived to that age. In an experiment on memory recall we might be interested in estimating the probability of recall between, say, ten and eleven seconds. Although linear models for response times have been developed by medical statisticians primarily for the analysis of controlled clinical trials, there are many areas of social or behavioural research where these methods might be extremely useful. Survival models can be used to describe data on the duration of marriages, the duration of periods of unemployment, the intervals between life events and the onset of psychiatric or social problems, and so on. As for any other type of data, these response times might be affected by, for example, the subject's age, sex or social class, and one therefore wishes to be able to model these response times as a function of the explanatory variables. But before analysing response-time data in detail, it is vital that the research worker explore the results using simple graphical methods and corresponding simple descriptive statistics.

To introduce some of the possibilities for investigating such data we shall consider the memory recall times given in Table 10.6, taken from

Table 10.6   *Memory recall times for one male subject (from Dunn and Master, 1982)*

Pleasant	Unpleasant	$\hat{S}(t)$
1.07	1.45	0.96
1.17	1.67	0.92
1.22	1.90	0.88
1.42	2.02	0.83
1.63	2.32	0.79
1.98	2.35	0.75
2.12	2.43	0.71
2.32	2.47	0.67
2.56	2.57	0.63
2.70	3.33	0.58
2.93	3.87	0.54
2.97	4.33	0.50
3.03	5.35	0.46
3.15	5.72	0.42
3.22	6.48	0.38
3.42	6.90	0.33
4.63	8.68	0.29
4.70	9.47	0.25
5.55	10.00	0.21
6.17	10.93	0.17
7.78	15+	0.13/0.17*
11.55	15+	0.08/0.17*
15+	15+	0.08/0.17*
15+	15+	0.08/0.17*

* The first number refers to pleasant memories, the second to unpleasant ones.

Dunn and Master (1982). These data arise from a study where a male subject was told that he would be presented with a series of stimulus words on a computer screen, one at a time, and each word would be preceded by an instruction on the screen asking him to recall either a pleasant or an unpleasant memory associated with the next word. Requests to recall pleasant and unpleasant memories alternated in the sequence, and successful recall of a memory was acknowledged by pressing the bar on the computer keyboard. If the subject was unable to recall a memory within fifteen seconds, the experimenter moved on to another stimulus word. In other words, the memory recall times were censored at fifteen seconds, and where appropriate these are represented by '15+' in Table 10.6. The latencies for twenty-four pleasant memories are to be compared with those for the same number of unpleasant ones.

The first thing that might be of interest about such data is the *survival function*, which is defined as the probability that an individual latency, *T*, is longer than a given time, *t*. That is,

$$S(t) = \Pr(T > t) \tag{10.9}$$

The survival function $S(t)$ can be estimated by the proportion of latencies found to be longer than each of the observed recall times, *t*. Graphs of $S(t)$ against *t* for both pleasant and unpleasant memories are plotted in Figure 10.1. Such plots are known as *survival curves*. (Note that they are step functions, although they are often represented by smooth curves.)

Table 10.7 gives some examples of the way in which the data in Table 10.6 can be summarised. For each type of memory are given *median recall times*. Clearly, since the memory recall times are censored, the mean recall time is not a very sensible descriptive statistic to compute. As a measure of variation of the latencies the *interquartile range*, or *midspread*, is also given for the two types of response. Table 10.7 also gives the number of observed latencies that are greater than 2, 5, 10 and 15 seconds respectively. The choice of these times is to some extent arbitrary, but is obviously influenced by the shape of survival surves such as those in Figure 10.1. As would be expected, these counts convey very similar information to the curves in Figure 10.1. Both Table 10.7 and Figure 10.1 show clearly that the latencies for unpleasant memories are, on average, longer than those for pleasant ones. The grouping of latencies in Table 10.7 has been done to aid the visual

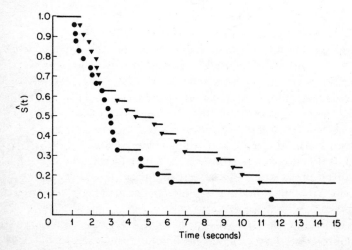

Figure 10.1   *Survival curves for the pleasant (●) and unpleasant (▼) memories from Table 10.6*

Table 10.7   *Summary statistics for the latencies in Table 10.6*

| Time (t) | Number of latencies greater than or equal to t | |
	Pleasant	*Unpleasant*
2	18	21
5	6	12
10	3	6
15	2	4

Median response time for pleasant memories: 2.97 seconds

Interquartile range: 1.98–4.70 seconds

Median response time for unpleasant memories: 4.33 seconds

Interquartile range: 2.35–9.47 seconds

interpretation of the data and to illustrate how models for grouped latencies or survival times can easily be constructed. The latter is the subject of the next section, but it is worthwhile noting here the similarity of the grouped data in Table 10.7 with that for the ordinal or counted response variables in Chapter 9 (see Tables 9.8 and 9.16), and in addition to note that the models about to be described are virtually identical to those described by Fienberg and Mason (1978) for ordinal response variables.

10.4   Linear-Logistic Latency Models

The aim of this section is to introduce simple linear models for survival time or latencies that have been grouped into discrete intervals. Once the reader has understood the philosophy of the approach introduced here, it should be fairly straightforward to move on to the models appropriate for ungrouped data given in Section 10.5.

Consider, again, the information given in Table 10.7. Taking only the pleasant memories, $S(2)$ can be estimated by the fraction 18/24, that is, 0.75; $S(5)$ is estimated by 6/24, or 0.25, and so on. Note that these values are close to the estimates that would have been found using the raw data in Table 10.6. Now, $S(5)$ is the product of $S(2)$ and the conditional probability of the latency being over 5 seconds given that it is more than 2 seconds; that is $\hat{S}(5) = \frac{18}{24} \times \frac{6}{18}$, or 0.25, as before. Similarly, $S(10)$ is the product of $S(5)$ and the conditional probability of the latency being over 10 seconds given that it is more than 5 seconds. Hence $\hat{S}(10) = \frac{18}{24} \times \frac{6}{18} \times \frac{3}{6}$, or 0.125. $S(15)$ is estimated in a similar way. It should be clear to the reader that all of the required information needed to compare the survival curves is contained in the above conditional probabilities and $S(2)$, which is itself a special case of one of these conditional probabilities. We symbolise the conditional probability of a latency being greater than t_i given that it is greater than t_{i-1}, by p_i. Here i ranges from 1 ($t = 2$) to 4 ($t = 15$). So, in general,

$$S(t_i) = p_1 p_2 \ldots p_{i-1} p_i \qquad (10.10)$$

where, by definition, $p_1 = S(t_1)$.

Now, we introduce linear-logistic models for the conditional probability p_i (that is, linear for $\log(p_i/(1 - p_i))$). We define a dummy variable, Pleasure, that takes the value 0 for pleasant memories, and 1 for unpleasant ones. We also define a qualitative factor, Time (i), that indicates which of the i conditional probabilities is under consideration. The simplest linear-logistic model for the data in Table 10.6 could have the form:

$$\log(\text{true odds}) = C + \text{Time}(i) \qquad (10.11)$$

This implies that there is no difference between the latencies for pleasant and unpleasant words, and that the joint p_i vary with time, t_i, in an arbitrary, but defined, way. When fitting this model using a computer package such as GLIM, Time (1) is constrained to be zero, so that $\log p_1/(1 - p_1) = C$, where C is a constant. If one now assumes that there is a constant effect of word type on the conditional probability, p_1, the model now becomes:

$$\log(\text{true odds}) = C + C' \times \text{Pleasure} + \text{Time}(i) \qquad (10.12)$$

The new parameter or constant, C', is a measure of the effect of word type on the conditional probability of the latency being longer than t_i, given that it is longer than t_{i-1}. As before, Time (1) is constrained to be 0 so that, for pleasant memories, $\log p_1/(1 - p_1) = C$, and for unpleasant ones, $\log p_1/(1 - p_1) = C + C'$.

Fitting model (10.11) to the two sets of data in Table 10.6 yields a likelihood ratio statistic (G^2) of 3.49 with 4 degrees of freedom. Fitting model (10.12) yields a G^2 of 0.92 with 3 degrees of freedom. Clearly both models provide an adequate fit, and the difference in G^2 (2.57 with 1 d.f.) indicates that there are insufficient data collected from this one subject to show a statistically significant difference between the latencies for pleasant and unpleasant words.

10.5   Log-linear Hazard Models
Here we introduce models that are applicable to latencies measured on

a continuous time scale, as opposed to those discussed in the last section that are used for latencies or survival times that are measured in, or are subsequently grouped into, discrete intervals. The survival function is defined as before, that is, $S(t) = P(T > t)$. Instead of dealing with the conditional probability, p_i, however, we will introduce h_i, where h_i is defined as the conditional probability of recall (or of death or failure) in the time interval between t_{i-1} and t_i, given that recall has not occurred before the beginning of this interval. It should be clear to the reader that $h_i = 1 - p_i$, and so a linear-logistic model for h_i is logically equivalent to the corresponding model for p_i. It should also be noted that h_i will depend on the size of the interval $t_i - t_{i-1}$, and so it would make more sense if $h_i/(t_i - t_{i-1})$ were modelled instead of h_i itself.

This leads to the concept of a *hazard function*. The hazard function, $h(t)$, is defined as follows:

$$h(t) = \underset{\delta t \to 0}{\text{limit}} \left[\frac{P(T \leqslant t + \delta t \mid T > t)}{\delta t} \right] \qquad (10.13)$$

The simplest linear model for this function assumes that it is constant for all possible time intervals $(t, t + \delta t)$, that is, $h(t) = C$ for all values of t. This is characteristic of the *exponential distribution*. A physical process that has a constant hazard function is radioactive decay. The survival function for the exponential distribution has the form $S(t) = \exp(-Ct)$, so that a plot of $\log(\hat{S}(t))$ against t will be a straight line with slope $-C$. If the hazard function is dependent on time then a *Weibull distribution* may be appropriate, but a detailed discussion of this and other more complex distributions is beyond the scope of this chapter.

Consider the situation where we may wish to compare latencies for two types of memory (assuming that they are measured in a single individual). We can construct a *log-linear hazard model* for the expected value of $h(t)$ as follows:

$$\log(h(t)) = C + C' \times \text{Pleasure} \qquad (10.14)$$

Pleasure is a dummy variable as defined before, and C and C' are the parameters of the model. Note that this model implies a constant ratio of hazards for the two memory types.

For the memory recall data presented in Table 10.6 a preliminary exploratory analysis (a plot of $\log(\hat{S}(t))$ against t) indicates that a log-linear exponential model describes the data adequately, except that there is a period of up to about one second during which the hazard function appears to be zero. That is, there is a short period during which it is impossible to recall a memory (the *guarantee time*). This period will be symbolised by G. The modified exponential distribution has a hazard given by

$$h(t) = 0 \quad \text{for } 0 \leqslant t < G \qquad (10.15)$$

$$h(t) = C \quad \text{for } T > G$$

The equivalent survival function is

$$S(t) = \exp(-C(t - G)) \quad \text{for } t \leqslant G \qquad (10.16)$$

$$S(t) = 1 \quad \text{for } t > G$$

If the data in Table 10.7 are transformed by replacing t by $t - 1$ (assuming that here $G = 1$, approximately), a log-linear exponential model (equation (10.14)) can be fitted to the latencies using GLIM (Aitken and Clayton, 1980). Removal of the term $C \times$ Pleasure from the model increases G^2 by 3.07 (with $d.f. = 1$). This should be compared with the increase in G^2 given in the last section. Neither is statistically significant.

In the log-linear hazard models described above it is implicit that there is a constant ratio between the hazards for the different types of memory (pleasant or unpleasant). These models are examples of the general class of *proportional hazards* models. In the above analysis we have assumed that, apart from a guarantee time of about one second (when the hazard is 0), the hazard remains constant over time. However, it is easy to visualise a situation where a subject becomes less likely to recall a memory as the time from the presentation of the stimulus word increases. This might be due to the fact that he, or she, is likely to give up trying.

In the analysis of life-tables we find that a plot of hazard against age is U-shaped. Here the hazard (or the probability of dying at a particular age, given that the individual has survived that long) is relatively high for young babies, decreases for older children and young adults, and then rises steeply in old age. As another example, if one considers patterns of divorce, it is easy to imagine a situation where the hazard might increase for the first few years of married life, and then slowly decrease. Each phenomenon has its own characteristic hazard distribution, and many of these distributions can be modelled using methods similar to those described in this chapter. In each case, groups of subjects can be compared by fitting a proportional hazards model, the most general of which allows for any arbitrary effect of time on the hazard (Cox, 1972). These models will not be described in detail here, and the interested reader is referred to Lee (1980) and Kalbfleisch and Prentice (1980) for a general discussion of the analysis of survival curves.

10.6   Summary

In this chapter we have introduced a few specialised uses of the generalised linear model that can be used to describe, for example, time series or survival or failure time data. There are large areas of this field that we have avoided discussing (econometric modelling, age-period-cohort models, theories of competing risks, and so on), but hope to have introduced enough examples of the use of the generalised linear model for the reader to be able to move on to more specialised texts with a much better grasp of the rationale behind the use of particular types of statistical model than would otherwise have been the case. In particular, we have avoided time-domain and frequency-domain models for time series where the variable or variables of interest are measured on an interval scale. Here, it is often the trends and periodicities that are of interest, as well as the random or stochastic components of the time series. This field is too large and specialised to be adequately introduced in a text such as this, and the reader is referred to Gottman (1981) for a comprehensive treatment.

EXERCISES

10.1   Consider a binary time series in which the probability of success at any trial depends on the outcomes of the previous three trials. How many independent transition probabilities are there? Specify a linear-logistic model to describe this series.

10.2   By splitting the data in Table 10.1 into two separate halves, test whether a stationary Markov chain is a sensible description of the process generating the full sequence of behavioural states.

10.3   Consider the lengths of sequences of 2's in Table 10.1. Plot a survival curve for these lengths and explain your results.

10.4   Use a linear-logistic survival model to examine the effects of age and sex on the first episodes of depression given in Table 10.8.

Table 10.8   *The effects of age and sex on the first episodes of depression (after Dunn and Skuse, 1981)*

Year	Sex	Age group	No. diagnosed as depressed for first time in study	No. at risk
1962	Male	1	0	56
1963	Male	1	0	56
1964	Male	1	0	56

Table 10.8   *continued*

Year	Sex	Age group	No. diagnosed as depressed for first time in study	No. at risk
1965	Male	1	1	56
1966	Male	1	0	55
1962	Male	2	3	193
1963	Male	2	4	190
1964	Male	2	4	186
1965	Male	2	7	182
1966	Male	2	3	175
1962	Male	3	5	213
1963	Male	3	3	208
1964	Male	3	3	205
1965	Male	3	5	202
1966	Male	3	1	197
1962	Male	4	1	67
1963	Male	4	1	66
1964	Male	4	1	65
1965	Male	4	1	64
1966	Male	4	0	63
1962	Female	1	0	28
1963	Female	1	1	28
1964	Female	1	0	27
1965	Female	1	0	27
1966	Female	1	1	27
1962	Female	2	10	142
1963	Female	2	8	132
1964	Female	2	8	124
1965	Female	2	10	116
1966	Female	2	7	106
1962	Female	3	13	126
1963	Female	3	11	113
1964	Female	3	2	102
1965	Female	3	8	100
1966	Female	3	5	92
1962	Female	4	9	84
1963	Female	4	7	75
1964	Female	4	2	68
1965	Female	4	0	66
1966	Female	4	5	66

PART IV
Latent Variable Models

One of the key assumptions in fitting linear regression models such as those described in Chapter 8 is that all of the variables other than the response variable have been measured without error. Clearly, in areas such as sociology and psychology this is very rarely the case. More importantly, perhaps, research workers in the social sciences are often also interested in modelling variation and covariation of traits that by definition cannot be measured directly. These, so-called, *latent variables* are often theoretical concepts such as intelligence, psychoticism or social class, so that, in practice, we have to make measurements on manifest variables that are assumed to be indicators for the measures that one is really interested in.

In the last two chapters of this text we introduce statistical methods that are suitable for the exploration of the relationships between latent variables and manifest variables or between sets of latent variables, where the latent variables can represent concepts that cannot be measured directly or measurements that cannot be made without error.

Factor analysis is essentially a regression model for the observed variables on the unobserved latent variables or factors. *Structural equation models* are more general and are specified in terms of tentative causal relations between a set of latent dependent and latent independent variables. In both cases one is interested in exploring or describing the structure of a covariance matrix.

---

11. Factor Analysis

11.1 Introduction

In many areas of psychology, sociology and the like it is often not possible to measure directly the concepts that are of major interest. Two obvious examples are intelligence and social class. In such cases the researcher will often collect information on variables likely to be indicators of the concepts in question and then try to discover whether the relationships between these observed variables are consistent with their being measures of a single underlying, latent variable, or whether some more complex structure has to be postulated. For example, the psychologist interested in intelligence may record the examination scores for a number of students in a variety of different subjects, and the sociologist attempting to assess social class may note a person's occupation, educational background, whether or not they own their own home, and so on.

In such studies the most frequently used method of analysis is some form of *factor analysis*, a term which subsumes a fairly large variety of procedures all of which have the aim of ascertaining whether the interrelations between a set of observed variables are explicable in terms of a small number of underlying, unobservable variables or factors. The basic factor analysis model is essentially the same as that of multiple regression discussed in Chapters 7 and 8 except that here the observed variables are regressed on the unobservable factors. Such a model has implications for the structure of the observed covariance or correlation matrix as we shall see later, but first we shall illustrate the model by means of a simple example.

11.2 A Simple Example of the Factor Analysis Model

Spearman (1904) considered children's examination marks in three subjects, classics (x_1), French (x_2) and English (x_3), and found the following correlations

$$
\begin{array}{c c c c}
 & x_1 & x_2 & x_3 \\
x_1 & \begin{bmatrix} 1.00 & & \\ \end{bmatrix} \\
\end{array}
$$

$$
\begin{array}{cc}
 & \begin{matrix} x_1 & \;\; x_2 & \;\; x_3 \end{matrix} \\
\begin{matrix} x_1 \\ x_2 \\ x_3 \end{matrix} &
\begin{bmatrix} 1.00 & & \\ 0.83 & 1.00 & \\ 0.78 & 0.67 & 1.00 \end{bmatrix}
\end{array}
$$

If we assume that a single underlying factor, f, is adequate for explaining these correlations then the appropriate factor model would be of the form

$$
\begin{aligned}
x_1 &= \lambda_1 f + u_1 \\
x_2 &= \lambda_2 f + u_2 \\
x_3 &= \lambda_3 f + u_3
\end{aligned}
\tag{11.1}
$$

where λ_1, λ_2 and λ_3 are regression coefficients of each observed variable on factor f, and u_1, u_2 and u_3 represent random disturbance terms. In the factor analysis context the λ_i are more commonly referred to as *factor loadings*, f is known as a *common factor* and the u_i as *specific factors*. The model is illustrated in Figure 11.1

In this example the common factor, f, might be equated with intelligence or general intellectual ability, and the specific factors, u_i will have small variances if the corresponding observed variable is closely

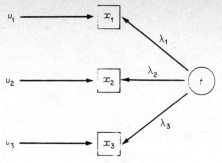

Figure 11.1   *Diagram illustrating the factor analysis model specified by equation (11.1)*

related to f. In theory the variation in u_i could be partitioned into two parts. The first would represent the extent to which an individual's ability at classics, say, differs from his general intellectual ability; the second would represent the fact that the examination is only an approximate measure of ability in the particular subject. In practice, however, this division is generally of little interest and so, in subsequent discussions of factor analysis in this chapter, will be ignored.

11.3   The Factor Model

Let our observed variables be denoted by the vector $\mathbf{x}' = (x_1, x_2, \ldots, x_p)$. The factor model for $\mathbf{x}$, assuming k underlying factors (the problem of choosing a suitable value for k will be taken up in Section 11.5), can be written as

$$
\begin{aligned}
x_1 &= \lambda_{11} f_1 + \lambda_{12} f_2 + \cdots + \lambda_{1k} f_k + u_1 \\
x_2 &= \lambda_{21} f_1 + \lambda_{22} f_2 + \cdots + \lambda_{2k} f_k + u_2 \\
x_p &= \lambda_{p1} f_1 + \lambda_{p2} f_2 + \cdots + \lambda_{pk} f_k + u_p
\end{aligned}
\tag{11.2}
$$

or

$$
\mathbf{x} = \Lambda \mathbf{f} + \mathbf{u}
\tag{11.3}
$$

where

$$
\Lambda = \begin{bmatrix} \lambda_{11} & \cdots & \lambda_{1k} \\ \vdots & & \vdots \\ \lambda_{p1} & & \lambda_{pk} \end{bmatrix}, \quad \mathbf{f} = \begin{bmatrix} f_1 \\ \vdots \\ f_k \end{bmatrix} \quad \text{and} \quad \mathbf{u} = \begin{bmatrix} u_1 \\ \vdots \\ u_p \end{bmatrix}
$$

(We have assumed that the mean vector of $\mathbf{x}$ is the null vector; this is of no consequence since we are essentially interested only in the covariance or correlational structure of the variables.) The factor 'loadings' Λ, are essentially standardised regression coefficients and in the case of orthogonal factors are equivalent to correlations between factors and variables.

Before we can consider the estimation of the parameters in this model we need to make a number of assumptions about the specific and common factors, namely that:

(a) the specific factors are independent of one another;
(b) the specific factors are independent of the common factors;
(c) the common factors are in standardised form with means zero and standard deviations unity.

For the present we shall also assume that the common factors are independent of one another, but this assumption will be relaxed in later discussions.

With these assumptions the factor model given by equation (11.3) implies that the variance of variable x_i, σ_i^2 is given by

$$\sigma_i^2 = \sum_{j=1}^{k} \lambda_{ij}^2 + \phi_i \tag{11.4}$$

where ψ_i is the variance of u_i, and the covariance of variables x_i and x_j, σ_{ij}, is given by

$$\sigma_{ij} = \sum_{l=1}^{k} \lambda_{il}\lambda_{jl} \tag{11.5}$$

Equation (11.4) shows that the factor model implies that the variance of an observed variable can be split into two parts. The first

$$h_i^2 = \sum_{j=1}^{k} \lambda_{ij}^2 \tag{11.6}$$

is known as the *communality* of the variable and represents the variance shared with the other variables via the common factors. The second part, ψ_i, is called the *specific* or *unique* variance and relates to the variability in x_i not shared with the other variables.

Equation (11.5) indicates that the factor model also implies that the covariance between two variables arises solely from their relationship with the common factors. The specific factors play no part.

Equations (11.4) and (11.5) can be summarised in the form

$$\Sigma = \Lambda \Lambda' + \Psi \tag{11.7}$$

where

$$\Psi = \begin{bmatrix} \psi_1 & & & \\ & \psi_2 & & \\ & & \ddots & \\ & & & \psi_p \end{bmatrix}$$

and Σ is the population covariance matrix of **x**.

So the k-factor model given by equation (11.3) implies that the covariance matrix of the observed variables has the form indicated by (11.7). The converse also holds; if Σ can be decomposed into the form given in (11.7) then the k-factor model of (11.3) holds for **x**.

In practice, Σ will be estimated by the sample covariance matrix, **S**, and from this we shall want to obtain estimates of Λ and Ψ, which might then be used to ascertain whether a k-factor model is appropriate for the data under investigation (see Section 11.5). Unfortunately the factor loading matrix, Λ, is not uniquely determined by equations (11.3) and (11.7). To illustrate this, suppose **M** is any orthogonal matrix of order k; then (11.3) can be written as

$$x = (\Lambda M)(M'f) + u \qquad (11.8)$$

Since it is easy to show that the vector **M'f** satisfies the same conditions required of **f**, then (11.8) is a valid k-factor model with new factors **M'f** and a new factor loadings, ΛM. Consequently we can write

$$\Sigma = (\Lambda M)(M'\Lambda') + \Psi \qquad (11.9)$$

which again reduces to equation (11.7).

Post multiplying Λ by an orthogonal matrix, **M**, is known as a *rotation* of the factors (see Section 11.6), and is often used as an aid in interpretation. However, to find an initial matrix of loadings it is necessary to impose some form of constraint to make them unique. In general this constraint takes the form of requiring the matrix given by

$$G = \Lambda'\Psi^{-1}\Lambda \qquad (11.10)$$

to be diagonal, with its elements arranged in descending order of magnitude. This constraint leads to factors such that the first one makes a maximum contribution to the variance in **x**, the second makes a maximum contribution subject to being uncorrelated with the first, and so on. (Compare principal components analysis in Chapter 4.)

11.4 Estimating the Parameters in the Factor Model

The estimation problem in factor analysis is essentially that of finding estimates Λ and Ψ satisfying the constraint (11.10), and for which

$$\mathbf{S} \doteq \hat{\mathbf{\Lambda}} \hat{\mathbf{\Lambda}}' + \hat{\mathbf{\Psi}} \tag{11.11}$$

is satisfied. The estimation procedures that will be considered here operate by first finding $\hat{\mathbf{\Lambda}}$ and then use

$$\hat{\psi}_i = s_i^2 - \sum_{j=1}^{k} \hat{\lambda}_{ij}^2 \tag{11.12}$$

to find the elements of $\hat{\mathbf{\Psi}}$ where s_i^2 is the sample variance of variable x_i.

It is easy to show that if $(p-k)^2 = (p+k)$ then equation (11.11) may be solved exactly. But in such cases the factor model contains as many parameters as the covariance matrix $\mathbf{\Sigma}$, and therefore offers no simplification of the original data. Consequently such cases are of no practical interest.

In general we shall only be interested in fitting the factor model when $(p-k)^2 > (p+k)$, when it is not possible for (11.11) to be satisfied exactly. For such cases a number of estimation procedures have been developed. We shall consider just two of them, namely *principal factor analysis* and *maximum likelihood factor analysis*.

11.4.1   Principal factor analysis

Principal factor analysis is essentially equivalent to a principal components analysis (see Chapter 4) performed on the *reduced covariance matrix* $\mathbf{S}^*$, obtained by replacing the diagonal elements of $\mathbf{S}$ with estimated communalities. Two frequently used estimates of the latter are:

(a) the square of the multiple correlation coefficient of the i-th variable with all other variables (see Chapter 7);

(b) the largest of the absolute values of the correlation coefficients between the i-th variable and one of the other variables.

Each of these estimates will give higher communality values when x_i is highly correlated with the other variables as we would expect.

The first k eigenvalues and eigenvectors of $\mathbf{S}^*$ are now found (remember that we are assuming that we know that the appropriate number of common factors is k; the difficult problem of deciding what is an appropriate value is discussed in Section 11.5). The i-th column of $\hat{\mathbf{\Lambda}}$ is then given by

$$\hat{\lambda}_i = \gamma_i^{1/2} \mathbf{a}_i \tag{11.13}$$

where $\gamma_1, \gamma_2, \ldots, \gamma_k$ and $a_1, \ldots, a_k$ are the first k eigenvalues and eigenvectors of $\mathbf{S}^*$. (Compare the scaling introduced in Section 4.5, and also see Exercise 4.5.) Since these eigenvectors are orthogonal we see that $\Lambda'\Lambda$ is diagonal and so condition (11.10) is satisfied. Estimates of the specific variances, ψ_i, are now obtained from equation (11.12) and a principal factor analysis is considered permissible if all of these are non-negative.

A commonly used version of principal factor analysis does not stop at this point but instead computes revised communality estimates from $\hat{\Lambda}$, uses these to find a revised, reduced covariance matrix, and, from this, a new set of estimated loadings. The iterative process is continued until the differences between successive communality estimates are negligible. Difficulties can arise, however, if at any time communality estimates exceed the variance of the corresponding observed variable, since this gives rise to negative estimates of the specific variances (see equation (11.12)). Some numerical examples of principal factor analysis appear in Section 11.4.3.

1.4.2 Maximum likelihood factor analysis

If we assume that our raw data matrix, $\mathbf{X}$, arises from a multivariate normal distribution, then we can apply the method of maximum likelihood to derive estimates of factor loadings and specific variances. This method was first applied to factor analysis by Lawley (1940, 1941, 1943), but its routine use had to await the development of satisfactory numerical optimisation methods and the provision of suitable computer programs. These were provided in the late 1960s, notably by Jöreskog (1967), Jöreskog and Lawley (1968) and Lawley (1967). The likelihood function that must be maximised is

$$L = -\tfrac{1}{2}n\left[\log_e |\Sigma| + \text{trace}\,(\mathbf{S}\Sigma^{-1})\right] \qquad (11.14)$$

This likelihood is regarded as a function of the elements of Σ and hence under the factor model as a function of the elements of Λ and Ψ. For various reasons it is more convenient to *minimise* the function F given by

$$F = \log_e |\Sigma| + \text{trace}\,(\mathbf{S}\Sigma^{-1}) - \log |\mathbf{S}| - p \qquad (11.15)$$

This is equivalent to maximising L, since $L = -\tfrac{1}{2}nF + $ a function of the observations. The function F is a positive quantity that approaches zero as $\mathbf{S}$ and Σ become identical. Details of the minimisation of F are provided in Lawley and Maxwell (1971), and Mardia, Kent and Bibby (1979).

One of the main advantages of using the maximum likelihood method of estimation is that it enables us to test the hypothesis that k common factors are sufficient to describe the observed relationships in the data. This test will be described in Section 11.5. Here we pass on to consider some numerical examples of principal factor analysis (PFA) and maximum likelihood factor analysis (MLFA).

11.4.3   Numerical examples of PFA and MLFA

It is easy to show that, unlike principal components analysis, the parameters in the factor model derived from a covariance matrix differ from those derived from a correlation matrix only by a simple scaling. Consequently all the procedures described above apply equally well to the correlation matrix, and the numerical examples in this section use the correlation matrix.

To illustrate the two estimation procedures outlined in Section 11.4 we shall again use the examination data previously described in Chapter 4, Section 4.6. The relevant correlation matrix is given in Table 4.2. First, principal factor analysis was applied to this matrix with $k = 1$ and $k = 2$ (without iterating). Communality estimates were the largest absolute correlation. The results are shown in Table 11.1

Table 11.1   *Non-iterative principal factor solution for the open/closed book data with $k = 1$ and $k = 2$ factors*

	$k = 1$		$k = 2$		
Variable	h_i^2	$\hat{\lambda}_1$	h_i^2	$\hat{\lambda}_1$	$\hat{\lambda}_2$
1	0.417	0.646	0.543	0.646	0.354
2	0.506	0.711	0.597	0.711	0.303
3	0.746	0.864	0.749	0.864	−0.051
4	0.698	0.786	0.680	0.786	−0.249
5	0.551	0.742	0.627	0.742	−0.276

Next, principal factor analysis was applied using multiple correlations as initial communalities, and iterating as described in Section 11.4.1. The results are shown in Table 11.2. For this example the difference in parameter estimates is only small.

The first factor is easily recognised as one of overall performance and the second as a contrast between open and closed book examinations. The communalities are all much less than unity, and so a fair proportion of the variance of each variable is left unexplained by the common factors. The maximum likelihood estimates for these data are shown in Table 11.3, and are seen to be fairly similar to those obtained from the principal factor analysis.

Table 11.2   *Iterative principal factor solution for the open/closed book data with k=1 and k=2 factors*

| | k = 1 | | k = 2 | | |
Variable	h_i^2	$\hat{\lambda}_1$	h_i^2	$\hat{\lambda}_1$	$\hat{\lambda}_2$
1	0.377	0.614	0.519	0.640	0.331
2	0.471	0.686	0.592	0.710	0.296
3	0.839	0.915	0.812	0.897	-0.086
4	0.579	0.761	0.647	0.770	-0.232
5	0.505	0.711	0.570	0.719	-0.230

Table 11.3   *Maximum likelihood factor solutions for the open/closed book data with k=1 and k=2 factors*

| | k = 1 | | k = 2 | | |
Variable	h_i^2	$\hat{\lambda}_1$	h_i^2	$\hat{\lambda}_1$	$\hat{\lambda}_2$
1	0.359	0.599	0.539	0.630	0.377
2	0.446	0.668	0.579	0.696	0.308
3	0.837	0.915	0.806	0.893	-0.048
4	0.597	0.773	0.653	0.782	-0.205
5	0.524	0.724	0.571	0.729	-0.201

11.5   Determination of the Number of Factors

An important question which arises when using factor analysis is, 'How well does the model with a particular number of common factors fit the data?' This question has been considered by a number of workers who have suggested a variety of techniques for providing an answer. Many are fairly informal procedures based on experience and intuition rather than any formal sampling model. For example, one of the most popular criteria for indicating number of factors is to retain only the factors associated with eigenvalues greater than unity. This simple criterion appears to work well when applied to samples from artificially created population models, and generally gives results consistent with investigators' expectations (although this may not be a particularly objective judgement!).

Another informal method for determining the number of factors is the so-called scree-test suggested by Cattell (1965). This method uses the graph of eigenvalues and chooses the number of factors corresponding to the point where the eigenvalues begin to level off to form an almost horizontal straight line. For example, see Figure 11.2. (This test has been met previously in Chapter 4.)

A more formal procedure is the large-sample chi-squared test associated with the maximum likelihood solution. From a statistical point of view this is the most satisfactory method, provided that the assumptions are adequately met. The form of the test statistic is as follows:

$$U = n' \min (F) \qquad (11.16)$$

where $n' = n - 1 - \frac{1}{6}(2p + 5) - \frac{2}{3}k$ and F is given by equation (11.15). If k common factors are sufficient to describe the data then U is asymptotically distributed as a χ^2 with v degrees of freedom where

$$v = \frac{1}{2}(p - k)^2 - \frac{1}{2}(p + k)$$

In most exploratory studies k cannot be specified in advance and so a sequential procedure is used to determine k. Starting with some small value for k (usually 1), the parameters in the factor model are estimated using the maximum likelihood method. If the test statistic, U, is not significant we accept the model with this number of factors, otherwise we increase k by one and repeat the process, until an acceptable solution is reached. If at any stage the degrees of freedom, v, become zero then either no non-trivial solution is appropriate, or alternatively

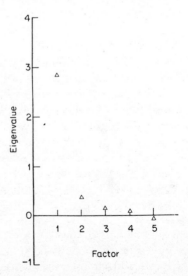

Figure 11.2   *Example of a 'scree' plot*

the factor model itself, with its assumption of linear relationships between observed and latent variables, is questionable.

As an example of this test, U was calculated for the one factor solution to the open/closed book example considered in the previous section. This gave $U = 8.59$. Since for these data $p = 5$ we test U as a chi-square variable with 5 degrees of freedom, which at the 5 per cent level leads to the acceptance of the one-factor solution as adequate for these data.

11.6 Rotation of Factors

The constraint on the factor loadings given by equation (11.10) was introduced to make the parameter estimates in the factor analysis model unique, and leads to orthogonal factors that are arranged in descending order of importance. These properties are not, however, inherent in the factor model, and merely considering such solutions can lead to difficulties in interpreting factors. For example, two consequences of making these arbitrary impositions are: (1) that the factorial complexity of variables is likely to be greater than one, regardless of the underlying true model, that is, variables will have substantial loadings on more than one factor; and (2) that, except for the first factor, the remaining factors may be *bipolar*—some variables have positive loadings on a factor while others have negative loadings. Both of these can make interpretation more difficult since this is most straightforward if each variable is loaded highly on at most one factor, and if all factor loadings are either large and positive or near zero, with few intermediate values. The variables are then split into disjoint sets, each of which is associated with one factor.

Consequently after an initial factoring has determined the number of common factors necessary, and the communalities of each variable, a further step is made, in which the factors are rotated, as outlined in Section 11.3 (equations (11.8) and (11.9)), in an attempt to find simpler and more easily interpretable factors, whilst keeping the number of factors and the communalities as determined previously.

Various methods of rotation seeking to give more readily interpretable factors are available. The simplest approach is to examine the pattern of loadings graphically and then to rotate the axes in such a way to best simplify the factors. For example, Figure 11.3 shows a plot of the factor loadings in the two-factor solution to the open/closed book example, given by principal factor analysis without iterating. A rotation of the axis by 21°, as shown, leads to the new set of loadings shown in Table 11.4. (The new axes are still orthogonal, but this is not necessary.) Such graphical rotation is simple and efficient when dealing

Table 11.4 *Rotated principal factor solution for open/closed book example obtained by simple graphical analysis*

	Rotated loadings	
Variable	F_1	F_2
1	0.45	0.59
2	0.60	0.54
3	0.81	0.30
4	0.80	0.04
5	0.79	0.01

with two-factor solutions in which there are clear clusters of variables. But whenever the pattern is not very clear or there are many factors to examine the method is no longer practicable.

Hence we are led to consider more formal approaches to the rotation of factors, and perhaps the most common is the varimax method originally proposed by Kaiser (1958). This leads to orthogonal factors and has as its rationale to provide factors with a few large loadings and as many near-zero loadings as possible. This is accomplished by an iterative maximisation of a quadratic function of the loadings, details of which are given in Mardia *et al.* (1979). As an example, we shall consider the factor analysis of the correlation matrix shown in Table 11.5. This arises from a study of the selection of airmen reported by Fleishman

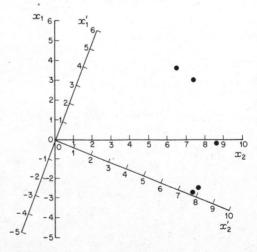

Figure 11.3 *Principal factor analysis two-factor solution for open/ closed book examination data*

Table 11.5 *Intercorrelations among test variables** (Fleishman and Hempel, 1954)*

Test	1	2	3	4	5	6	7	8	9	10	11	12	13	14	15	16	17	18
1 Numerical operations—II	—	63	32	23	44	34	23	45	42	31	37	40	22	08	39	13	09	12
2 Dial and table reading		—	54	43	61	59	40	61	51	54	49	50	38	22	54	28	05	24
3 Mechanical principles			—	52	46	52	34	43	30	44	33	26	27	22	37	27	−05	12
4 General mechanics				—	29	30	17	32	30	32	17	23	26	29	30	30	02	04
5 Speed of identification					—	57	44	58	40	58	55	48	31	23	52	31	15	22
6 Pattern comprehension						—	43	60	44	49	45	39	32	31	54	30	03	26
7 Visual pursuit							—	33	35	46	32	39	29	20	38	24	10	16
8 Decoding								—	53	59	41	32	24	19	55	22	08	18
9 Instrument comprehension									—	46	34	22	28	29	47	31	11	24
10 Spatial orientation										—	49	37	40	21	41	26	06	15
11 Speed of marking											—	55	26	18	43	20	14	28
12 Log book accuracy												—	27	19	33	18	23	26
13 Rotary pursuit													—	35	34	28	26	28
14 Plane control														—	36	20	20	20
15 Discrimination reaction time															—	22	23	23
16 Nut and bolt																—	05	14
17 Reaction time																	—	30
18 Rate of movement																		—

* Decimal points omitted.

and Hempel (1954), in which eighteen tests were given to a sample of 197 individuals. The tests were concerned with mechanical aptitude, rate of movement, the comprehension of spatial relations, and similar problems of a technical nature. An iterative principal factor analysis was applied to the correlation matrix, and three factors had eigenvalues greater than unity. The loadings for these three factors appear in Table 11.6.

Table 11.6   *Principal factor solution for Fleishman and Hempel (1954) data*

	Factor 1	Factor 2	Factor 3
1 Numerical operations—II	.56082	−.10029	−.23775
2 Dial and table reading	.82083	−.16609	−.10479
3 Mechanical principles	.61578	−.29572	.21514
4 General mechanics	.47462	−.19384	.36465
5 Speed of identification	.76445	−.02352	−.16021
6 Pattern comprehension	.73499	−.08461	.03454
7 Visual pursuit	.53487	.02808	.00957
8 Decoding	.72363	−.17187	−.08801
9 Instrument comprehension	.61669	−.00944	.07185
10 Spatial orientation	.69869	−.08962	−.01696
11 Speed of marking	.63414	.11689	−.29033
12 Log book accuracy	.56917	.18366	−.25384
13 Rotary pursuit	.49391	.28130	.23530
14 Plane control	.38742	.26064	.37226
15 Discrimination reaction time	.68545	.10088	.03372
16 Nut and bolt	.39170	.00626	.22949
17 Reaction time	.19026	.55580	−.00698
18 Rate of movement	.33136	.38843	−.01969

This solution does not easily lead to a clear classification of the tests and so all three factors were subjected to a varimax rotation in the hope that a clearer picture would emerge. The result of such a rotation appears in Table 11.7. It now becomes much simpler to attach reasonable labels to the three factors. Factor 1, which has high loadings on tests such as dial and table reading, speed of identification, decoding and pattern comprehensive, might be associated with the ability to understand spatial relations. Factor 2, which loads highly on tests such as mechanical principles, general mechanics and plane control, might be labelled mechanical aptitude. Factor 3 has high loadings only on rotary pursuit, reaction time and rate of movement, and should obviously be labelled a speed factor. Consequently it appears that the eighteen tests administered tap information on only three underlying dimensions: spatial relationships, mechanical aptitude and speed.

Table 11.7 *Varimax rotated factors for Fleishman and Hempel (1954) data*

	Factor 1	Factor 2	Factor 3
1 Numerical operations—II	.60228	.12713	.04686
2 Dial and table reading	.74613	.38898	.06568
3 Mechanical principles	.42520	.56830	−.09575
4 General mechanics	.20724	.59333	−.02843
5 Speed of identification	.70498	.28324	.18271
6 Pattern comprehension	.58205	.43965	.12839
7 Visual pursuit	.41489	.28818	.17827
8 Decoding	.66026	.35190	.03381
9 Instrument comprehension	.45176	.39087	.16939
10 Spatial orientation	.58361	.37917	.11007
11 Speed of marking	.64815	.07729	.27207
12 Log book accuracy	.56243	.05817	.32001
13 Rotary pursuit	.20342	.39705	.42358
14 Plane control	.04430	.45640	.38255
15 Discrimination reaction time	.50669	.37308	.29195
16 Nut and bolt	.17931	.39597	.13110
17 Reaction time	.04645	−.02185	.58526
18 Rate of movement	.19890	.07882	.46400

Other methods of rotation are available which do not necessarily lead to orthogonal factors. Such *oblique rotation* methods are more general since they do not impose the restriction that the factors be uncorrelated. An advantage over orthogonal rotations is that, after allowing oblique rotations, if the resulting factors are found to be orthogonal, we can be sure that orthogonality is not an artifact of the rotation procedure. However, because oblique solutions involve the introduction of correlations between factors, a different type of complexity in the interpretation of factor analysis is introduced. To illustrate the oblique rotation of factors a method known as *oblimin* (see Nie *et al.*, 1975) was applied to the three-factor solution shown in Table 11.6 for the correlation matrix of Table 11.5. The result is shown in Table 11.8. For these data the oblique factors are very similar to the orthogonal ones reported earlier. It is unlikely that they would be preferred to the varimax solution, because of the added complexity introduced by their correlations, which are also given in Table 11.8. It has been suggested that this correlation matrix might also be subjected to a factor analysis to derive so-called *second-order factors*. However, this procedure cannot be recommended since the results are, in general, very difficult.

Table 11.8 *Oblique factor solution for Fleishman and Hempel (1954) data*

	Factor 1	Factor 2	Factor 3
1 Numerical operations—II	.67701	−.06410	−.10575
2 Dial and table reading	.79689	−.10372	.12026
3 Mechanical principles	.40620	−.24184	.43477
4 General mechanics	.14006	−.14319	.55583
5 Speed of identification	.75563	.03578	.03068
6 Pattern comprehension	.58967	−.02166	.24669
7 Visual pursuit	.41598	.07585	.15454
8 Decoding	.70629	−.11745	.11306
9 Instrument comprehension	.44179	.04691	.25006
10 Spatial orientation	.60407	−.03208	.17928
11 Speed of marking	.71660	.16358	−.16293
12 Log book accuracy	.61489	.22811	−.14522
13 Rotary pursuit	.12447	.34205	.37606
14 Plane control	−.06796	.31713	.50269
15 Discrimination reaction time	.49673	.16484	.21677
16 Nut and bolt	.12618	.04994	.36453
17 Reaction time	−.00126	.58812	−.00218
18 Rate of movement	.17149	.42768	.03602

Factor correlations

	Factor 1	Factor 2	Factor 3
Factor 1	1.00000	.25167	.50678
Factor 2	.25167	1.00000	.13862
Factor 3	.50678	.13862	1.00000

11.7 Confirmatory Factor Analysis

The factor methods discussed in the previous sections may be described as exploratory, since they are concerned not only with the problem of determining the number of factors required for a data set, but also with the problem of rotation to facilitate the interpretation of factors. In some situations, however, an investigator, perhaps on the basis of previous research, may wish to postulate in advance the number of factors and the pattern of zero and non-zero loadings on them. Testing such a specific hypothesis about the factorial composition of a set of variables in some population involves specifying a number of parameters in the model as *fixed* and a number as *free*. Those designated as free are then estimated (generally by maximum likelihood methods), and the fit of the model assessed. For example, an investigator might postulate a three-factor model for a set of eight variables, where the factors have the following pattern:

	var 2	var 2	var 3	var 4	var 5	var 6	var 7	var 8
Factor 1	X	X	X	X	X	X	X	X
Factor 2	X	X	X	0	0	0	0	X
Factor 3	0	X	X	X	X	X	0	0

Here the X represents free parameters to be estimated; the remaining loadings are considered fixed with, in this case, values of zero.

If the factors were postulated to be orthogonal there would be a further six fixed parameters in the model, since the elements of the correlation matrix between factors are either zeros or ones. If the orthogonality restriction is relaxed then there would be three fixed parameters (the diagonal elements of this correlation matrix), and three free parameters (the off-diagonal elements, i.e. the inter-factor correlations). Intermediates between these two extremes might also be considered.

Such *confirmatory factor analysis models* are essentially part of the general covariance structure and structural equation models to be discussed in Chapter 12, and so we shall leave details of fitting the models and testing their fit until then.

11.8   Factor Analysis and Principal Components Analysis Compared

Factor analysis, like principal components analysis, is an attempt to explain a set of data in a smaller number of dimensions than one starts with, but the procedures used to achieve this goal are essentially quite different in the two methods.

Factor analysis, unlike principal components analysis, begins with a hypothesis about the covariance (or correlational) structure of the variates. Formally, this hypothesis is that a covariance matrix Σ, of order and rank p, can be partitioned into two matrices $\Lambda \Lambda'$ and Ψ. The first is of order p but rank k (the number of common factors), whose off-diagonal elements are equal to those of Σ. The second is a diagonal matrix of full rank, p, whose elements when added to the diagonal elements of $\Lambda \Lambda'$ give the diagonal elements of Σ. In other words, the hypothesis is that a set of k latent variables exist ($k < p$), and these are adequate to account for the interrelationships of the variates, though not for their full variances.

Principal components analysis, on the other hand, is merely a transformation of the data, and no assumptions are made about the form of the covariance matrix from which the data arise. This type of analysis has no part corresponding to the specific variates of factor analysis. Consequently if the factor model holds but the specific variances are small we would expect both forms of analysis to give similar results. However, if the specific variances are large they will be absorbed into all the principal components, both retained and rejected, whereas factor analysis makes special provision for them. Factor analysis also has the advantage that there is a simple relationship between the results obtained by analysing a covariance matrix and those obtained from a correlation matrix.

It should be remembered that principal components analysis and factor analysis are similar in one other respect, namely that they are both pointless if the observed variables are almost un-correlated—factor analysis, because it has nothing to explain and principal components analysis because it would simply lead to components which are similar to the original variables.

11.9 Summary

Factor analysis has probably attracted more critical comment than any other statistical technique. Because the factor loadings are not determined uniquely by the basic factor model many statisticians have complained that investigators can choose to rotate factors in such a way as to get the answer they are looking for. Indeed, Blackith and Reyment (1971) suggest that the method has persisted precisely because it allows the experimenter to impose his preconceived ideas on the raw data. Other criticisms have been concerned with the acceptability of the concept of underlying, unobservable variables; in psychology such a concept may be reasonable, but in other areas far less appealing. Hills (1977) has gone so far as to suggest that factor analysis is not worth the time necessary to understand it and carry it out, and Chatfield and Collins (1980) recommend that factor analysis should not be used in most practical situations.

However, we feel that these criticisms are, on the whole, too extreme. Factor analysis should be regarded as simply an additional tool for investigating the structure of multivariate observations. The main danger in its use is taking the model too seriously, since it is only likely to be a very idealised approximation to the truth in the situations in which it is generally applied. Such an approximation may, however, prove a valuable starting point for further investigations.

EXERCISES

11.1   Explain the similarities and differences between factor analysis and principal component analysis.

11.2   The matrix shown below gives the correlation coefficients between the scores for a sample of 220 boys on six school subjects, namely French, English, history, arithmetic, algebra and geometry (Lawley and Maxwell, 1971).

1	2	3	4	5	6
1.000	0.439	0.410	0.288	0.329	0.248
	1.000	0.351	0.354	0.320	0.329
		1.000	0.164	0.190	0.181
			1.000	0.595	0.470
				1.000	0.464
					1.000

A maximum likelihood factor analysis gives the following two factor solution.

	Factor loadings		
Subject	*I*	*II*	*Communality*
1 French	0.553	0.429	0.490
2 English	0.568	0.288	0.406
3 History	0.392	0.450	0.356
4 Arithmetic	0.740	−0.273	0.623
5 Algebra	0.724	−0.211	0.569
6 Geometry	0.595	−0.132	0.372

By plotting these loadings find an orthogonal rotation which makes the solution easier to interpret.

11.3   For the Spearman examination correlation matrix shown in Section 11.2, a one-factor model will fit exactly. Find the values of $\lambda_1, \lambda_2, \lambda_3$, and ψ_1, ψ_2, ψ_3 for this solution.

11.4   For the analysis considered in Exercise 11.2, the value of the function F for the solution given is 0.010867. Use the test criterion given by equation 11.16 to test the hypothesis that two common factors are sufficient to account for the data (the value of n is 219).

11.5   The matrix shown below gives the correlations between nine measures of body dimension made on 2400 males. Try to find a three-factor solution, first by rearranging the rows and columns of the matrix to bring large correlations together (see Chapter 2), and then by one of the methods of factor analysis discussed in this chapter. Examine the residual correlations from both solutions (i.e. the matrix $\mathbf{R} - \hat{\mathbf{\Lambda}}\hat{\mathbf{\Lambda}}'$). (From Bennett and Bowers, 1976.)

Variable		1	2	3	4	5	6	7	8	9
Standing height	1									
Sitting height	2	0.81								
Arm length	3	0.59	0.67							
Leg length	4	0.58	0.29	0.19						
Thigh length	5	0.53	0.25	0.16	0.67					
Abdomen girth	6	0.17	0.13	0.08	0.23	0.29				
Hip girth	7	0.33	0.39	0.28	0.17	0.22	0.70			
Shoulder girth	8	0.22	0.29	0.21	0.08	0.12	0.52	0.59		
Weight	9	0.40	0.41	0.29	0.28	0.33	0.77	0.83	0.62	

12. Structural Equation Models

12.1 Introduction

In the models considered in the previous chapter the observed variables were considered to be linear functions of a number of unobservable latent variables. In this chapter these ideas will be extended to situations involving both response and explanatory latent variables, linked by a series of linear equations. Again models will be considered which attempt to explain the statistical properties, generally covariances and correlations, of the measured variables (which will now also be divided into response and explanatory), in terms of the hypothetical latent variables. As with factor analysis models, the primary statistical problem is one of estimating the parameters of the model and determining the goodness-of-fit.

The type of procedure to be described in this chapter is often referred to as *causal* modelling. We prefer, however, not to talk about causes since this has implications for the models that in most applications cannot be justified. As an alternative we might talk about the 'influence' that one variable has on another, and we might suggest that this influence is directional in the sense that x influences y, but not vice versa. For example, in most multiple regression situations it would be natural to assume that the explanatory variables are influencing the response variable, but that the latter does not influence any of $x_1, \ldots, x_p$.

12.2 A Simple Structural Equation Model

In the models to be considered in this chapter we imagine that the underlying latent variables may be divided into response and explanatory variables, and that these are linked by a series of linear relationships known as *structural equations*. For example, consider a hypothetical model in which there is a single latent response variable, η_1, and two latent explanatory variables, ζ_1 and ξ_2, related as follows:

$$\eta_1 = \gamma_{11}\xi_1 + \gamma_{12}\xi_2 + \zeta_1 \tag{12.1}$$

where ζ_1 is a random disturbance term. (We shall assume that the means of η_1, ξ_1, ξ_2 and ζ_1 are all zero.)

The latent variables, η_1, ξ_1 and ξ_2 cannot be observed directly. Instead measurements are taken on say four variables, x_1, x_2, x_3 and x_4, thought to be indicators of ξ_1 and ξ_2, and on, say, two variables y_1 and y_2, thought to be indicators of η_1. The observed variables are considered to be related to the latent variables as follows:

$$y_1 = \lambda^y_{11}\eta_1 + \varepsilon_1$$

$$y_2 = \lambda^y_{21}\eta_1 + \varepsilon_2$$

$$x_1 = \lambda^x_{11}\xi_1 + \lambda^x_{12}\xi_2 + \delta_1 \qquad (12.1)$$

$$x_2 = \lambda^x_{21}\xi_1 + \lambda^x_{22}\xi_2 + \delta_2$$

$$x_3 = \lambda^x_{31}\xi_1 + \lambda^x_{32}\xi_2 + \delta_3$$

$$x^4 = \lambda^x_{41}\xi_1 + \lambda^x_{42}\xi_2 + \delta_4$$

These can be written more conveniently in terms of matrices and vectors as

$$\mathbf{y} = \boldsymbol{\Lambda}_y\boldsymbol{\eta} + \boldsymbol{\varepsilon} \qquad (12.3)$$

and

$$\mathbf{x} = \boldsymbol{\Lambda}_x\boldsymbol{\xi} + \boldsymbol{\delta} \qquad (12.4)$$

where $\mathbf{y}' = (y_1, y_2)$, $\mathbf{x}' = (x_1, x_2, x_3, x_4)$, $\boldsymbol{\eta}' = (\eta_1)$, $\boldsymbol{\xi}' = (\xi_1, \xi_2)$, $\boldsymbol{\varepsilon}' = (\varepsilon_1, \varepsilon_2)$, $\boldsymbol{\delta}' = (\delta_1, \delta_2, \delta_3, \delta_4)$ and

and

$$\boldsymbol{\Lambda}_y = \begin{bmatrix} \lambda^y_{11} \\ \lambda^y_{21} \end{bmatrix}, \quad \boldsymbol{\Lambda}_x = \begin{bmatrix} \lambda^x_{11} & \lambda^x_{12} \\ \lambda^x_{21} & \lambda^x_{22} \\ \lambda^x_{31} & \lambda^x_{32} \\ \lambda^x_{41} & \lambda^x_{42} \end{bmatrix}$$

Equation (12.1) is seen to be of the same form as the linear regression models discussed in Chapter 8. Here, however, it is known as the *structural model*, and the parameters γ_{11} and γ_{12} can be considered to represent relatively invariant effects in the underlying process generating relationships between the observed variables $\mathbf{y}$ and $\mathbf{x}$.

Equations (12.3) and (12.4), relating the observed response and explanatory variables to the appropriate latent variables, are seen to be of exactly the same form as the factor analysis model of the previous chapter (see equation 11.3). These are known as the *measurement model*.

Diagrams representing the structural model, the measurement model, and the complete model are shown in Figure 12.1. These diagrams, which were introduced in the previous chapter, are known as

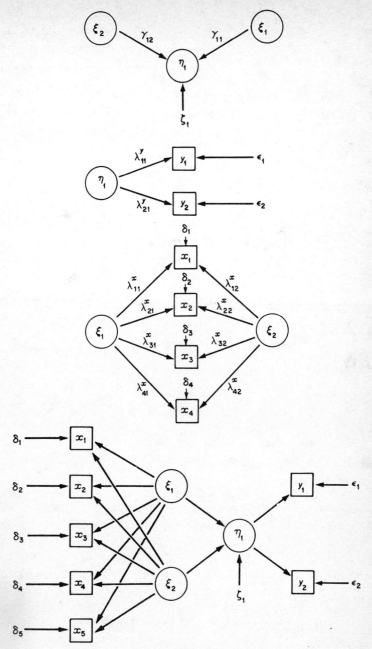

Figure 12.1 *Illustration of structural model, measurement model and complete model specified by equations (12.1) and (12.2)*

path diagrams, and are extremely useful aids in visualising complex models. (Such diagrams and the related concept of path analysis were introduced by Wright, 1934).

12.3 General Structural Equation Models

In general we shall assume that we have a set of latent response or dependent variables, $\boldsymbol{\eta}' = [\eta_1, \eta_2, \ldots, \eta_r]$, and a set of latent explanatory variables, $\boldsymbol{\xi}' = [\xi_1, \xi_2, \ldots, \xi_s]$, and that these are related by the following system of linear structural equations:

$$\boldsymbol{\eta} = \mathbf{B}\boldsymbol{\eta} + \boldsymbol{\Gamma}\boldsymbol{\xi} + \boldsymbol{\zeta} \tag{12.5}$$

where $\mathbf{B}(r \times r)$ and $\boldsymbol{\Gamma}(r \times s)$ are coefficient matrices and $\boldsymbol{\zeta}' = [\zeta_1, \zeta_2, \ldots, \zeta_r]$ is a vector of random disturbance terms. We shall assume that the means of $\boldsymbol{\eta}$, $\boldsymbol{\xi}$ and $\boldsymbol{\zeta}$ are zero. The elements of $\mathbf{B}$ represent direct influences of response variables on other response variables and the elements of $\boldsymbol{\Gamma}$ represent direct influences of explanatory variables on response variables.

As an illustration of the structural equations given in (12.5), consider the path diagram shown in Figure 12.2. Here the complete form of

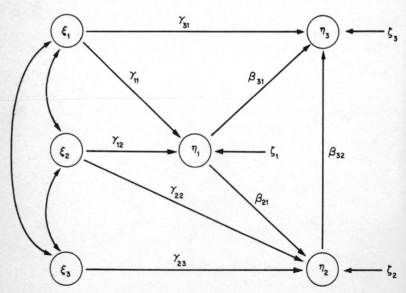

Figure 12.2 *Path diagram for model specified in equation (12.6) (Taken with permission from Jöreskog and Sörbom, 1981)*

(12.5) would be

$$
\begin{bmatrix} \eta_1 \\ \eta_2 \\ \eta_3 \end{bmatrix} = \begin{bmatrix} 0 & 0 & 0 \\ \beta_{21} & 0 & 0 \\ \beta_{31} & \beta_{32} & 0 \end{bmatrix} \begin{bmatrix} \eta_1 \\ \eta_2 \\ \eta_3 \end{bmatrix} + \begin{bmatrix} \gamma_{11} & \gamma_{12} & 0 \\ 0 & \gamma_{22} & \gamma_{23} \\ \gamma_{31} & 0 & 0 \end{bmatrix} \begin{bmatrix} \xi_1 \\ \xi_2 \\ \xi_3 \end{bmatrix} + \begin{bmatrix} \zeta_1 \\ \zeta_2 \\ \zeta_3 \end{bmatrix}
$$

$$(12.6)$$

$$\eta = \mathbf{B}\eta + \Gamma\xi + \zeta$$

Measured response variables $\mathbf{y}' = [y_1, \ldots, y_q]$ and measured explanatory variables $\mathbf{x}' = [x_1, \ldots, x_p]$ are related to the latent variables η and ξ by the equations

$$\mathbf{y} = \Lambda_y \eta + \varepsilon \qquad (12.7)$$

and

$$\mathbf{x} = \Lambda_x \xi + \delta \qquad (12.8)$$

where the elements of $\Lambda_y(q \times r)$ and $\Lambda_x(p \times s)$ are regression coefficients, and ε and δ are vectors of random disturbance terms. Equations (12.7) and (12.8) are of course directly analogous to the factor analysis models met in the previous chapter.

Since η and ξ are unobserved they do not have a definite scale. Both the origin and the unit of measurement in each latent variable are arbitrary, and to define the model completely the origin and unit of measurement of each latent variable must be assigned. The origin has already been taken care of by the assumption that each latent variable has zero mean. Various methods may be employed to fix the scale of the latent variables. The one used in factor analysis is to assume that they are standardised to have unit variance. However, in the programs used for fitting more complex structural equation models it is generally more convenient to define the unit of measurement of the latent variable as that of one of the observed variables. This may be arranged by simply finding one of the elements in each column of Λ_x and Λ_y to be unity. The numerical examples given in Section 12.6 should help to clarify this procedure.

In the following section we shall consider how we can estimate the parameters in such a model and test its fit. In later sections we shall describe some numerical examples. An important point to note here, however, is that a theory to be tested via such models will have to be specified mathematically, that is, translated into structural equations and a measurement model.

12.4　Estimating the Parameters of Structural Equation Models and Testing their Fit

We begin by making a number of assumptions about the terms in the structural and measurement model. These are as follows:

(a) ζ is uncorrelated with ξ.

(b) $\mathbf{I} - \mathbf{B}$ is non-singular and $\mathbf{B}$ has zeros in the diagonal.

(c) ε and δ are uncorrelated and uncorrelated with the latent variables.

(d) $\mathbf{\Psi}(r \times r)$ is the covariance matrix of ζ.

(e) $\mathbf{\Phi}(s \times s)$ is the covariance matrix of ξ.

(f) θ_ε is the covariance matrix of ε.

(g) θ_δ is the covariance matrix of δ.

From these assumptions it follows that the covariance matrix $\mathbf{\Sigma}[(p+q) \times (p+q)]$ of the observed response and explanatory variables is given by

$$\mathbf{\Sigma} = \begin{bmatrix} \mathbf{\Lambda}_y(\mathbf{I} - \mathbf{B})^{-1}(\mathbf{\Gamma}\mathbf{\Phi}\mathbf{\Gamma}' + \mathbf{\Psi})(\mathbf{I} - \mathbf{B})'^{-1}\mathbf{\Lambda}_y' + \theta_\varepsilon, & \mathbf{\Lambda}_y(\mathbf{I} - \mathbf{B})^{-1}\mathbf{\Gamma}\mathbf{\Phi}\,\mathbf{\Lambda}_x' \\ \mathbf{\Lambda}_x\mathbf{\Phi}\mathbf{\Gamma}'(\mathbf{I} - \mathbf{B})'^{-1}\mathbf{\Lambda}_y', & \mathbf{\Lambda}_x\mathbf{\Phi}\,\mathbf{\Lambda}_x' + \theta_\delta \end{bmatrix}$$

$$(12.9)$$

The elements of $\mathbf{\Sigma}$ are functions of the elements of $\mathbf{\Lambda}_y, \mathbf{\Lambda}_x, \mathbf{B}, \mathbf{\Gamma}, \mathbf{\Phi}, \mathbf{\Psi}, \theta_\varepsilon$ and θ_δ. In a particular application some of these elements will be fixed and equal to previously assigned values (often zero or unity); others will be unknown but *constrained* to be equal to one or more other parameters, and the remainder will be free parameters that are unknown and not constrained to be equal to any other parameter.

The estimation of the parameters in the model is completely analogous to maximum likelihood factor analysis described in Chapter 11. A sample of n observed response vectors, $\mathbf{y}_1, \ldots, \mathbf{y}_n$, and explanatory vectors, $\mathbf{x}_1, \ldots, \mathbf{x}_n$ are available and these are used to compute the $(p+q) \times (p+q)$ sample covariance matrix $\mathbf{S}$. The fitting problem is then essentially that of fitting the $\mathbf{\Sigma}$ imposed by the model to the sample covariance matrix. The maximum likelihood approach uses a fitting function of the form

$$F = \log |\mathbf{\Sigma}| + \text{trace}\,(\mathbf{S}\mathbf{\Sigma}^{-1}) - \log |\mathbf{S}| - (p+q) \qquad (12.10)$$

(cf. equation 11.15).

Programs are available for minimising F, the most well known being LISREL, produced by Jöreskog and Sörbom (1981). This will be used in the numerical examples described in Section 12.6. It is important to bear in mind, however, that the program is complex and may yield meaningless results even when the user sets up the problem correctly. For example, an identification problem (see Section 12.5) may preclude obtaining a solution, or the initial parameter values supplied may be so far off the optimum that the program may not converge to a final solution, and so some parameter estimates may be completely unreasonable (i.e., negative variances). If some parameters do fall outside their admissible range, either the model is fundamentally wrong or the data are not informative enough.

After a model has been fitted satisfactorily, a chi-square statistic may ·be obtained to evaluate the goodness-of-fit of the model to the data. In addition, standard errors of each parameter estimate can be calculated which can be used to provide an indication of the importance of that parameter in the model as a whole.

The value of the chi-square statistic should be interpreted very cautiously because of its sensitivity to various model assumptions, and also because in large samples the most trivial discrepancy between model and data may lead to the rejection of the model. In practice it is the difference between chi-square values for competing models with different numbers of parameters which are important. If the drop in chi-square when fitting a model with more parameters is large compared to the difference in degrees of freedom, this is an indication that the change made in the model represents a real improvement. If, on the other hand, the drop in chi-square is close to the difference in the number of degrees of freedom, this is an indication that the improvement in fit is obtained by 'capitalising on chance' and the added parameters may not have any real significance or meaning. Some more detailed comments about how to assess the goodness-of-fit of these models are given by Bentler and Bonet (1980).

12.5 Identification of Parameters

Before an attempt can be made to estimate the parameters in structural equation models the identification problem must be considered. Essentially this concerns whether a knowledge of Σ (in terms of its sample estimate, S) allows one to find unique estimates of the unknown elements in the matrices $\mathbf{B}, \mathbf{\Gamma}, \mathbf{\Phi}, \Lambda_y, \Lambda_x, \mathbf{\Psi}, \theta_\varepsilon$ and θ_δ. If Σ is generated by one and only one set of parameters the model is said to be *identifiable*. (We have seen in the previous chapter that the parameters in the factor analysis model are not identifiable unless we introduce some constraints, since different sets of factor loadings, corresponding to different rotations, will give rise to the same Σ.)

Identifiability depends on the choice of model and on the specification of fixed, constrained and free parameters. Under a given specification, a given set of matrices $\mathbf{B}, \mathbf{\Gamma}, \ldots, \boldsymbol{\theta}_\varepsilon$ and $\boldsymbol{\theta}_\delta$ generates one and only one $\mathbf{\Sigma}$, but there may be several structures generating the same $\mathbf{\Sigma}$. If two or more structures generate the same $\mathbf{\Sigma}$ they are said to be *equivalent*. If a parameter has the same value in all equivalent structures, the parameter is said to be identified. If all the parameters of the model are identified the whole model is said to be identified. If a parameter is not identified it is not possible to find a consistent estimator of it.

Unfortunately there do not appear to be simple, practicable methods for evaluating identification in the various special cases that might be entertained under the general model. A necessary (but not a sufficient) condition for the identification of all parameters is that

$$s < \tfrac{1}{2}(p+q)(p+q+1) \tag{12.11}$$

where s is the number of parameters to be estimated.

In practice it may be necessary to use empirical means to evaluate each particular situation. For example, Jöreskog and Sörbom (1981) suggest that if the information matrix is positive definite it is almost certain that the model is identified. They also demonstrate how the identifiability of a model can be examined in particular cases.

12.6   Numerical Examples

The general structural equation model introduced in Section 12.3 subsumes a large number of other models met in the social and behavioural sciences. For example, the usual factor analysis model described in Chapter 11 is obtained by setting $q = 0$ and $r = 0$ so that there are only ξ variables and x variables in the model; in this case there is no structural equation model of the form (12.5) and no measurement model of the form (12.7). The covariance matrix of the observed variables is thus given by

$$\mathbf{\Sigma}(p \times p) = \mathbf{\Lambda}_x \mathbf{\Phi} \mathbf{\Lambda}_x' + \boldsymbol{\theta}_\delta \tag{12.12}$$

(If $\mathbf{\Phi}$ were constrained to be the identity matrix then we would have a model with orthogonal factors.) If some elements of $\mathbf{\Lambda}_x$ are fixed according to some hypothetical structure for the factor loadings then we have the so-called confirmatory or restricted factor analysis model mentioned briefly in Section 11.7. Let us consider fitting such a model to the correlation matrix shown in Table 12.1, taken from Child (1970), involving correlations between eight tests of mental ability. Tests 1 and

Table 12.1 *Correlations between eight tests of mental ability (from Child, 1970)*

		1	2	3	4	5	6	7	8
1	AH5—verbal	1.00							
2	AH5—spatial	0.54	1.00						
3	Uses—F	0.08	0.01	1.00					
4	Uses—O	0.18	0.05	0.58	1.00				
5	Consequences—F	0.20	0.07	0.51	0.46	1.00			
6	Consequences—O	0.13	−0.01	0.26	0.40	0.46	1.00		
7	Circles—F	0.10	0.08	0.24	0.27	0.40	0.11	1.00	
8	Circles—O	0.05	0.00	0.22	0.22	0.21	0.18	0.51	1.00

2 are conventional 'intelligence tests' purporting to measure convergent thinking. The others are tests of fluency (F) and originality (O) in divergent thinking. Tests 3 to 6 require verbal responses, whilst tests 7 and 8 require non-verbal responses. On the basis of psychological theory we believe that these tests measure three relatively distinct aspects of mental behaviour: convergent thinking, verbal divergent thinking and non-verbal divergent thinking. That is, we believe that there are three underlying latent variables the first of which is indicated by variables 1 and 2, the second by variables 3, 4, 5 and 6, and the third by variables 7 and 8. We also wish to include in our model a possible correlation between factors two and three since these both contain variables which are tests of divergent thinking.

The proposed model and the parameters to be estimated are shown in Figure 12.3. Use of the LISREL program gives the parameter estimates shown in Table 12.2. The chi-square goodness-of-fit statistic takes the value 45.64 with 25 degrees of freedom, indicating that the model does not provide a particularly good fit.

As a more complex example of a structural equation model we shall consider the longitudinal study reported by Wheaton *et al.* (1977), and analysed previously by Jöreskog and Sörbom (1981), on the stability of alienation. This study was concerned with the stability over time of attitudes such as alienation and the relation to background variables such as education and occupation. Data on attitude scales were collected from 932 people in two rural regions in Illinois in 1967 and 1971. Jöreskog and Sörbom concentrate their analysis on the *anomia* subscale and the *powerlessness* subscale, taken to be indicators of alienation. The observed background variables were respondents' education (years of schooling completed) and Duncan's socioeconomic index (SEI); these were taken to be indicators of the respondents' socioeconomic status (SES). The covariance matrix of the six observed

Table 12.2 *Parameter estimates for model of Figure 12.3 fitted to correlation matrix in Table 12.1*

Variable		$\hat{\Lambda}_x$	
1	1	0	0
2	0.54 (0.08)	0	0
3	0	1	0
4	0	0.58 (0.08)'	0
5	0	0.51 (0.09)	0
6	0	0.26 (0.10)	0
7	0	0	1
8	0	0	0.51 (0.09)

$$
\begin{array}{c} 1 \\ 2 \\ 3 \end{array}
\begin{array}{ccc} 1 & 2 & 3 \\ \end{array}
\begin{bmatrix} 1.00 & & \\ 0 & 1.00 & \\ 0 & 0.46\,(0.07) & 1.00 \end{bmatrix} = \hat{\Phi}
$$

				$\hat{\theta}_\delta$			
1	2	3	4	5	6	7	8
0	0.71 (0.10)	0	0.66 (0.09)	0.74 (0.10)	0.93 (0.13)	0	0.74 (0.10)

The standard errors of free parameters are shown in brackets after their estimates. All other parameters in the model take fixed values.

variables is given in Table 12.3. The first model considered by Jöreskog and Sörbom was as follows:

Structural model

$$
\begin{bmatrix} \eta_1 \\ \eta_2 \end{bmatrix} = \begin{bmatrix} 0 & 0 \\ \beta & 0 \end{bmatrix} \begin{bmatrix} \eta_1 \\ \eta_2 \end{bmatrix} + \begin{bmatrix} \gamma_1 \\ \gamma_2 \end{bmatrix} \xi + \begin{bmatrix} \zeta_1 \\ \zeta_2 \end{bmatrix} \tag{12.13}
$$

where the latent variables η_1 and η_2 are equated with alienation in 1967 and in 1971 respectively, and the explanatory latent variable, ξ, is socioeconomic status.

Measurement model

$$
\begin{bmatrix} y_1 \\ y_2 \\ y_3 \\ y_4 \end{bmatrix} = \begin{bmatrix} 1 & 0 \\ \lambda_1 & 0 \\ 0 & 1 \\ 0 & \lambda_2 \end{bmatrix} \begin{bmatrix} \eta_1 \\ \eta_2 \end{bmatrix} + \begin{bmatrix} \varepsilon_1 \\ \varepsilon_2 \\ \varepsilon_3 \\ \varepsilon_4 \end{bmatrix} \tag{12.14}
$$

$$
\begin{bmatrix} x_1 \\ x_2 \end{bmatrix} = \begin{bmatrix} 1 \\ \lambda_3 \end{bmatrix} \xi + \begin{bmatrix} \delta_1 \\ \delta_2 \end{bmatrix} \tag{12.15}
$$

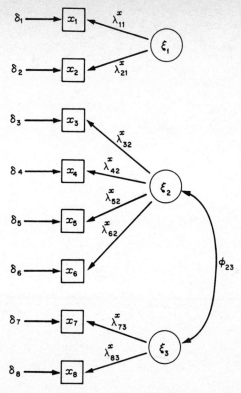

Figure 12.3 *Path diagram of proposed model for the data shown in Table 12.1*

where $y_1 =$ anomia 67, $y_3 =$ anomia 71,

  $y_2 =$ powerlessness 67, $y_4 =$ powerlessness 71,

  $x_1 =$ education, and $x_2 =$ socioeconomic index

We shall assume that the covariance matrices, Ψ, θ_ε, and θ_ε are all diagonal. The unities in Λ_y and Λ_x are needed to prevent identification problems, and imply that we are assuming that the scales for η_1 and η_2 have been chosen to be the same as for y_1 and y_2, and similarly that for ξ to be the same as for x_1.

The complete model is illustrated in Figure 12.4.

The maximum likelihood estimates of the parameters and their standard errors are shown in Table 12.4. The stability of alienation

Table 12.3   *The covariance matrix of the six observed variables in the stability of alienation example (from Wheaton et al., 1977)*

	y_1	y_2	y_3	y_4	x_1	x_2
y_1	11.83					
y_2	6.94	9.36				
$\mathbf{S} = y_3$	6.82	5.09	12.53			
y_4	4.78	5.03	7.49	9.99		
x_1	−3.84	−3.89	−3.84	−3.62	9.61	
x_2	−21.90	−18.83	−21.75	−18.77	35.52	450.20

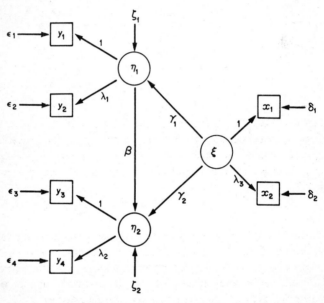

Figure 12.4   *Path diagram of the model specified in equations (12.13), (12.14) and (12.15) for stability of alienation example (Taken with permission from Jöreskog and Sörbom, 1981)*

over time is reflected is the parameter β, and we see that the influence of socioeconomic status on alienation at the two occasions is significant. The negative sign of the γ-coefficients indicates that for high socio-economic status the alienation is low and vice versa. The chi-square goodness-of-fit statistic for this model has the value 71.54 which, with 6 degrees of freedom, is significant, indicating that the overall fit of the

Table 12.4 *Parameter estimates obtained when fitting the model specified by Figure 12.4 to the covariance matrix of Table 12.3*

Parameter	Estimate	Standard Error
λ_1	0.89	0.04
λ_2	0.85	0.04
λ_3	5.33	0.43
β	0.70	0.05
γ_1	-0.61	0.06
γ_2	-0.17	0.05
ψ_{11}	5.31	0.47
ψ_{22}	3.74	0.39
$\emptyset$	6.67	0.64
$\theta_{11}^{(\delta)}$	2.94	0.50
$\theta_{22}^{(\delta)}$	260.98	18.24
$\theta_{11}^{(\varepsilon)}$	4.01	0.34
$\theta_{22}^{(\varepsilon)}$	3.19	0.27
$\theta_{44}^{(\varepsilon)}$	3.62	0.29

model is not acceptable. Jöreskog and Sörbom (1981) consider an extension of the model which allows the error terms ε_1 and ε_3, and ε_2 and ε_4 to be correlated. This leads to a substantially improved fit, having a chi-square value of 4.73 with 4 degrees of freedom.

12.7 Summary
This chapter has provided a very brief introduction to the estimation of parameters in linear structural models. The subject now has an extensive and expanding literature and can perhaps be identified as one of the 'fashionable' techniques with which research workers in the social and behavioural sciences can become associated. This is not without its dangers, however. Although the approach allows the fitting of very complex models, these will often only be, at best, useful approximations to the real mechanisms underlying the relationships between a set of observed variables.

The formulation of these models as outlined in Section 12.3 is the most popular, but not the only way in which they may be specified. An alternative representation, which in some respects is even more general, is given by McDonald (1978), who also provides an alternative computer program known as COSAN (see Appendix A). The models have also been extended to incorporate binary and categorical variables. For details the reader is referred to Muthen (1981).

EXERCISES

1 Show that the factor analysis model can be derived from equations (12.5) and (12.7) when p and s are set to zero.

2 Write out the structural equations and the measurement model corresponding to the following path diagram.

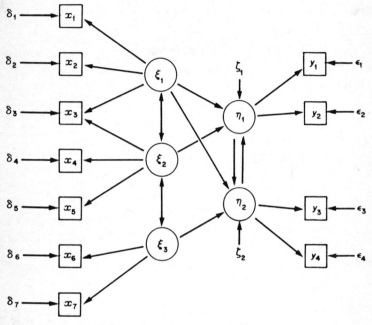

Figure 12.5 *Path diagram for Exercise (12.2)*

3 Construct a path diagram corresponding to the following set of structural equations and measurement model equations.

The structural equations are

$$\eta_1 = \beta_1 \eta_2 + \gamma_1 \xi_1 + \gamma_2 \xi_2 + \zeta_1$$

$$\eta_2 = \beta_2 \eta_1 + \gamma_3 \xi_1 + \gamma_4 \xi_3 + \zeta_2$$

or

$$\begin{bmatrix} \eta_1 \\ \eta_2 \end{bmatrix} = \begin{bmatrix} 0 & \beta_1 \\ \beta_2 & 0 \end{bmatrix} \begin{bmatrix} \eta_1 \\ \eta_2 \end{bmatrix} + \begin{bmatrix} \gamma_1 & \gamma_2 & 0 \\ \gamma_3 & 0 & \gamma_4 \end{bmatrix} \begin{bmatrix} \xi_1 \\ \xi_2 \\ \xi_3 \end{bmatrix} + \begin{bmatrix} \zeta_1 \\ \zeta_2 \end{bmatrix}$$

The measurement model equations are

$$
\begin{bmatrix} y_1 \\ y_2 \\ y_3 \\ y_4 \end{bmatrix} = \begin{bmatrix} 1 & 0 \\ \lambda_1 & 0 \\ 0 & 1 \\ 0 & \lambda_2 \end{bmatrix} \begin{bmatrix} \eta_1 \\ \eta_2 \end{bmatrix} + \begin{bmatrix} \varepsilon_1 \\ \varepsilon_2 \\ \varepsilon_3 \\ \varepsilon_4 \end{bmatrix}
$$

and

$$
\begin{bmatrix} x_1 \\ x_2 \\ x_3 \\ x_4 \\ x_5 \\ x_6 \\ x_7 \end{bmatrix} = \begin{bmatrix} 1 & 0 & 0 \\ \lambda_3 & 0 & 0 \\ \lambda_4 & \lambda_5 & 0 \\ 0 & 1 & 0 \\ 0 & \lambda_6 & 0 \\ 0 & 0 & 1 \\ 0 & 0 & \lambda_7 \end{bmatrix} \begin{bmatrix} \xi_1 \\ \xi_2 \\ \xi_3 \end{bmatrix} + \begin{bmatrix} \delta_1 \\ \delta_2 \\ \delta_3 \\ \delta_4 \\ \delta_5 \\ \delta_6 \\ \delta_7 \end{bmatrix}
$$

Appendix A Computer Programs and Packages

Most of the methods of analysis that are described in this text have to be performed with the aid of a computer and a suitable program. Fortunately, many of the programs needed for these analyses have been collected and made available as standard statistical packages, and in this appendix we give a brief description of the most commonly used of these. In addition we describe a number of more specialised packages and collections of programs. We make no attempt to evaluate any of these packages, nor do we claim to have produced an exhaustive list. Many useful addresses are given at the end of the appendix.

General Statistical Packages

(1)   SPSS (Statistical Package for the Social Sciences)
This widely-used package is very useful for the routine management of data and for analysing data using the more common statistical procedures. The package includes programs for linear regression and the analysis of variance, principal components analysis, canonical variates analysis, factor analysis, and multivariate analysis of variance (MANOVA). One of its advantages is the associated documentation (a manual and a simpler primer) which provides the non-specialist with well-written introductions to many areas of statistical analysis.

(2)   BMDP (Biomedical Computer Programs)
This package includes programs for the use of statistical methods that are similar to those covered by SPSS. In addition the package includes methods for fitting log-linear and linear-logistic models to categorical data, and also proportional hazard models for survival data. Cluster analysis algorithms are also found within BMDP.

(3)   GENSTAT (A General Statistical Package)
GENSTAT is a statistical package for the manipulation of data and subsequent statistical analysis. It contains algorithms for matrix manipulation, fitting generalised linear models, principal components and principal co-ordinates analysis, canonical variates analysis, and cluster analysis.

Specialised Packages and Programs

Chapter 2 There are several programs available for matrix manipulation. Examples include programs from the NAG library and GENSTAT. The NAG library contains several numerical optimisation techniques. CERN also provides algorithms for matrix manipulation and numerical optimisation.

Chapter 3 Most general statistical packages include procedures for simple bivariate plots, and BMDP provides facilities for stem-and-leaf displays. Algorithms for Andrews plots are not yet included in any of the general packages but they are relatively easy to program. A FORTRAN listing of a version producing output on a microfilm plotter is available from the authors of this text.

A FORTRAN listing of a faces algorithm (originating from Dr C. Frith), again producing output on a microfilm plotter, is also available from the authors. A program producing faces on a line printer is available from Dr W. Turner at Baylor University. Another program that can be used to draw asymmetric faces (Flury and Riedwyl, 1981) can be obtained from Dr B. Flury at the University of Berne.

Chapter 4 Most general statistical packages (including SPPS, BMDP and GENSTAT) include programs for principal components analysis.

Chapter 5 Classical multidimensional scaling (principal co-ordinates analysis) can be performed using GENSTAT. Perhaps the most comprehensive package of scaling programs is MDS(X), produced by Coxon and Omond. This has a control language similar to SPSS, and includes algorithms for metric and nonmetric multidimensional scaling, multidimensional unfolding, individual differences scaling, and several others. Other major programs are ALSCAL and MULTISCAL. ALSCAL can be used as part of the general statistical package SAS (Statistical Analysis System).

Chapter 6 CLUSTAN (originating from Dr D. Wishart) is the most comprehensive package of clustering algorithms. Within this package there is a choice of one of many similarity or distance measures as the starting point for a large variety of clustering procedures. A number of very useful plotting methods are also included. A program for analysing multivariate mixtures, called NORMIX, is available from Dr J. Wolfe. FORTRAN listings for a number of clustering techniques can also be found in the books by Anderberg (1973) and Hartigan (1975).

Chapters 7 to 10   The methods described in these chapters are included in most of the standard statistical packages. However, we recommend the package of interactive programs called GLIM (Generalised Linear Interactive Modelling) which arose from a project sponsored by the Royal Statistical Society and developed by R. J. Baker, M. R. B. Clarke and J. A. Nelder. By specifying the appropriate link function and error distribution for the random disturbance terms, a wide variety of linear models can be fitted. These include those for multiple regression and analysis of variance, as well as log-linear and linear-logistic models for data contained within multidimensional contingency tables.

MULTIVARIANCE is a statistical package for univariate and multivariate analysis of variance, covariance, regression and the analysis of repeated measures designs. ECTA (originating from Dr L. Goodman) is a program often used for fitting log-linear models to contingency tables. FORTRAN listings of a number of programs relevant to the analysis of survival data are described in Lee (1980) and Kalbfleisch and Prentice (1980). Time series analysis for continuous response variables can be carried out using GENSTAT and BMDP.

Chapter 11   Principal factor analysis is available within SPSS and BMDP. Maximum likelihood factor analysis is also available within SPSS.

Chapter 12   The main package for fitting structural equation models (including factor analysis) is LISREL V (Jöreskog and Sörbom, 1981). COSAN (McDonald, 1978), which is in many respects more flexible than LISREL, can also be used for these models.

ADDRESSES FOR INFORMATION ON PACKAGES

ALSCAL

Professor F. W. Young
Psychometric Laboratory
Davie Hall 013A
University of North Carolina
Chapel Hill
NC 27514 USA

BMDP

BMDP Statistical Software
Box 24A26 Los Angeles
CA 90024 USA

CERN
Program Library
Data Handling Division
Cern
CH-1211 Geneva 23

CLUSTAN
Program Library Unit
University of Edinburgh
18 Buccleuch Place
Edinburgh EH8 9LN
Scotland

Dr D. Wishart
c/o Department of Computational Science
University of St Andrews
North Haugh
St Andrews KY16 9SX
Scotland

Documentation can be obtained from the first
address, details of the package from the second.

COSAN
Department of Measurement, Evaluation
and Computer Applications
The Ontario Institute for Studies in Education
252 Bloor Street West
Toronto
Canada M5S IV6

ECTA
Professor L. Goodman
Department of Statistics
University of Chicago
5734 University Avenue
Chicago
Illinois 60637 USA

GENSTAT
The Programs Secretary
Statistics Department
Rothamsted Experimental Station
Harpenden
Hertfordshire
England

GLIM
The GLIM Coordinator
NAG Central Office
7 Banbury Road
Oxford OX2 6NN England

LISREL   International Educational Services
                         1525 East 53rd Street
                         Suite 829
                         Chicago
                         Illinois 60615 U S A

MDS(X)   Program Library Unit
                         University of Edinburgh
                         18 Buccleuch Street
                         Edinburgh EH8 9LN
                         Scotland

                         Professor A. P. M. Coxon
                         Sociological Research Unit
                         University College
                         P O Box 78
                         Cardiff CF1 1XL
                         Wales

                         Documentation can be obtained from the first
                         address, details of the package from the second.

MULTISCAL   International Educational Services
                         1525 East 53rd Street
                         Suite 829
                         Chicago
                         Illinois 60615 U S A

MULTIVARIANCE As above

NAG   Numerical Algorithms Group
                         NAG Central Office
                         7 Banbury Road
                         Oxford OX2 6NN
                         England

NORMIX   Dr J. Wolfe
                         U S Naval Personnel Research Laboratory
                         San Diego
                         California U S A

SAS

SAS Institute Inc.
Box 8000
Cary
North Carolina 27511 USA

SPSS

SPSS Inc.
Suite 3300, 444 North Michigan Ave.
Chicago
Illinois 60611 U S A

Other useful addresses

Mr B. S. Everitt
Biometrics Unit
Institute of Psychiatry
De Crespigny Park
Camberwell
London SE5 8AF
England

Dr B. Flury
Department of Statistics
University of Berne
Sidlestrasse 5 Ch-3012
Berne
Switzerland

Dr W. Turner
Department of Mathematics
Baylor University
Waco
Texas 76703 USA

Appendix B Answers to Selected Exercises

Chapter 2

2.1   Matrix **A** is of rank 5.

2.4 $$f(x) = \frac{1}{\sqrt{2\pi}\sigma} \exp{-\tfrac{1}{2}\left(\frac{x-\mu}{\sigma}\right)^2}$$

$$\log_e f = -\tfrac{1}{2}\log_e(2\pi) - \tfrac{1}{2}\log_e \sigma^2 - \tfrac{1}{2}\left(\frac{x-\mu}{\sigma}\right)^2$$

$$\frac{\partial \log_e f}{\partial \mu} = \frac{x-\mu}{\sigma^2}. \quad E\left(\frac{\partial \log_e f}{\partial \mu}\right)^2 = \frac{1}{\sigma^2}.$$

$$\frac{\partial \log_e f}{\partial \sigma^2} = -\frac{1}{2\sigma^2} + \frac{1}{2\sigma^4}(x-\mu)^2.$$

$$E\left(\frac{\partial \log_e f}{\partial \sigma^2}\right)^2 = E\left\{\frac{(x-\mu)^4}{4\sigma^8} - \frac{(x-\mu)^2}{2\sigma^6} + \frac{1}{4\sigma^4}\right\}$$

$$= \frac{1}{2\sigma^4}$$

(Since for a normal distribution $E(x-\mu)^4 = 3\sigma^4$.)

$$E\left(\frac{\partial \log_e f}{\partial \sigma^2}\right)\left(\frac{\partial \log_e f}{\partial \mu}\right) = E\left(\frac{x-\mu}{\sigma^2}\right)\left\{\frac{(x-\mu)^2}{2\sigma^2} - \frac{1}{2\sigma^2}\right\}$$

$$= 0$$

(Since for a normal distribution $E(x-\mu)^3 = 0$.)

Consequently the information matrix, **I**, is given by

$$\mathbf{I} = \begin{bmatrix} \dfrac{1}{\sigma^2} & 0 \\ 0 & \dfrac{1}{2\sigma^4} \end{bmatrix}$$

and the covariance matrix, $(n\mathbf{I})^{-1}$, would be

232

$$(n\mathbf{I})^{-1} = \begin{bmatrix} \dfrac{\sigma^2}{n} & 0 \\ 0 & \dfrac{2\sigma^4}{n} \end{bmatrix}$$

An estimate of this matrix would be obtained by substituting the m.l.e. of σ^2, so that

$$\text{vâr}\,(\bar{x}) = s^2/n; \quad \text{vâr}\,(s^2) = 2s^4/n$$

$$\text{Côv}\,(\bar{x}, s^2) = 0.$$

2.5
$$f(x) = x^2 + 2x + 3$$

$$\frac{df(x)}{\partial x} = 2x + 2$$

Setting
$$\frac{df(x)}{\partial x} = 0$$

gives $x = -1$

$$\frac{d^2f(x)}{\partial x^2} = 2$$

so that $x = -1$ corresponds to a minimum value of $f(x)$.

2.7   Variables y_1 and y_2 are linear functions of $\mathbf{x}$ and the result in Section 2.4 is easily extended to show that if

$$y_1 = \mathbf{a}'\mathbf{x} \quad \text{and} \quad y_2 = \mathbf{b}'\mathbf{x}$$

then
$$\text{Cov}\,(y_1, y_2) = \mathbf{a}'\Sigma\mathbf{b}$$

Here
$$\mathbf{a}' = [1, 1, 1], \qquad \mathbf{b}' = [1, 0, -1],$$

so that

$$\text{Cov}\,(y_1, y_2) = \begin{bmatrix} 1 & 1 & 1 \end{bmatrix} \begin{bmatrix} \sigma_{11} & \sigma_{12} & \sigma_{13} \\ \sigma_{21} & \sigma_{22} & \sigma_{23} \\ \sigma_{31} & \sigma_{32} & \sigma_{33} \end{bmatrix} \begin{bmatrix} 1 \\ 0 \\ -1 \end{bmatrix}$$

$$= \sigma_{11} + \sigma_{21} - \sigma_{23} - \sigma_{33}.$$

Chapter 4

4.3   The eigenvalues of $\mathbf{R}$ are defined to be the roots of the equation

$$|\mathbf{R} - \lambda\mathbf{I}| = 0$$

that is

$$\begin{vmatrix} 1-\lambda & r \\ r & 1-\lambda \end{vmatrix} = 0$$

$$(1-\lambda)^2 - r^2 = 0$$

so that

$$\lambda_1 = 1-r, \qquad \lambda_2 = 1+r.$$

To find the eigenvector corresponding to λ_1 we need to solve

$$\begin{bmatrix} 1 & r \\ r & 1 \end{bmatrix}\begin{bmatrix} x_1 \\ x_2 \end{bmatrix} = (1-r)\begin{bmatrix} x_1 \\ x_2 \end{bmatrix}$$

leading to $x_1/x_2 = -1$. Setting $x_1 = 1$ gives the eigenvector as $[1, -1]$.
    Similarly we could find the eigenvector corresponding to λ_2.

4.6   We first need to find the expected value of **x**

$$E(\mathbf{x}) = \begin{bmatrix} E(x_1) \\ E(x_2) \end{bmatrix} = \begin{bmatrix} p \\ q \end{bmatrix}$$

The covariance matrix of x is defined to be

$$E(\mathbf{x} - E(\mathbf{x}))(\mathbf{x} - E(\mathbf{x}))'$$

$$= E\begin{bmatrix} x_1 - p \\ x_2 - q \end{bmatrix}[x_1 - p \quad x_2 - q]$$

$$= E\begin{bmatrix} (x_1 - p)^2 & (x_1 - p)(x_2 - q) \\ (x_2 - q)(x_1 - p) & (x_2 - q)^2 \end{bmatrix}$$

$$= \begin{bmatrix} p(1-p) & -pq \\ -pq & q(1-p) \end{bmatrix}$$

Chapter 5

5.5   For missing data simply omit, both in the numerator and the denominator of the stress goodness-of-fit measure, the terms which correspond to the missing dissimilarities.
    Kruskal (1964a) suggests two approaches to ties. One is to say that when $\delta_{ij} = \delta_{kl}$ we do not care which of d_{ij} and d_{kl} is larger nor whether they are equal or not. The second approach is to say that when $\delta_{ij} = \delta_{kl}$, d_{ij} should be equal to d_{kl}, and to downgrade a configuration if this is not so.
    Both approaches can be accommodated by small alterations in the goodness-of-fit criterion, and are described in Kruskal, *op. cit.*

Chapter 6

6.1   Let x, y and z be any three objects, and suppose that, at fusion level α_j, x and y are in the same cluster, and at fusion level α_k, y and z are in the same cluster. Since the clusters are hierarchical, one of these includes the other. This will be the cluster corresponding to the larger of j and k. Let this be the integer e so that at α_e, x, y and z are all in the same cluster. Then,

$$d(x, z) \leqslant \alpha_1$$

but since

$$e = \max \{j, k\}$$

$$\alpha_e = \max \{\alpha_j, \alpha_k\}$$

so that

$$d(x, z) \leqslant \max \{\alpha_j, \alpha_k\}$$

i.e.

$$d(x, z) \leqslant \max \{d(x, y), d(y, z)\}.$$

6.2   The single linkage distance between cluster k and the cluster formed by the fusion of clusters i and j is defined to be $\min \{d_{ki}, d_{kj}\}$. According to the formula given in Exercise 6.2 this distance, $d_{k(ij)}$ is

$$d_{k(ij)} = \tfrac{1}{2}d_{ki} + \tfrac{1}{2}d_{kj} - \tfrac{1}{2}|d_{ki} - d_{kj}|$$

if

$$d_{ki} > d_{kj}, \quad |d_{ki} - d_{kj}| = d_{ki} - d_{kj}$$

therefore

$$d_{k(ij)} = d_{kj}$$

If

$$d_{ki} < d_{kj}, \quad |d_{ki} - d_{kj}| = d_{kj} - d_{ki}$$

and therefore

$$d_{k(ij)} = d_{ki}$$

i.e. the formula gives $d_{k(ij)} = \min \{d_{ki}, d_{kj}\}$, as required.

Chapter 7

7.1

$$\log m_{ij} = \log N + \log p_{i.} + \log p_{.j} \tag{1}$$

since $m_{i.} = Np_{i.}$ and $m_{.j} = Np_{.j}$, this may be rewritten as

$$\log m_{ij} = \log m_{i.} + \log m_{.j} - \log N \tag{2}$$

Summing (2) over i we have

$$\sum_{i=1}^{r} \log m_{ij} = \sum_{i=1}^{r} \log m_{i.} + r \log m_{.j} - r \log N$$

Summing (2) over j we have

$$\sum_{j=1}^{r} \log m_{ij} = c \log m_{i.} + \sum_{j=1}^{c} \log m_{.j} - c \log N$$

Finally summing (2) over i and j we have

$$\sum_{i=1}^{r} \sum_{j=1}^{c} \log m_{ij} = c \sum_{i=1}^{r} \log m_{i.} + r \sum_{j=1}^{c} \log m_{.j} - rc - \log N.$$

By setting

$$u = \frac{1}{rc} \sum \sum \log m_{ij},$$

$$u_{1(i)} = \frac{1}{c} \sum_{i=1}^{c} \log m_{ij} - u,$$

and

$$u_{2(j)} = \frac{1}{r} \sum_{i=1}^{r} \log m_{ij} - u,$$

it is now a matter of simple algebra to show that equation (2) may be written in the form

$$\log m_{ij} = u + u_{1(i)} + u_{2(j)}$$

7.3 $$\log m_{ijk} = u + u_{1(i)} + u_{2(j)} + u_{3(k)} + u_{12(ij)}$$ (saturated

$$+ u_{13(ik)} + u_{23(jk)} + u_{123(ijk)}$$ model)

$$\log m_{ijk} = u + u_{1(i)} + u_{2(j)} + u_{3(k)}$$ (minimal

model)

Chapter 11

11.3   For this example $p = 3$, $k = 1$ and so $(p-k)^2 = (p+k)$ which implies that equation (11.11) has an exact solution (see Section 11.4). Writing out this equation explicitly we have

1.00			$\hat{\lambda}_1^2 + \hat{\psi}_{11}$		
0.83	1.00	$=$	$\hat{\lambda}_1 \hat{\lambda}_2$	$\hat{\lambda}_2^2 + \psi_{22}$	
0.78	0.67	1.00	$\hat{\lambda}_1 \hat{\lambda}_3$	$\hat{\lambda}_2 \hat{\lambda}_3$	$\hat{\lambda}_3^2 + \psi_{33}$

The unique solution (except for the sign of $\hat{\lambda}_1$, $\hat{\lambda}_2$ and $\hat{\lambda}_3$) is given by

$$\hat{\lambda}_1^2 = r_{12} r_{13} / r_{23}, \qquad \hat{\lambda}_2^2 = r_{12} r_{23} / r_{13}, \qquad \hat{\lambda}_3^2 = r_{13} r_{23} / r_{12},$$

$$\hat{\psi}_{11} = 1 - \hat{\lambda}_1^2, \qquad \hat{\psi}_{22} = 1 - \hat{\lambda}_2^2, \qquad \hat{\psi}_{33} = 1 - \hat{\lambda}_3^2.$$

leading to

$$\hat{\lambda}_1 = 0.983, \qquad \hat{\lambda}_2 = 0.844, \qquad \hat{\lambda}_3 = 0.794,$$

$$\hat{\psi}_{11} = 0.034, \qquad \hat{\psi}_{22} = 0.287, \qquad \hat{\psi}_{33} = 0.370.$$

Bibliography and References

AITKEN, M. (1978), 'The analysis of unbalanced cross-classifications', *Journal of the Royal Statistical Society*, A, **141**, 195–223.

AITKEN, M. (1979), 'A simultaneous test procedure for contingency table models', *Applied Statistics*, **28**, 233–42.

AITKEN, M. and CLAYTON, D. (1980), 'The fitting of exponential, Weibull and extreme value distributions to complex censored survival data using GLIM', *Applied Statistics*, **29**, 156–63.

AITKEN, M., ANDERSON, D. and HINDE, J. (1981), 'Statistical modelling of data on teaching styles', *Journal of the Royal Statistical Society*, A, **144**, 419–48.

ALLEN, D. M. (1971), 'Mean square error of prediction as a criterion for selecting variables', *Technometrics*, **13**, 469–75.

ANDERBERG, M. R. (1973), *Cluster Analysis for Applications*, New York: Academic Press.

ANDREWS, D. F. (1972), 'Plots of high dimensional data', *Biometrics*, **28**, 125–36.

ANSCOMBE, F. J. (1973), 'Graphs in statistical analysis', *The American Statistician*, **27**, 17–21.

BAKER, R. J. and NELDER, J. A. (1978), *The GLIM System, Release 3: Generalized Linear Interactive Modelling*, London: Royal Statistical Society.

BARNETT, V. (ed.) (1981), *Interpreting Multivariate Data*, London: John Wiley & Sons.

BARNETT, V. and LEWIS, T. (1978), *Outliers in Statistical Data*, London: John Wiley & Sons.

BAUM, B. R. (1977), 'Reduction of dimensionality for heuristic purposes', *Taxon*, **26**, 191–95.

BENNETT, N. (1976), *Teaching Styles and Pupil Progress*, London: Open Books.

BENNETT, S. and BOWERS, D. (1976), *An Introduction to Multivariate Techniques for Social and Behavioural Sciences*, London: Macmillan.

BENTLER, P. M. and BONETT, D. G. (1980), 'Significance tests and goodness-of-fit in the analysis of covariance structures', *Psychological Bulletin*, **88**, 588–606.

BINDER, D. A. (1978), 'Bayesian cluster analysis', *Biometrika*, **65**, 31–8.

BIRCH, M. W. (1963), 'Maximum likelihood in three-way contingency tables', *Journal of the Royal Statistical Society*, B, **25**, 220–33.

BISHOP, Y. M. M., FIENBERG, S. E. and HOLLAND, P. W. (1975), *Discrete Multivariate Analysis: Theory and Practice*, Cambridge, Mass.: MIT Press.

BLACKITH, R. E. and REYMENT, R. A. (1971), *Multivariate Morphometrics*, London: Academic Press.

BLALOCK, H. M. (1972), *Social Statistics*, New York: McGraw-Hill.

BLUMEN, I., KOGAN, M. and McCARTHY, P. J. (1955), *The Industrial Mobility of Labor as a Probability Process*, Ithaca, New York: Cornell University Press.

BOX, M. J., DAVIES, D. and SWANN, W. H. (1969), *Non-linear Optimization Techniques*, Edinburgh: Oliver and Boyd.

BRUNTZ, S. M., CLEVELAND, W. S., KLEINER, B. and WARNER, J. L. (1974), 'The dependence of ambient ozone on solar radiation, wind temperature and mixing height', *Proceedings of a Symposium on Atmospheric Diffusion and Air Pollution—American Meteorological Society*, 125–28.

BURTON, M. (1972), 'Semantic dimensions of occupation names', in *Multidimensional Scaling*, vol. 11, eds. A. K. Romney, R. N. Shepard and S. B. Nerlove, New York: Seminar Press, 55–71.

BUSS, A. H. and DURKEE, A. (1957), 'An inventory for assessing different kinds of hostility', *Journal of Consulting Psychology*, **21**, 343–49.

BUTLER, D. and STOKES, D. (1975), *Political Change in Britain* (2nd ed.), London: Macmillan.

CARROLL, J. D. and CHANG, J. J. (1970), 'Analysis of individual differences in multidimensional scaling via an N-way generalization of Eckart–Young decomposition', *Psychometrika*, **35**, 283–319.

CATTELL, R. B. (1965), 'Factor analysis: an introduction to essentials', *Biometrics*, **21**, 190–215.

CHATFIELD, C. and COLLINS, A. J. (1980), *Introduction to Multivariate Analysis*, London: Chapman and Hall.

CHATTERJEE, S. and PRICE, B. (1977), *Regression Analysis by Example*, New York: John Wiley & Sons.

CHERNOFF, H. (1973), 'Using faces to represent points in k-dimensional space graphically', *Journal American Statistical Association*, **68**, 361–68.

CHILD, D. (1970), *The Essentials of Factor Analysis*, London: Holt, Rinehart Winston.

COHEN, A., GNANADESIKAN, R., KETTENRING, J. R. and LANDWEHR, J. M. (1977), 'Methodological developments in some applications of clustering', in *Proceedings of Symposium on Applications of Statistics*, ed. P. R. Krishnaiah, Amsterdam: North Holland Publishing Co.

CONSTANTINE, A. G. and GOWER, J. C. (1978), 'Graphical representation of asymmetric matrices', *Applied Statistics*, **27**, 297–304.

COOMBS, C. H. (1964), *A Theory of Data*, New York: John Wiley & Sons.

CORMACK, R. M. (1971), 'A review of classification', *Journal of the Royal Statistical Society*, A, **134**, 321–67.

COX, D. R. (1970), *Analysis of Binary Data*, London: Chapman and Hall.

COX, D. R. (1972), 'Regression models and life tables', *Journal of the Royal Statistical Society*, B, **34**, 187–220.

CUNNINGHAM, K. M. and OGILVIE, J. C. (1972), 'Evaluation of hierarchical grouping techniques: a preliminary study', *Computer Journal*, **15**, 209–13.

DAY, N. E. (1969), 'Estimating the components of a mixture of normal distributions', *Biometrika*, **56**, 463–74.

DRAPER, N. R. and SMITH, H. (1981), *Applied Regression Analysis* (2nd ed.), New York: John Wiley & Sons.

DUBES, R. and JAIN, A. K. (1979), 'Validity studies in clustering methodologies', *Pattern Recognition Journal*, **11**, 235–54.

DUDA, R. and HART, P. (1973), *Pattern Classification and Scene Analysis*, New York: John Wiley & Sons.

DUNN, G. (1981), 'The role of linear models in psychiatric epidemiology', *Psychological Medicine*, **11**, 179–84.

DUNN, G. and CLARK, P. (1982) (in preparation).

DUNN, G. and EVERITT, B. S. (1982), *An Introduction to Mathematical Taxonomy*, Cambridge: Cambridge University Press.

DUNN, G. and MASTER, D. (1982), 'Latency models: the statistical analysis of response times', *Psychological Medicine*, **12**, 659–65.

DUNN, G. and SKUSE, D. (1981), 'The natural history of depression in general practice: stochastic models', *Psychological Medicine*, **11**, 755–64.

EHRENBERG, A. S. C. (1977), 'Rudiments of numeracy', *Journal of the Royal Statistical Society*, A, **140**, 277–97.

EKMAN, G. (1954), 'Dimensions of colour vision', *Journal of Psychology*, **38**, 467–74.

ERICKSON, B. H. and NOSANCHUK, T. A. (1979), *Understanding Data*, Milton Keynes: Open University Press.

EVERITT, B. S. (1977a), *The Analysis of Contingency Tables*, London: Chapman and Hall.

EVERITT, B. S. (1977b), 'Cluster analysis', in *The Analysis of Survey Data, Volume*

1, Exploring Data Structures, eds. C. A. O'Muircheartaigh and C. Payne, London: John Wiley & Sons.

EVERITT, B. S. (1978), *Graphical Techniques for Multivariate Data*, London: Heinemann Educational Books.

EVERITT, B. S. (1980), *Cluster Analysis* (2nd ed.), London: Heinemann Educational Books.

EVERITT, B. S. (1981), 'A Monte Carlo investigation of the likelihood ratio test for the number of compositions in a mixture of normal distributions', *Multiv. Behav. Res.*, **16**, 171–80.

EVERITT, B. S. and HAND, D. J. (1981), *Finite Mixture Distributions*, London: Chapman and Hall.

FEYERABEND, P. (1975), *Against Method*, London: Verso.

FIENBERG, S. E. (1980), *The Analysis of Cross-Classified Categorical Data* (2nd ed.), Cambridge, Mass.: MIT Press.

FIENBERG, S. A. and MASON, W. M. (1978), 'Identification and estimation of age-period-cohort effects in the analysis of discrete archival data', *Sociological Methodology, 1979*, ed. K. F. Schuessler, San Francisco: Jossey-Bass, 1–67.

FINN, J. D. (1974), *A General Model for Multivariate Analysis*, New York: Holt, Rinehart and Winston.

FISHER, R. A. (1936), 'The use of multiple measurements on taxonomic problems', *Ann. Eugen.*, **7**, 179–88.

FLEISHMAN, E. A. and HEMPEL, W. E. (1954), 'Changes in factor structure of a complex psychomotor test as a function of practice', *Psychometrika*, **19**, 239–52.

FLOREK, K., LUKASZEWICZ, J., PERKAL, J., STEINHAUS, H., and ZUBRZYCKI, S. (1951), 'Sur la liason et la division des points d'un ensemble fini', *Colloguium Math.*, **2**, 282–85.

FLURY, B. and RIEDWYL, H. (1981), 'Graphical representation of multivariate data by means of asymmetrical faces', *Journal American Statistical Association*, **76**, 757–65.

FRANCIS, I. (1973), 'Comparison of several analysis of variance programs', *Journal American Statistical Association*, **68**, 860–65.

FRCKA, G. F., BEYTS, J. P., MARTIN, I. M. and LEVEY, A. B. (1982), unpublished data.

FREIREICH, E. J., GEHAN, E. and FREI, E. (1963), 'The effect of 6-mercapto-purine on the duration of steroid-induced remissions in acute leukemia: a model for evaluation of other potentially useful therapy', *Blood*, **21**, 699–716.

GABRIEL, K. R. (1981), 'Biplot display of multivariate matrices for inspection of data and diagnosis', in *Interpreting Multivariate Data*, ed. V. Barnett, London: John Wiley & Sons, 147–73.

GNANADESIKAN, R. (1977), *Statistical Data Analysis of Multivariate Observations*, New York: John Wiley & Sons.

GNANADESIKAN, R. and WILK, M. B. (1969), 'Data analytic methods in multivariate statistical analysis', in *Multivariate Analysis*, vol. II, ed. P. R. Krishnaiah, New York: Academic Press, 593–638.

GOLDBERG, D. P. (1972), *The Detection of Psychiatric Illness by Questionnaire*, Maudsley Monographs No. 21, London: Oxford University Press.

GOTTMAN, J. M. (1981), *Time Series Analysis: A Comprehensive Introduction for Social Scientists*, Cambridge: Cambridge University Press.

GOWER, J. C. (1966), 'Some distance properties of latent root and vector methods used in multivariate analysis', *Biometrika*, **53**, 325–38.

GOWER, J. C. (1967), 'Multivariate analysis and multidimensional geometry', *The Statistician*, **17**, 13–25.

GOWER, J. C. (1975), 'Goodness-of-fit criteria for classification and other patterned structures', in *Proceedings of the 8th International Conference on Numerical Taxonomy*, ed. G. Estabrook, London: Freeman, 38–62.

240 *Latent Variable Models*

GOWER, J. C. (1977), 'The analysis of asymmetry and orthogonality', in *Recent Developments in Statistics*, ed. J. Barra, Amsterdam: North-Holland, 109–23.

GOWER, J. C. and DIGBY, P. G. N. (1981), 'Expressing complex relationships in two dimensions', in *Interpreting Multivariate Data*, ed. V. Barnett, London: John Wiley & Sons, 83–118.

GREENACRE, M. J. (1981), 'Practical correspondence analysis', in *Interpreting Multivariate Data*, ed. V. Barnett, London: John Wiley & Sons, 119–46.

GUTTMAN, L. A. (1954), 'A new approach to factor analysis: the radex', in *Mathematical Thinking in the Social Sciences*, ed. P. F. Lazarsfeld, New York: Columbia University Press, 258–348.

HAND, D. J. (1981a), 'Branch and bound in statistical data', *The Statistician*, **30**, 3–16.

HAND, D. J. (1981b), *Discrimination and Classification*, London: John Wiley & Sons.

HARSHMAN, R. A. (1972), 'PARAFAC 2: mathematical and technical notes', in *Working Papers in Phonetics*, **22**, Los Angeles: University of California.

HARTIGAN, J. A. (1975), *Clustering Algorithms*, New York: John Wiley & Sons.

HARTWIG, F. and DEARING, B. E. (1979), *Exploratory Data Analysis*, Beverley Hills/London: Sage Publications.

HILLS, M. (1977), (Book review), *Applied Statistics*, **26**, 339–40.

HOERL, A. E. and KENNARD, R. W. (1970), 'Ridge regression: biased estimation for nonorthogonal problems', *Technometrics*, **12**, 55–67.

HUBERT, L. J. (1974), 'Approximate evaluation techniques for the single-link and complete-link hierarchical clustering procedures', *Journal American Statistical Association*, **69**, 698–704.

JARDINE, N. and SIBSON, R. (1968), 'The construction of hierarchic and non-hierarchic classifications', *Computer Journal*, **11**, 117–84.

JOHNSON, S. C. (1967), 'Hierarchical clustering schemes', *Psychometrika*, **32**, 241–54.

JÖRESKOG, K. G. (1967), 'Some contributions to maximum likelihood factor analysis', *Psychometrika*, **32**, 443–82.

JÖRESKOG, K. G. and LAWLEY, D. N. (1968), 'New methods in maximum likelihood factor analysis, *Br. J. Math. and Statist. Psychol.*, **21**, 85–96.

JÖRESKOG, K. G. and SÖRBOM, D. (1981), *LISREL V: Analysis of linear structural relationships by maximum likelihood and least squares methods*, Research Report 81–8, Department of Statistics, Uppsala, Sweden.

KAISER, H. F. (1958), 'The varimax criterion for analytic rotation in factor analysis', *Psychometrika*, **23**, 187–200.

KALBFLEISCH, J. D. and PRENTICE, R. L. (1980), *The Statistical Analysis of Failure Time Data*, New York: John Wiley & Sons.

KENDALL, D. G. (1975), 'The recovery of structure from fragmentary information, *Phil. Trans. Roy. Soc. (A)*, **279**, 547–82.

KENDALL, M. G. (1975), *Multivariate Analysis*, London: Griffin.

KENDALL, M. G. and STUART, A. (1963), *The Advanced Theory of Statistics*, London: Griffin.

KIHLBERG, J. K., NARRAGON, E. A. and CAMPBELL, B. J. (1964), 'Automobile crash injury in relation to car size', *Cornell Aero. Lab. Report* No. VJ-1823-R11.

KLEINER, B. and HARTIGAN, J. A. (1981), 'Representing points in many dimensions by trees and castles', *Journal American Statistical Association*, **76**, 260–69.

KRUSKAL, J. B. (1964a), 'Multidimensional scaling by optimizing goodness-of-fit to non-metric hypotheses', *Psychometrika*, **29**, 1–27.

KRUSKAL, J. B. (1964b), 'Non-metric multidimensional scaling: a numerical method', *Psychometrika*, **29**, 115–29.

KRUSKAL, J. B. and WISH, M. (1978), *Multidimensional Scaling*, Beverley Hills/London: Sage Publications.

LAWLEY, D. N. (1940), 'The estimation of factor loadings by the method of maximum likelihood', *Proceedings of the Royal Society of Edinburgh*, **A60**, 64–82.

LAWLEY, D. N. (1941), 'Further investigations in factor estimation', *Proceedings of the Royal Society of Edinburgh*, **A61**, 176–85.

LAWLEY, D. N. (1943), 'The application of the maximum likelihood method to factor analysis', *British Journal of Psychology*, **33**, 172–75.

LAWLEY, D. N. (1967), 'Some new results in maximum likelihood factor analysis', *Proceedings of the Royal Society of Edinburgh*, **A67**, 256–64.

LAWLEY, D. N. and MAXWELL, A. E. (1971), *Factor Analysis as a Statistical Method* (2nd ed.), London: Butterworths.

LAZARSFELD, P. L. and HENRY, N. W. (1968), *Latent Structure Analysis*, Boston: Houghton Mifflin.

LEE, E. T. (1980), *Statistical Methods for Survival Data Analysis*, California: Wadsworth.

LING, R. F. (1973), 'A computer generated aid for cluster analysis', *Communications of the ACM*, **16**, 355–61.

MACDONELL, W. R. (1902), 'On criminal anthropometry and the identification of criminals', *Biometrika*, **1**, 177–227.

MAHON, B. H. (1977), 'Statistics and decisions: the importance of communication and the power of graphical presentation', *Journal of the Royal Statistical Society, A*, **140**, 298–306.

MALLOWS, C. L. (1973), 'Some comments on C_p', *Technometrics*, **15**, 661–75.

MARDIA, K. V., KENT, J. T. and BIBBY, J. M. (1979), *Multivariate Analysis*, London: Academic Press.

MAXWELL, A. E. (1977), *Multivariate Analysis in Behavioural Research*, London: Chapman and Hall.

MCCULLAGH, P. (1980), 'Regression models for ordinal data', *Journal of the Royal Statistical Society, B*, **42**, 109–27.

MCDONALD, R. P. (1978), 'A simple comprehensive model for the analysis of covariance structures', *Br. J. Math. Statist. Psychol.*, **31**, 59–72.

MCQUITTY, L. L. (1957), 'Elementary linkage analysis for isolating orthogonal and oblique types and typal relevances', *Educ. Psychol. Measurmt.*, **17**, 207–29.

MELZAK, R. (1975), 'The McGill pain questionnaire: major properties and scoring methods', *Pain*, **1**, 277–99.

MILLIGAN, G. W. (1981), 'A Monte Carlo study of thirty internal criterion measures for cluster analysis', *Psychometrika*, **46**, 187–99.

MOJENA, R. (1977), 'Hierarchical grouping methods and stopping rules: an evaluation', *Computer Journal*, **20**, 359–363.

MORGAN, B. J. T. (1981), 'Three applications of methods of cluster analysis', *The Statistician*, **30**, 205–24.

MORRISON, D. F. (1967), *Multivariate Statistical Methods*, New York: McGraw-Hill.

MOSTELLER, F. and TUKEY, J. W. (1977), *Data Analysis and Regression*, Reading, Mass.: Addison-Wesley.

MURRAY, J., DUNN, G. and TARNOPOLSKY, A. (1982), 'Self-assessment of health: an exploration of the effects of physical and psychological symptoms', *Psychological Medicine*, **12**, 371–378.

MURRAY, J., DUNN, G., WILLIAMS, P. and TARNOPOLSKY, A. (1981), 'Factors affecting the consumption of psychotropic drugs', *Psychological Medicine*, **11**, 551–60.

MUTHEN, B. (1981), *A general structural equation model with ordered categorical and continuous latent variable indicators*, Research Report 81-9, Department of Statistics, Uppsala, Sweden.

NELDER, J. A. (1977), 'A reformulation of linear models', *Journal of the Royal Statistical Society, A*, **140**, 48–63.

NELDER, J. A. and WEDDERBURN, R. W. M. (1972), 'Generalized linear models, *Journal of the Royal Statistical Society, A*, **135**, 370–84.

NIE, N. H., HULL, C. H., JENKINS, J. G., STEINBRENNER, K. and BENT, D. H. (1975), SPSS: *Statistical Package for the Social Services* (2nd Edition), New York: McGraw-Hill.

PAYKEL, E. S. and RASSABY, E. (1978), 'Classification of suicide attempters by cluster analysis', *Brit. J. Psychiat.*, **133**, 45–52.

POWELL, G. E., CLARK, E. and BAILEY, S. (1979), 'Categories of aphasia: a cluster analysis of Schuell test profiles', *British Journal of Disorders of Communications*, **14**, 111–22.

RAMSAY, J. O. (1977), 'Maximum likelihood estimation in multidimensional scaling', *Psychometrika*, **42**, 241–66.

READING, A. E., EVERITT, B. S. and SLEDMERE, C. M. (1982), 'The McGill pain questionnaire: a replication of its construction', *British Journal of Clinical Psychology*, **21**, 339–49.

RIES, P. N. and SMITH, H. (1963), 'The use of chi-square for preference testing in multidimensional problems', *Chemical Engineering Progress*, **59**, 39–43.

ROHLF, F. J. (1970), 'Adaptive hierarchical clustering schemes', *Syst. Zool.*, **19**, 58–82.

ROHLF, F. J. and FISHER, D. L. (1968), 'Test for hierarchical structure in random data sets', *Syst. Zool.*, **17**, 407–12.

ROMNEY, A. K., SHEPARD, R. N. and NERLOVE, S. B. (1972), *Multidimensional Scaling*, volumes I and II, New York: Seminar Press.

ROTHKOPF, E. Z. (1957), 'A measure of stimulus similarity and errors in some paired associate learning tasks', *Journal of Experimental Psychology*, **53**, 94–101.

SAMMON, J. W. (1969), 'A non-linear mapping for data structure analysis', *IEEE Trans. Computers*, **C18**, 401–9.

SATTATH, S. and TVERSKY, A. (1977), 'Additive similarity trees', *Psychometrika*, **42**, 319–45.

SCHUELL, H. (1965), *Differential Diagnosis of Aphasia*, Minneapolis: University of Minnesota Press.

SEARLE, S. R. (1971), *Linear Models*, New York: John Wiley & Sons.

SHEPARD, R. N. (1962), 'The analysis of proximities: multidimensional scaling with an unknown distance function, 1', *Psychometrika*, **27**, 219–46.

SIEGEL, S. (1956), *Nonparametric Statistics*, New York: McGraw-Hill.

SMITH, S. P. and DUBES, R. (1980), 'Stability of a hierarchical clustering', *Pattern Recognition*, **12**, 177–87.

SNEATH, P. H. A. (1957), 'The application of computers to taxonomy', *J. Gen. Microbiol.*, **17**, 201–26.

SPEARMAN, C. (1904), '"General Intelligence", objectively determined and measured', *Amer. J. Psychol.*, **15**, 201–93.

SPENCE, I. (1970), *Multidimensional scaling: an empirical and theoretical investigation*, Ph.D. thesis, University of Toronto.

SPENCE, I. (1972), 'An aid to the estimation of dimensionality in nonmetric multidimensional scaling', University of Western Ontario Research Bulletin No. 229.

SPENCE, I. and GRAEF, J. (1974), 'The determination of the underlying dimensionality of an empirically obtained matrix of proximities', *Multiv. Behav. Res.*, **9**, 331–42.

SROLE, L., LANGNER, T. S., MICHAEL, S. T., OPLER, M. K. and RENNIE, T. A. C. (1962), *Mental Health in the Metropolis: The Midtown Manhattan Study*, New York: McGraw-Hill.

TARNOPOLSKY, A. and MORTON-WILLIAMS, J. (1980), *Aircraft and Prevalence of Psychiatric Disorders*, London: Social and Community Planning Research.

TUCKER, L. R. (1964), 'The extension of factor analysis to three-dimensional matrices', in *Contributions to Mathematical Psychology*, ed. N. Fredriksen and H. Gulliksen, New York: Holt, Rinehart and Winston, 109–27.

TUCKER, L. R. (1972), 'Relations between multidimensional scaling and three-mode factor analysis', *Psychometrika*, **37**, 3–27.

TUCKER, L. R. and MESSICK, S. (1963), 'An individual differences model for multidimensional scaling', *Psychometrika*, **28**, 333–67.

TUKEY, P. A. and TUKEY, J. W. (1981a), 'Preparation; pre-chosen sequence of views', in *Interpreting Multivariate Data*, ed. V. Barnett, London: John Wiley & Sons, 189–213.

TUKEY, P. A. and TUKEY, J. W. (1981b), 'Data-driven view selection; agglomeration and sharpening', in *Interpreting Multivariate Data*, ed. V. Barnett, London: John Wiley & Sons, 215–43.

TUKEY, P. A. and TUKEY, J. W. (1981c), 'Summarization smoothing; supplemented views', in *Interpreting Multivariate Data*, ed. V. Barnett, London: John Wiley & Sons, 245–75.

WAGENAAR, W. A. and PADMOS, P. (1971), 'Quantitative interpretation of stress in Kruskal's multidimensional scaling technique', *Brit. J. Math. and Statist. Psychol.*, **24**, 101–10.

WARD, J. H. (1963), 'Hierarchical grouping to optimize an objective function', *Journal of the American Statistical Association*, **58**, 236–44.

WHEATON, B., MUTHEN, B., ALWIN, D. and SUMMERS, G. (1977), 'Assessing reliability and stability in panel models', in D. R. Heise (ed.), *Sociological Methodology*, San Francisco: Jossey Bass, 84–136.

WILLIAMS, W. T., LANCE, G. N., DALE, M. B. and CLIFFORD, H. T. (1971), 'Controversy concerning the criteria for taxonometric strategies', *Computer Journal*, **14**, 162–65.

WINER, B. J. (1971), *Statistical Principles in Experimental Design*, 2nd ed., New York: McGraw-Hill.

WOESE, C. R. (1981), 'Archaebacteria', *Scientific American*, **244**, 94–106.

WOLFE, J. H. (1970), 'Pattern clustering by multivariate mixture analysis', *Multiv. Behav. Res.*, **5**, 329–50.

WOLFE, J. H. (1971), 'A Monte Carlo study of the sampling distribution of the likelihood ratio for mixtures of multinormal distributions' (Naval Personnel and Training Research Laboratory), *Technical Bulletin*, STB 72-2 (San Diego, California, 92152).

WONNACOTT, R. J. and WONNACOTT, T. H. (1981), *Regression: A Second Course in Statistics*, New York: John Wiley & Sons.

WRIGHT, S. (1934), 'The method of path coefficients', *Annals of Math. Statist.*, **5**, 161–215.

YULE, W., BERGER, M., BUTLER, S., NEWHAM, V. and TIZARD, J. (1969), 'The WPPSI: an empirical evaluation with a British sample', *Brit. J. Educ. Psychol.*, **39**, 1–13.

Author Index

Subject Index